How Computers Play Chess

How Computers Play Chess

David Levy and Monty Newborn

Computer Science Press
An imprint of
W. H. Freeman and Company
New York

Library of Congress Cataloging-in-Publication Data

Levy, David N. L.
    How computers play chess / by David Levy and Monty Newborn.
        p.   cm.
    Includes bibliographical references and index.
    1. Chess—Computer programs.   I. Newborn, Monroe.   II. Title.

    GV1449.3.L477   1991
    794.1'72416—dc20
    ISBN 0-7167-8239-1   90-39244
    ISBN 0-7167-8121-2 (pbk.)   CIP

Computer Science Press
An imprint of W. H. Freeman and Company
41 Madison Avenue, New York, NY 10010
20 Beaumont Street, Oxford OX1 2NQ, England

1 2 3 4 5 6 7 8 9 0 RRD 9 9 8 7 6 5 4 3 2 1

Contents

Preface

It now appears possible—even likely—that within a few decades and within certain specialized domains, *the computer will be more intelligent than we ourselves.* What was unimaginable a few years ago is happening today with alarming rapidity. A small piece of silicon, no larger than a thumbnail, can exhibit more "intelligence" than the best human brains.

This book attempts to satisfy two different goals. It presents a comprehensive history of computer chess along with many rare examples of the play of early programs. These examples contain both amazing strokes of brilliance and inexplicable catastrophes; they will give the reader a clear perspective of the pioneer days of computer chess. In contrast, contemporary programs are capable of defeating International Grandmasters; the text contains several recent examples including a remarkable victory over former World Champion Anatoly Karpov.

The remainder of the book is devoted to an explanation of how the various parts of a chess program are designed and how they function. Readers who have no knowledge of computers will gain insight into how they "think." Readers who own a personal computer and who want to write their own chess programs will find sufficient information in this book to enable them to make a good start.

In many areas of human intellectual endeavor it is difficult to assess accomplishment accurately. There is no scientifically quantifiable technique for determining who is better: Cézanne or Warhol, Brahms or the Beatles. But in chess there is a reliable, accurate method of determining playing strength. The *Elo System* is a statistically reliable rating scale developed in the late 1950s by Professor Arpad Elo of Marquette University. It has been used by the United States Chess Federation (USCF) since 1960 and universally since 1970, both for rating of chess players in international competition and as the basis of international title awards. Along this rating scale there are landmark points such as the titles of National Master, International Master, and International Grandmaster. And above all, there is the supreme chess title—World Chess Champion. In chess, therefore, it *is* possible to give a numerical representation of playing strength. Perhaps for this reason chess has been used as the touchstone of Artificial Intelligence (AI). Successes at the chessboard have often been cited as proof that AI is a real science, that computerized intelligence is with us, like it or not.

The authors of this work have been involved in computer chess for more than 20 years, but from slightly different perspectives. Monty Newborn is a professor of Computer Science at McGill University; his programs have competed successfully in many computer chess tournaments since 1970. David Levy is an International Master who has a professional interest in computers. He has provided the chess expertise for a number of commercially available programs since 1979. Both authors have been present at most of the computer chess events held in North America and Europe.

David Levy, *London*
Monty Newborn, *Montreal*
April 1990

A Note on Notation

Algebraic notation is a simple, unambiguous system for recording chess moves. Each square on the board is identified by a single designation, which may be seen in the following diagram.

Black

8	a8	b8	c8	d8	e8	f8	g8	h8
7	a7	b7	c7	d7	e7	f7	g7	h7
6	a6	b6	c6	d6	e6	f6	g6	h6
5	a5	b5	c5	d5	e5	f5	g5	h5
4	a4	b4	c4	d4	e4	f4	g4	h4
3	a3	b3	c3	d3	e3	f3	g3	h3
2	a2	b2	c2	d2	e2	f2	g2	h2
1	a1	b1	c1	d1	e1	f1	g1	h1

| | a | b | c | d | e | f | g | h |

White

The chess games in this book are described in *long form* algebraic notation. In this system, moves are written with the symbol for the piece first (see the list of symbols below), then the square the piece moves *from*, followed by the square it moves *to* (example: Ng1–f3). For pawn moves there is no piece symbol (example: e2–e4). Captures are designated by an "x" (example: Nf3xe5).

Symbols

K	king
Q	queen
B	bishop
N	knight
R	rook
0–0	castles kingside
0–0–0	castles queenside
+	check
++	double check
!?	interesting, speculative move
!	good move
!!	excellent, beautiful move
?!	dubious move
?	bad move
??	terrible move, blunder

Many people "grew up" with descriptive notation; this system is still widely used at the club and tournament level. A comparison of the following game score (the classic miniature Reti–Tartakower, Vienna 1910) will help the reader understand the mechanics of long form algebraic notation.

Long form algebraic		Descriptive	
1 e2–e4	c7–c6	1 P–K4	P–QB3
2 d2–d4	d7–d5	2 P–Q4	P–Q4
3 Nb1–c3	d5xe4	3 N–QB3	PxP
4 Nc3xe4	Ng8–f6	4 NxP	N–B3
5 Qd1–d3	e7–e5	5 Q–Q3	P–K4
6 d4xe5	Qd8–a5+	6 PxP	Q–R4+
7 Bc1–d2	Qa5xe5	7 B–Q2	QxKP
8 0–0–0	Nf6xe4	8 0–0–0	NxN
9 Qd3–d8+	Ke8xd8	9 Q–Q8+	KxQ
10 Bd2–g5++	Kd8–c7	10 B–N5++	K–B2
11 Bg5–d8 mate		11 B–Q8 mate	

How Computers Play Chess

1

The Challenge Is World Champion Kasparov

We all understand that computers can help a jumbo jet land safely in the worst of weather, aid astronauts in complex maneuvers in space, and assist physicians in creating cross-sectional drawings of the interior of the human body. We are delighted to have computers perform these functions for us. In doing them, they are showing no intelligence, but merely carrying out lengthly complex calculations while serving as our obedient helpers. Yet the question of whether computers are able to think, whether they can show any true intelligence, has been a controversial one from the day humans first realized the potential power of their new ingenious creation. Exactly what intelligence is, how it is created, and how we test for it or measure it have become issues central to computer science and, more specifically, to artificial intelligence. In searching for a domain in which to study these issues, many scientists have selected the game of chess; it serves the world of artificial intelligence just as the fruit fly serves the world of genetics. Chess requires what is generally understood to be a high level of intelligence, and through its rating system, performance levels can be measured and compared.

From the beginning, some have argued that computers would never play strong chess until humans first understood how they themselves played and then modeled computers to play the same way. In the early 1960s, Carnegie Mellon University professors Alan Newell, John Shaw and Herbert Simon followed the eyes of human experts hoping to shed light on man's techniques. Most computer scientists felt that humans carried out highly selective searches, and programmers initially set out to have their programs do the same. It was believed that special-purpose computer languages in which chess concepts could be easily expressed and manipulated were necessary. The Dutch scientist Adrian de Groot argued that although human intuition could not be programmed, it was required for top level play. Computers have improved gradually over a 30-year period from the point where they barely were able to make legal moves to their current state of grandmasterhood. On the surface, they do not seem to imitate the human thought process, but upon closer examination, one begins to sense that they do. They, in fact, mimic human play just as man's flying craft mimic the flight of birds.

Because the approach of the computer has seemed so different than that of humans, there has been a large lobby who have contended that computers will never play "good chess." Once upon a time, "good" chess meant "Class A level," the level of a good university player. Around 1976 when CHESS 4.6 started playing chess at the Expert level, the definition of "good" was raised to "master level chess." In 1983, when BELLE was awarded the title of U. S. Master, good was redefined as "grandmaster." Today, with DEEP THOUGHT playing grandmaster level chess and HITECH playing just a touch weaker, and with a number of other programs playing at the master level, good has finally been made equivalent to the "world chess champion." There are still those who refuse to believe a computer will ever beat a human world champion.

The twentieth century will be remembered for many great scientific and intellectual advances. One of the most important will be humanity's improved understanding of our own intellectual capabilities and those of the creatures that cohabit this planet with us. Human intelligence is not as unique as we once imagined. At the beginning of the twentieth century, we believed our intellect was not possessed by any other living creature and certainly not by any machine. But science has made a number of amazing discoveries in the last 100 years. Language, once thought to be unique to man, can be learned by monkeys and dolphins. Moreover, they can express abstract concepts in these languages, and even more surprising, they can teach language to one another. Tools are used by animals for gathering food and building homes in ways humans once did not believe possible. Mysterious instincts give birds sufficient information to journey great distances from their summer homes in Canada to their winter ones in Mexico. And from the opposite side, humanity's creation, the computer, metallic and lifeless, has been programmed to play chess, the human intellectual game par excellence and most likely will soon play better than any of its creators.

Humans are not likely to resign their position of intellectual supremacy without some anguish. Our self-image has had several setbacks before and we have been very slow to accept them. Once it was believed that the earth, humanity's planet, was at the center of the universe. When Galileo showed that this was not the case, he was thrown in jail. At the beginning of the twentieth century when Darwin showed that man was a relative of all the other creatures on this planet, he was attacked by those who disagreed. Now our intellect is under attack and we are attempting to defend it with arguments that are more emotional than substantive. In 1983, at the 4th World Computer Chess Championship, Bernard Zuckerman, a New York night owl and International Chess Master nicknamed "Zuck the book" because of his phenomenal knowledge of the openings, sat down at 3:00 A. M. to play BELLE a few speed games. Zuckerman asked Ken Thompson, BELLE's captain, whether he "owned BELLE's soul if I beat it ten in a row." Thompson smiled. Ten minutes later, BELLE won the first game. Thompson smiled to himself this time. Zuckerman fell silent, struggling for several more games, finishing two hours later with a hard-fought near-even score.

Let us also recount a fable that began, indirectly, with Mikhail Botvinnik, World Chess Champion for 12 years and one of the pioneers in the struggle to create a strong chess program. In 1960 Botvinnik lost his world crown to a brilliant young Grandmaster from Riga called Mikhail Tal. In the qualifying events that lead to a match for the World Championship, Tal had swept away all opposition, including such famous names in the chess world as Vassily Smyslov, Paul Keres, and Bobby Fischer. Tal had won the title match with Botvinnik in brilliant style and was hailed as a great new star in the chess firmament.

As he was leaving the playing hall on his great day of triumph, Tal noticed in the crowd thronging around him a wiry haired young man in thick glasses who was tugging at the new champion's jacket. Thinking that the young man was trying to congratulate him, Tal shook hands with him. "But you don't understand," said the young man. "I am a computer scientist at the university, and I can tell you for certain that within a generation, 30 years at the most, there will be a computer program that will play chess better than you." Tal was incredulous, as were the other fans who were jostling for autographs or struggling to have their picture taken with the new king of chess. How could this crazy looking youth be serious? Everyone began to laugh and within a few moments the young man had been taken away, later to be sent to a comfortable rest home on the shores of the Black Sea. There he would be able to avoid all the pressures of life that had so obviously deranged him, and he could while away the years reading the latest chess magazines and computer journals.

Almost everyone forgot about this crazy scientist, but not Tal. Every time something was published in the chess literature about computers, Tal would remember this young man and his crazy prophecy. As time went by computer programs became a little stronger. In 1977 one of them won the Minnesota Open Championship. Four years later another won the Mississippi State Championship. Occasionally grandmasters would drop a draw or even lose a game against a program in a simultaneous exhibition, but none of the programs was anywhere near to grandmaster strength. In 1983 there was a report in the American magazines that something called BELLE had been awarded the title of U. S. Master, but in America anything can happen. And then, near the end of 1988, Tal had an opportunity to see for himself how these computers played. He was invited to a tournament in Long Beach, California, together with many of his grandmaster colleagues. There was the ebullient Walter Browne, many times champion of the Unted States. There was the Englishman Tony Miles who once had the audacity to play 1 ... a7–a6 against Karpov's 1 e2–e4, and win the game. There was Bent Larsen, the Danish grandmaster who had been one of the most successful tournament players of all time. Tal watched as the DEEP THOUGHT computer demolished one opponent after another. Even Larsen was unable to survive against it. Only Browne could beat the electronic monster. And when the dust had cleared the first place in the tournament was shared by ... Tony Miles and DEEP THOUGHT!

One of the grandmasters who finished with fewer points than the computer was Tal, who immediately placed a call to that nice rest home on the Black Sea, demanding the release of the brilliant computer scientist who had been wrongly sent there 28 years earlier.

Well, it almost could have happened, couldn't it? Grandmasters and world champions have for years been claiming that computers would "never" rise to their lofty heights. Even as recently as the end of 1985 Kasparov doubted that it would happen in his lifetime. Now he feels that his mission in life during the latter half of the 1990s will be to defend man against the machine.

If prediction is a science, then the Elo system for rating players is the foundation stone in chess. Out of all of man's intellectual endeavours almost none offers such a convenient measure of merit as does chess. The Elo system, devised by Professor Arpad Elo of Brookfield, Wisconsin, assigns to each chess player on the tournament circuit a numerical rating to indicate his current strength or, more accurately, his level of performance in recent events. It is said that the average Elo rating of all those in the world who know how to play chess would be around 800. Most club players would be rated between 1400 and 2000. Anyone with a rating of 2200 in the United States* is automatically given the title of U.S. Master, while to become an International Master one needs to be at least 2450 strength and most grandmasters are 2550 or above. At the end of 1989 Gary Kasparov had just exceeded Bobby Fischer's all time high of 2785 on the international rating list, which corresponded to

---

* The versions of the Elo rating system used by the United States Chess Federation (USCF) in the USA and by FIDE, the International Chess Federation, differ. A player's rating on the USCF scale is usually 100 pointer higher than it would be on the international (FIDE) rating list. This discrepancy appears to become smaller near the top of the rating list but for the purposes of this chapter we shall assume that it remains constant. In this chapter we use USCF ratings as our basis and have converted Kasparov's international ratings to the USCF scale by adding 100 points.

a 2885 USCF rating. Kasparov's rating in the January 1990 list published by FIDE was 2800, equivalent to approximately 2900 on the USCF scale.

The rating system is based on the following simple principles. If your rating is X and you are playing in a tournament where the average rating of your opponents is Y, you are statistically expected to make a score which is related to X and Y. If your final score in the tournament exceeds your expectation your rating goes up. If you perform worse than expected it goes down.

Computer programs have been competing in human chess tournaments since 1967, when Greenblatt's MACHACK VI achieved a performance rating of 1640 at a tournament in the Boston area. By the end of 1985 the best performance rating achieved by a program had risen to 2530 — nearly the grandmaster level. This did not necessarily mean that the program in question, HITECH, was a consistent grandmaster level chess player, but it did mean that the program had shown itself capable of playing at a level commensurate with having the Grandmaster title. (In order to win a match against Kasparov a program merely needs to show itself capable of playing at the level of a 2911 rated player just once — in a match for the World Championship! A rating of at least 2911 is required to win a match against a 2900 rated player by the smallest possible margin, i.e., 12.5–11.5.)

Following earlier efforts by Ken Thompson and Monty Newborn to predict the future strength of chess programs based on their measured performances, David Levy, in 1986, plotted the progress that had been made since 1967, using the data below. Table 1.1 shows the best performance ratings achieved by chess programs in human tournaments in the indicated years, which covered the first two decades of computer participation in human events. For those years where no performance is indicated there were no computer results of significance.

Table 1.1 Progress of computer programs in rated human tournaments

Year	Program; Event(Score)	Perf. Rating
1967	MACHACK VI; Tournament in Massachusetts	1640
1974	CHESS 4.0; NW Univ. Winter Quarter Tourn. (4.5/6)	1730
1977	CHESS 4.5; Paul Masson Chess Classic, Sarasota (5/5)	2136
1977	CHESS 4.5; Minnesota Open Chess Championship (5/6)	2271
1980	CHESS 4.7; U. S. Amateur Team Championship (4/6)	2168
1981	CRAY BLITZ; Mississippi State Championship (5/5)	2258
1983	BELLE; United States Open Championship (8.5/12)	2363
1985	HITECH; Open tournament in Pittsburgh	2530

The data in Table 1.1 was fitted to a least squares straight line and is shown on the bottom of this page with the points encircled. The equation for the line is:

$$\text{Rating} = 49.2 \times (\text{year} - 1900) - 1697$$

This indicates an average increase in performance of almost 50 Elo points per year and extrapolates to a computer performance of 2911 or better in the year 1994.

When this graph was shown at the 1986 World Computer Chess Championship in Cologne, West Germany, the general view of the audience was predictable. "It will not continue like this. The graph will flatten out." Was this sound analysis or wishful thinking of the chess cognoscenti? We can go some way towards answering this question when we add the performance by DEEP THOUGHT when two years later in 1988 it shared first place at Long Beach. That result, a performance rating of 2745, is the square at the top of the

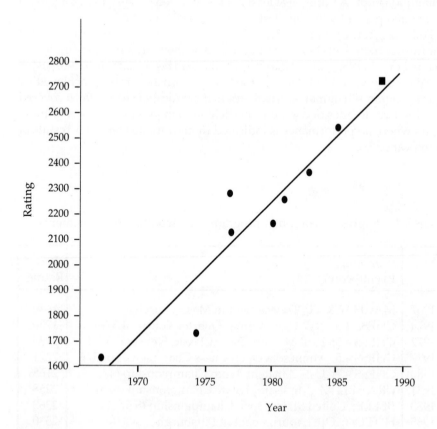

Figure 1.1 Best performance ratings of chess programs

graph, surpassing the expected achievement level for 1988 by 112 points! So much for the chess cognoscenti.

Whether or not 1994 will be the year is still an open question. It was certainly IBM's target when the company hired Feng–hsiung Hsu and some of his DEEP THOUGHT colleagues in the summer of 1989. In order to gauge the opinion of many leading computer science experts and some strong human chess players, your first author conducted a survey during the 1989 World Computer Chess Championship in Edmonton. The question was, "In what year do you think a chess program will be able to defeat the human World Champion?" Here are the answers. Excluding Cahlander, the mean of the predictions is the year 2005.

Table 1.2 Estimates of the year in which a computer will defeat the world human chess champion.

Year	Names
1992	Gyula Horvath; Monty Newborn.
1993	John McCarthy.
1994	I. M. Hans Berliner; Marty Hirsch; Feng–hsiung Hsu.
1995	Murray Campbell; Larry Kaufmann; David Kittinger; I. M. Danny Kopec, Donald Michie; David Slate; I. M. Mike Valvo.
1997	John Stanbeck.
1998	Kevin O'Connell.
1999	Ed Felton; Tom Pronk; Sidney Samole; Claude Shannon; Jos Uiterwijk.
2000	Robert Hyatt; G. M. Kevin Spraggett; Victor Vikhrev; Jaap van den Herik.
2001	Jurg Nievergelt; Mark Taylor.
2002	I. M. Julio Kaplan.
2005	Richard Lang; Pierre Nolot; Ard van Bergen.
2008	Harry Nelson.
2010	Don Dailey; Ossi Weiner.
2011	Lars Hjorth.
2013	Tony Scherzer.
2014	I. M. David Levy.
2020	Tony Marsland.
2025	Dap Hartmann.
2030	Franz Morsch.
2040	Jonathan Schaeffer.
2050	Harm Bakker.
2056	Helmut Horacek.
NEVER	David Cahlander.

World Champions Meet in New York: DEEP THOUGHT versus Kasparov

Gary Kasparov loves to play chess. He is also good at it — so good that many consider him the greatest player in the history of the game. He is better than his mentor Botvinnik, who held the world title for a total of 12 years, better than Fischer, the most frequent comparison, and certainly better than the best computer program. Until last year there was no question whether the human world champion, now Kasparov or before him Karpov, would find the best computer program even a match. But the incredible recent success of DEEP THOUGHT in games against grandmasters has raised the question of just how good computers are, whether they are in fact ready to challenge the human World Champion, how much better they are going to get, and at what rate might they be expected to improve. Kasparov would not let the world down by avoiding his important role of shedding light on these intriguing questions.

Figure 1.2 Gary Kasparov talking with Robert Byrne before playing DEEP THOUGHT, New York, October 1989

Strong chess players have frequently declined opportunities to play computers for a variety of reasons, but not Kasparov. With his intense love of the game and his fiercely competitive nature, Kasparov was more than willing to pit his talent against the world's best chess machine. Kasparov probably would be first to line up for a match with a Martian who happened to land on earth claiming he/it/she was that planet's best. And so when Shelby Lyman, New York chess promoter, approached Kasparov with an offer of $10,000 to take on DEEP THOUGHT, the champion accepted. On October 22, 1989, 400 chess enthusiasts and 100 people from the media gathered in the New York Academy of Art to see the human World Champion sit down to a two-game challenge match with the computer World Champion. It was the largest media event in chess since the Fischer—Spassky championship in Iceland in 1972. Grandmaster Robert Byrne, chess columnist for *The New York Times* and one of DEEP THOUGHT's recent sparring partners, was there as was Grandmaster Lev Alburt, a former Soviet citizen and now one of America's top players. Byrne had played DEEP THOUGHT five games in the months leading up to this event, three speed chess games and two games at tournament speeds. He lost one speed chess game and drew two. The two more slowly played games were split. The loss to DEEP THOUGHT was played on August 23, 1989 and appeared in his column in *The New York Times* on September 26, 1989. In a return game played on September 2, 1989, Byrne was victorious. Byrne, in his younger days, was ranked among the top players in the United States; his current USCF rating is 2548.

Game 1
White: **DEEP THOUGHT**
Black: **Byrne**
Carnegie Mellon University, August 23, 1989
Sicilian Defense

**1 e2–e4 c7–c5 2 c2–c3 b7–b6 3 d2–d4 Bc8–b7 4 Bf1–d3 e7–e6 5 Bc1–e3 Ng8–f6
6 Nb1–d2 Nb8–c6 7 a2–a3 d7–d6 8 Qd1–f3 g7–g6 9 Ng1–e2 Bf8–g7 10 O–O
O–O 11 b2–b4 c5xd4 12 c3xd4 Qd8–d7 13 Ra1–c1 Ra8–c8**
Byrne points out that his 13 ... Ra8–c8 "was not accurate; 13 ... Rf8–c8 would have kept the rooks united. Thus, quite soon, after 16 ... Nf6–e8, the black rook was out of action. DEEP THOUGHT's 17 Bd3–b5 cost Black more time in retreat."

**14 h2–h3 Nc6–e7 15 Be3–g5 Rc8xc1 16 Rf1xc1 Nf6–e8 17 Bd3–b5 Qd7–d8
18 Qf3–g3 h7–h6 19 Bg5–e3 d6–d5 20 f2–f3 Ne8–d6 21 Bb5–d3 b6–b5
22 Rc1–c5**
This seizes "on its one chance to keep the initiative," Byrne observed. "Of course, it ran the danger, after 22 ... a7–a6 23 Be3–f4 Nd6–c4 24 Bd3xc4 d5xc4, of having the rook trapped, but I could not figure out how to bring that off."

22 ... a7–a6 23 Be3–f4 Nd6–c4 24 Bd3xc4 d5xc4 25 Bf4–d6 Rf8–e8 26 Rc5–c7
Bb7–a8 27 Rc7–c5 Ne7–c8 28 Bd6–e5 Bg7xe5 29 Qg3xe5 Nc8–d6 30 a3–a4
Qd8–d7 31 Qe5–f4 Kg8–g7 32 h3–h4 Ba8–c6 33 d4–d5 Bc6–a8 34 d5xe6
Re8xe6 35 a4xb5 a6xb5 36 Nd2–f1

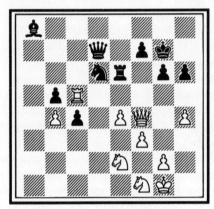

Figure 1.3 After 36 Nd2–f1

36 ... Nd6xe4 37 f3xe4 Re6xe4 38 Qf4–f2 c4–c3 39 Ne2xc3 Re4xb4 40 Nf1–e3
Ba8–c6 41 Ne3–d5 Bc6xd5 42 Nc3xd5 Rb4–b1+ 43 Kg1–h2 Qd7–d6+
44 g2–g3 Qd6–e5 45 Nd5–c3 Qe5–e1 46 Qf2–d4+ Kg7–g8 47 Nc3xb1 Qe1–e2+
48 Kh2–g1 **Black resigns.**
Byrne began to have serious problems when "DEEP THOUGHT put the
queenside under pressure with 30 a3–a4! and then broke open the center with
33 d4–d5! After 36 Nd2–f1, I could find no antidote to the coming Nf1–e3
followed by Ne2–c3 and Ne3–d5." He then gambled that DEEP THOUGHT
could be "shaken up or flustered or bluffed," but he failed with 36 . . . Nd6xe4
37 f3xe4 Re6xe4 38 Qf4–f2 c4–c3 which he hoped would "get enough pawns
off the board to draw various possible endings that might arrise."

Game 2
White: **Byrne**
Black: **DEEP THOUGHT**
Carnegie Mellon University, September 2, 1989
Queen's Gambit Accepted

1 d2–d4 d7–d5 2 c2–c4 d5xc4 3 Ng1–f3 Ng8–f6 4 Qd1–a4+ c7–c6 5 Qa4xc4
Bc8–f5 6 Nb1–c3 Nb8–d7 7 g2–g3 Nd7–b6 8 Qc4–b3 Bf5–e6 9 Qb3–d1
Nb6–d5 10 Bf1–g2 Nd5xc3 11 b2xc3 Qd8–a5 12 Qd1–c2 Nf6–e4 13 Bc1–b2
Qa5–f5 14 Qc2–a4 a7–a6 15 O–O Qf5–h5 16 Rf1–e1 Qh5–f5 17 c3–c4 f7–f6
18 Qa4–b4 O–O–O 19 Ra1–c1 Be6–f7 20 Qb4–b6 g7–g5 21 d4–d5 c6–c5

22 Bb2–c3 e7–e5 23 d5xe6 Bf7xe6 24 Rc1–b1 Rd8–d7 25 Nf3–d2 Ne4xc3
26 Bg2xb7+ Rd7xb7 27 Qb6–c6+ Kc8–d8 28 Rb1xb7 Be6–d7 29 Rb7xd7+
Qf5xd7 30 Qc6xf6+ Kd8–e8 31 Qf6xc3 Bf8–g7 32 Qc3–e3+ Qd7–e7
33 Nd2–e4 Bg7–d4 34 Qe3–d3 Rh8–f8 35 e2–e3 Bd4–e5 36 Qd3–d5 Rf8–f7
37 Ne4xc5 Qe7–d6 38 Qd5–a8+ Ke8–e7 39 Nc5–e4 Qd6–d3 40 Ne4xg5 Rf7–f5
41 Qa8–g8 Black resigns.

Kasparov and DEEP THOUGHT's programmers agreed that their games
would be played with each side having 90 minutes of clock time. This
format would ensure that there would be no adjournments and that games
would last at most three hours. This rate of play, slightly faster than in most
major tournaments, was to the advantage of the computer. They have performed relatively better at speed chess than at slower speeds, a phenomenon
that became apparent in the mid-seventies when CHESS 4.9 started to
beat masters in five-minute games but had less success in longer games.
Consistent with this pattern, beginning in late 1988 and continuing for the next
five months, Mike Valvo, with a USCF rating of 2488, defeated DEEP
THOUGHT in two postal games played at a rate of one move every three days,
a better performance than might be expected of Valvo when playing at usual
tournament speeds.

The chess community might learn something from the format of this match:
games of major tournaments should be played with the same time controls
used by Kasparov and DEEP THOUGHT. The slower speeds currently in
vogue benefit no one. Players get tired, adjudications are often incorrect, and
the media will not cover a competition that goes on indefinitely. The three-
hour format can be electrifying. Professional tennis, when it introduced the
tie-breaker, suddenly became a much more popular sport than ever before.

In fairness to Hsu and company — Thomas Anantharaman, Mike Browne,
Murray Campbell, and Andreas Nowatzyk — they realized DEEP THOUGHT
had little chance against Kasparov. They would have been more than satisfied
with a draw but understood even that was a longshot. Certainly they wanted
to play the match, but they would have preferred to wait until their new
version, which is expected to be ten times as fast, was ready. Hsu and
Campbell had only recently left CMU to join IBM's Thomas J. Watson
Research Center in Yorktown Heights, New York where they were hired to
complete the job they so successfully started as students, building a chess
machine better than any human. They had barely settled in at IBM, and their
chess machine was still at CMU, giving them two additional reasons for
wanting to wait. According to Gina Campbell, Murray's wife, Hsu, the
ultimate workaholic, had only recently found time to acquire a bed for his new
apartment near IBM. But the World Champion is hard to pin down to a
commitment, and the DEEP THOUGHT team realized it could not pass up
this historic opportunity.

Kasparov held a press conference at 12:00 noon, one hour before the
scheduled start of the match. He answered questions while Hsu and Campbell

sat alongside, listening and occasionally typing on a terminal connected to their computer at CMU. With the opportunity of asking the human champion all the questions they had always wanted to, and with Kasparov so obliging in his answers, Hsu and Campbell were completely forgotten by the media. Nobody thought of asking them a single question! Their computer was actually three SUN computers linked together, each housing Hsu's specially-designed dual-processor VLSI chess circuit. The dual-processor circuit shared the search of branches at positions deep in the tree, while the three SUNs divided up the search as dictated by the conventional principal variation splitting algorithm. Each dual-processor searched approximately 720,000 chess positions per second; the overall system searched 3 x 720,000 chess positions per second — somewhere between 200,000,000 and 500,000,000 per move!

At the press conference, it quickly became clear that Kasparov had done his homework. He admitted that he had reviewed about fifty of DEEP THOUGHT's games and felt confident he understood the machine. When questioned on the program's strength, he credited it with a 2480–2500 FIDE rating, considerably less than his own 2800 rating, and he estimated that he would garner 8 or 9 points in a ten game match. He found it played an

Figure 1.4 Gary Kasparov at press conference before the start of his match with DEEP THOUGHT, New York, October, 1989

aggressive, active game. Kasparov granted that some day a computer might outplay him, but he believes the day is not just over the horizon. "I don't know how we can exist knowing that there exists something mentally stronger than us," he said. He contended that the best human will improve when the day comes that a computer really challenges him.

The audience was 100 percent behind Kasparov — well, almost 100 percent. Of the 500 or so present, there were four DEEP THOUGHT supporters sitting in the front row, thanks to Lyman who had reserved seats for them so the media could film the few strange birds rooting for the computer. In addition to your second author, Hans Berliner had come from Pittsburgh, Jonathan Schaeffer happened to be passing through New York on his way to Boston, and Mike Valvo who lives in New Jersey dropped in for the first game. Kasparov said after the match that he missed having any interaction of energy with his opponent, but that the enthusiasm of the audience partly made up for this.

The games took place on the first floor of the academy amidst paintings and pieces of sculpture, providing a more intimate and esthetic environment than the usual sterile hotel meeting rooms where chess tournaments are often held; a kibitzing room was set up on the second floor where most of the audience gathered. Lyman acted as moderator with GM Edmar Mednis assisting him. A communication line connected the terminal at the game board with one in the kibitzing room upstairs. Photographers were permitted to photo Kasparov during the first eight minutes of each game. After that, silence was required.

Game 1
White: **DEEP THOUGHT**
Black: **Kasparov**
New York, October 23, 1989
Sicilian Defense

1 e2–e4 c7–c5 2 c2–c3
This variation of the Sicilian was used with great success by BELLE in the early 1980s at a time when computers were beginning to score victories over masters. It is not clear whether this line is sufficiently aggressive to be appropriate against someone of Kasparov's strength. Kasparov had seen DEEP THOUGHT play this line in many games, including the one against Byrne.

2 ... e7–e6 3 d2–d4 d7–d5 4 e4xd5 e6xd5 5 Ng1–f3 Bf8–d6 6 Bc1–e3
The bishop never moves again.

6 ... c5–c4
The champion gains space on the queenside with this move; Black already has a space advantage on the kingside with two strong bishops controlling many important squares.

7 b2–b3 c4xb3 8 a2xb3
This is DEEP THOUGHT's first move out of book.

8 ... Ng8–e7 9 Nb1–a3 Nb8–c6 10 Na3–b5
DEEP THOUGHT goes on a fishing expedition. Wasting a tempo against someone of Kasparov's strength can only lead to trouble.

10 ... Bd6–b8 11 Bf1–d3 Bc8–f5 12 c3–c4
Computers handle passed pawns terribly, especially when there are many pieces on the board to distract them. White's 12 c3–c4 invites a passed a–pawn, and in addition, weakens the b4 square. But the real problem here for DEEP THOUGHT is a bug in the castling code. From here until move 17, DEEP THOUGHT has several chances to castle but other moves are given priority. The bug caused DEEP THOUGHT to want to castle, but only at the end of the principal continuation. This bug remained in the program until after the first round of the 20th ACM North American Computer Chess Championship in Reno three weeks later when DEEP THOUGHT defeated PHOENIX after finding itself in a lost position midway through the game. The bug was related to a problem in the parallel code. When DEEP THOUGHT ran on one computer, the problem did not appear; but when running on more than one computer the bug materialized. A second bug in the parallel code also surfaced in this match: the program did not always choose the best move found by the processors. Which moves were adversely affected, however, is not clear.

12 ... O–O 13 Ra1–a4??
This is a strange way to protect b4, but computers have strange minds. Hsu and Campbell credit this move to the castling bug. Kasparov, meanwhile, continues with his systematic development.

13 ... Qd8–d7 14 Nb5–c3
DEEP THOUGHT thinks Black has a small edge at this point.

14 ... Bb8–c7 15 Bd3xf5 Qe7xf5 16 Nf3–h4
This is in the spirit of the earlier rook move. Campbell's immediate reaction was that this was also caused by a bug.

16 ... Qf5–d7
Black's pieces are now all on active squares. White has yet to castle, has placed one rook on an unbelievably bad square, one knight on almost as bad a square, and has traded off its good bishop.

17 O–O
The audience applauded!

17 ... Ra8–d8 18 Rf1–e1

DEEP THOUGHT imagines White has a small advantage now. In an interview after the game, Kasparov indicated the game was wrapped up after the next two moves.

18 ... Rf8–e8 19 c4–c5

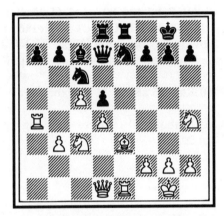

Figure 1.5 After 19 c4–c5

19 ... Bc7–a5
According to Kasparov, this was a particularly good move.

20 Qd1–d3 a7–a6 21 h2–h3 Ba5xc3 22 Qd3xc3 Ne7–f5 23 Nh4xf5 Qd7xf5
Black's rooks are now very strong and it has a good knight while White has a weak bishop and rooks that are poorly placed.

24 Ra4–a2 Re8–e6 25 Ra2–e2 Rd8–e8 26 Qc3–d2 f7–f6 27 Qd2–c3 h7–h5
Kasparov is gradually pulling the noose tighter.

28 b3–b4 Re8–e7 29 Kg1–h1
DEEP THOUGHT cannot find a move to improve White's position and decides to mark time in characteristically computer fashion. Kasparov continues with his theme:

29 ... g7–g5 30 Kh1–g1 g5–g4 31 h3–h4 Re6–e4 32 Qc3–b2 Nc6–a7 33 Qb2–d2 Re4–e6 34 Qd2–c1 Na7–b5 35 Qc1–d2
DEEP THOUGHT, the eternal optimist, thinks the game is about even.

35 ... Nb5–a3 36 Qd2–d1 Kg8–f7 37 Qd1–b3 Na3–c4 38 Kg1–h2 Re6–e4 39 g2–g3

Turning pessimistic, DEEP THOUGHT now concludes that White is down
about a half pawn.

39 ... Qf5–f3 40 b4–b5 a6–a5
Kasparov has finally created a passed a-pawn that eventually will be pushed
and lead to DEEP THOUGHT's demise. DEEP THOUGHT has about 34
minutes left while Kasparov has about 20.

**41 c5–c6 f6–f5 42 c6xb7 Re7xb7 43 Kh2–g1 f5–f4 44 g3xf4 g4–g3 45 Qb3–d1
Rb7–e7 46 b5–b6 g3xf2+ 47 Re2xf2 Qf3xd1 48 Re1xd1 Re4xe3**
A resignation is in order at this point but DEEP THOUGHT is programmed
to play on until it is behind 7 points (a rook and two pawns).

**49 Rf2–g2 Nc4xb6 50 Rg2–g5 a5–a4 51 Rg5xh5 a4–a3 52 Rd1–d2 Re3–e2
White resigns.**
Kasparov finished with about 10 minutes showing on his clock. DEEP
THOUGHT had about 20.

Figure 1.6 Feng–Hsiung Hsu enjoying watching DEEP THOUGHT — or
maybe the sculpture — during the DEEP THOUGHT—Kasparov match

Between games, Hsu and Campbell reprogrammed DEEP THOUGHT, at Jonathan Schaeffer's suggestion, to take slightly more time on early moves in the game. Kasparov's style in the first game was conservative and methodical. He never exposed himself, took no chances, and one step at a time, nailed DEEP THOUGHT into a coffin. The game lacked the dramatic, but Kasparov was devastating in his simplicity and clarity. The game left Kasparov knowing DEEP THOUGHT was no serious threat. In Kasparov's words, "after such a loss, no human would come back for more." But DEEP THOUGHT did come back for Game 2 after its programmers had had an early dinner.

Game 2
White: **Kasparov**
Black: **DEEP THOUGHT**
New York, October 23, 1989
Queen's Gambit Accepted

1 d2–d4
Kasparov has been using 1 d2–d4 as his primary weapon against the world's leading players, and thus he implicitly says here that he is all business.

1 ... d7–d5 2 c2–c4 d5xc4
Not a bad line for the computer, following the line played against Byrne. Since computers are naturally greedy, it makes good sense to use book lines consistent with this behavior. But DEEP THOUGHT's book is small, and the program's desire to hold the pawn quickly leads to trouble.

3 e2–e4
This is a sharp line that Kasparov knows well, and is more aggressive than Byrne's 3 Ng1–f3.

3 ... Nb8–c6 4 Ng1–f3 Bc8–g4 5 d4–d5 Nc6–e5
This is DEEP THOUGHT's first move out of book. It carried out an 11-ply search, concluding White was down about a tenth of a pawn.

6 Nb1–c3 c7–c6
The audience groaned when this move was made. One move out of book and the castling bug reappeared to haunt DEEP THOUGHT. Against someone at Kasparov's level, this move was sufficient to lose the game. DEEP THOUGHT met HITECH three weeks later at the 20th ACM North American Computer Chess Championship in Reno with the bug corrected. Berliner, having witnessed DEEP THOUGHT's 6 ... c7–c6 fiasco, had made extensive additions to HITECH's book anticipating that the two programs might meet and that HITECH might then waltz DEEP THOUGHT down the same or a similar garden path. This time DEEP THOUGHT played 6 ... Ng8–f6 and HITECH

was booked to the hilt on this alternative. The game continued: 7 Bc1–f4 Nf6–d7 8 Qd1–a4 Ne5xf3+ 9 g2xf3 Bg4xf3 10 Rh1–g1 a7–a6 11 Qa4xc4 Ra8–c8 12 Rg1–g3 Bf3–h5 13 Bf1–h3 f7–f6 14 Qc4–b4 (White's first move out of book and it wastes valuable time moving its queen. Instead *14 Bh3–e6* leaves Black in a very cramped position.) 14 ... g7–g5 15 Bf4–e3 b7–b5 16 Qb4–d4 (Once again HITECH passes up *16 Bh3–e6*, although Black can gain some freedom with *16 ... Nd7–e5* threatening *17 ... Ne5–d3+*) 16 ... c7–c5 17 d5xc6 Rc8xc6 18 Rg3xg5 f6xg5 19 Qd4xh8 Nd7–f6 (HITECH has seen the advantages gained by its book dissolve in six moves. White's queen is out of play while Black's queen, rook and bishop are well placed. DEEP THOUGHT is threatening *20 ... Qd8–d3, 21 ... Rc6xc3* followed by *22 ... Qd3–e2* mate) 20 Bh3–f1 Qd8–a5 21 Be3–d4 Qa5–b4! 22 Bd4xf6 Rc6xf6 23 Ra1–d1 Bh5xd1 24 a2–a3 Qb4xb2 25 Nc3xd1 Qb2xa3 26 Qh8xh7 Qa3–a5+ 27 Ke1–e2 Rf6–d6 28 Qh7–h5+ Ke8–d8 29 Qh5xg5 Bf8–h6 30 Qg5–g8+ Kd8–c7 White resigns.

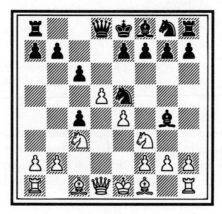

Figure 1.7 After 6 ... c7–c6

7 Bc1–f4 Ne5–g6 8 Bf4–e3 c6xd5
DEEP THOUGHT's scoring function returns a value of –0.29 pawns for this position. Kasparov thought for much longer than usual on 8 Bf4–e3, but replies almost instantaneously to DEEP THOUGHT's 8 ... c6xd5.

9 e4xd5 Ng6–e5
Black falls futher behind in development while trying to hang on to its c-pawn.

10 Qd1–d4
The first hard punch has been thrown in the guise of a pawn sacrifice. Black must reply 10 ... Ne5xf3+ 11 g2xf3 Bg4xf3 attacking the rook, but this leaves White with an even larger lead in development. Black cannot make up for the sins of past moves at this point, and decides to go deeper into the hole.

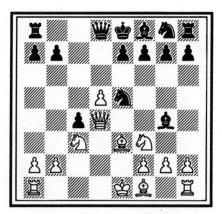

Figure 1.8 After 10 Qd1–d4

10 ... Ne5xf3+ 11 g2xf3 Bg4xf3

11 ... Bg4–d7 would be more circumspect.

12 Bf1xc4

Kasparov is threatening 13 Bc4–b5+, leaving DEEP THOUGHT in deep trouble.

12 ... Qd8–d6

DEEP THOUGHT naively thinks White is down a quarter of a pawn, while Kasparov prepares, and the audience eagerly awaits, the knockout blow. The alternative, 12 ... a7–a6, is met by 13 Rh1–g1 with an overwhelming advantage for White. For example, 13 ... Ng8–f6 14 Bc4–b3! b7–b5 15 a2–a4!, or 13 ... e7–e6 14 d5xe6 f7xe6 15 Qd4–f4 Bf3–d5 (*15 ... Bf3–h5 16 Bc4xe6*) 16 Bc4xd5 e6xd5 17 O–O–O.

13 Nc3–b5 Qd6–f6

Computers are good at encouraging exchanges when they find themselves in trouble. Note that 13 ... Qd6–d7 is refuted by 14 Nb5xa7, threatening 15 Bc4–b5.

14 Qd4–c5

The audience continues to expect mate shortly as Kasparov hammers away.

14 ... Qf6–b6

If 14 ... Bf3xh1 15 Nb5–c7+ Ke8–d8 16 Nc7xa8 Qb6–d6 17 Qc5xa7! with a killing attack.

15 Qc5–a3 e7–e6

DEEP THOUGHT now calculates that it is down the equivalent of two pawns. After only 15 moves the knockout seems imminent. Kasparov has two choices here: 16 Qa3–a4 Qb6–d8 or the line he followed.

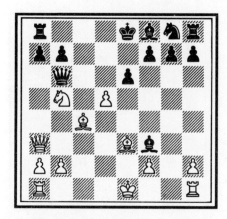

Figure 1.9 After 15 ... e7–e6

16 Nb5–c7+ Qb6xc7
Or 16 ... Ke8–d8 17 Qa3xf8+ Kd8xc7 18 Be3xb6+.

17 Bc4–b5+ Qc7–c6 18 Bb5xc6+ b7xc6 19 Be3–c5 Bf8xc5
If 19 ... Bf3xh1 20 Bc5xf8, threatening 21 Bf8xg7.

20 Qa3xf3 Bc5–b4+
DEEP THOUGHT finally manages one harmless lick at the champion's chin.
This is the only time Kasparov was placed in check in the two games.

21 Ke1–e2 c6xd5
Kasparov is ahead a queen for a knight, bishop and two pawns, but Black's
pieces have yet to develop. To DEEP THOUGHT's credit, it managed to
escape mate here. Certainly Kasparov would have liked to have capped his
performance with such a finale.

**22 Qf3–g4 Bb4–e7 23 Rh1–c1 Ke8–f8 24 Rc1–c7 Be7–d6 25 Rc7–b7 Ng8–f6
26 Qg4–a4 a7–a5 27 Ra1–c1 h7–h6 28 Rc1–c6 Nf6–e8 29 b2–b4 Bd6xh2
30 b4xa5 Kf8–g8 31 Qa4–b4 Bh2–d6 32 Rd6xe6 Ne8xd6 33 Rb7–b8+ Ra8xb8
34 Qb4xb8+ Kg8–h7 35 Qb8xd6 Rh8–c8 36 a2–a4 Rc8–c4 37 Qd6–d7 Black
resigns.**

Kasparov received a standing ovation for a job well done; the human race had
been given a reprieve. What did the match teach us? Certainly, Kasparov is
the better player, but DEEP THOUGHT is better than these games show. In
itself, the castling bug was sufficient to cost DEEP THOUGHT both games,
and the bug that caused nonoptimal moves to be selected didn't help either.
Furthermore, while Kasparov was familiar with DEEP THOUGHT's play,
Hsu and company hadn't taken adequate time to prepare an opening book for
Kasparov, something absolutely necessary next time.

Figure 1.10 Gary Kasparov in good spirits following his second victory over
DEEP THOUGHT, New York, October 1989

Karpov Struggles to Survive DEEP THOUGHT's Attack

A few months after the Kasparov—DEEP THOUGHT match it was the turn
of another great super-Grandmaster of the present era, Anatoly Karpov, who
had reigned as World Chess Champion from 1975 to 1985. Karpov had won
the title in 1975 by default when Bobby Fischer failed to defend his title. In
1985 he lost the title to Kasparov after the two giants had battled in Moscow
for 72 games over a 229 day period. Since giving up his title, Karpov has
clearly remained the world's second strongest player. His FIDE rating is over
2700.

Karpov took on DEEP THOUGHT in a one game encounter at Harvard
University, on February 2, 1990. To be fair to Karpov he had arrived in the
United States only the evening before the game, not having slept for the
previous 24 hours. To compensate for this state of fatigue Karpov insisted on
having White. The rate of play agreed upon was all moves in one hour by each
player. This was more to DEEP THOUGHT's advantage than the typically
slower rates used in most major games.

White: **Karpov**
Black: **DEEP THOUGHT**
Harvard University, February 2, 1990
Caro-Kann Defense

1 e2–e4 c7–c6 2 d2–d4 d7–d5 3 Nb1–d2 g7–g6 4 c2–c3 Bf8–g7 5 e4–e5
Another possibility is 5 Bf1–d3, or equivalently 5 e4xd5 c6xd5 6 Bf1–d3.

5 ... f7–f6!
An excellent move, and an unusual one for a computer to play. At the cost of
creating a slight weakening in its kingside pawn structure DEEP THOUGHT
immediately attacks the head of White's central pawn chain.

6 f2–f4 Ng8–h6 7 Ng1–f3?!
This move was criticized by the spectators and by DEEP THOUGHT, all of
whom considered 7 Nd2–f3 to be best, followed by Bf1–d3 and Ng1–e2. After
the move played, Karpov's knight does not have a great future.

7 ... O–O 8 Bf1–e2 f6xe5 9 f4xe5 c6–c5! 10 Nd2–b3
If 10 d4xc5 Nh6–g4 gives Black an active game.

10 ... c5xd4 11 c3xd4 Nb8–c6 12 O–O Qd8–b6 13 Kg1–h1 a7–a5! 14 a2–a4
Probably better was 14 Nb3–c5. Karpov's move weakens b3 and b2.

14 ... Bc8–f5 15 Bc1–g5 Bf5–e4 16 Nb3–c5
This move is active but perhaps not best. The young GM Patrick Wolff
suggested 16 Be2–b5. After the text move Black may have a slight edge.

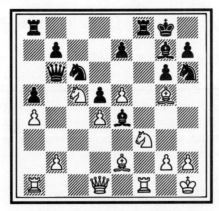

Figure 1.11 After 16 Nb3–c5

16 ... Qb6xb2?!
True to the nature of computer programs, DEEP THOUGHT grabs a pawn.

Instead the program could have played 16 ... Nh6–f5!, and if 17 Nc5–d7 Qb6xb2 18 Nd7xf8 Nc6xd4. Although Black is a down a rook for two pawns, he threatens 19 ... Nd4–b3, 19 ... Nd4xe2 as well as simply capturing the knight on f8.

17 Nc5xe4 d5xe4 18 Ra1–b1 Qb2–a3
Not 18 ... Qb2–c3?? 19 Rb1–b3, trapping the queen. Also bad is 18 ... Qb2–a2 because of 19 Nf3–d2.

19 Bg5–c1 Qa3–c3 20 Bc1–d2 Qc3–a3 21 Bd2–c1 Qa3–c3
Karpov has been repeating moves to gain time on the clock.

22 Rb1–b3 Qc3–a1 23 Be2–c4+ Kg8–h8 24 Bc1xh6! Qa1xd1 25 Bh6xg7+ Kh8xg7 26 Rf1xd1 e4xf3 27 g2xf3
Karpov could have tried for more with 27 Rb3xb7, putting the rook on the seventh rank. The computer's next move prevents that idea.

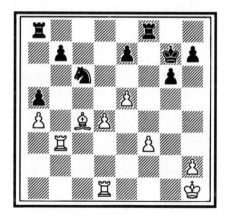

Figure 1.12 After 27 g2xf3

27 ... Ra8–a7!!
Although the spectators criticized this move, Karpov said after the game that it was the program's only chance.

28 Bc4–d5 Rf8–d8 29 Rb3–b5 Ra7–a6!
Intending to equalize with 30 ... Nc6–a7 31 Bd5xb7 Na7xb5 32 Bb7xa6 Rd8xd4.

**30 Bd5–c4 Ra6–a7 31 Bc4–d5 Ra7–a6 32 Rb5–c5 Rd8–d7 33 Kh1–g2 Ra6–b6!
34 Bd5xc6 b7xc6 35 Kg2–f2!**
If 35 Rc5xa5 Rb6–b4 equalizing.

35 ... Rd7–d5 36 Rc5xd5 c6xd5 37 Rd1–c1 Rb6–b4 38 Kf2–e3 Rb4xa4
38 ... Rb4–b3+ 39 Ke3–e2 Rb3–b4 also leads to a draw. White must submit to repetition of position since he cannot afford to give up his d-pawn.

39 Rc1–c5 e7–e6 40 Rc5–c7+ Kg7–g8 41 Rc7–e7 Ra4–a3+ 42 Ke3–f4 Ra3–d3
43 Re7xe6 Rd3xd4+ 44 Kf4–g5 Kg8–f7 45 Re6–a6

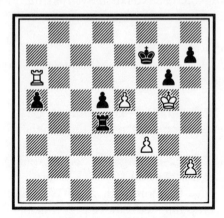

Figure 1.13 After 45 Re6–a6

45 ... a5–a4!?
DEEP THOUGHT could force an easy draw by 45 ... h7–h6+ 46 Kg5xh6
Rd4–h4+ 47 Kh6–g5 Rh4–h5+ 48 Kg5–f4 Rh5–f5+ followed by 49 ... Rf5xe5,
but the program thought that it held the advantage and so 45 ... a5–a4 is a
winning try!

46 f3–f4 h7–h6+ 47 Kg5–g4 Rd4–c4?
47 ... g6–g5 would draw, because it forces the exchange of pawns. Now
Karpov is able to mobilize his kingside pawns.

48 h2–h4 Rc4–d4 49 Ra6–f6+ Kf7–g7 50 Rf6–a6 Kg7–f7 51 h4–h5 g6xh5+?
A better drawing try was 51 ... g6–g5, though Karpov believed that he would
still have winning chances.

**52 Kg4–f5 Kf7–g7 53 Ra6–a7+ Kg7–f8 54 e5–e6 Rd4–e4 55 Ra7–d7 Re4–c4
56 Rd7xd5 h5–h4 57 Rd5–d3 Kf8–e7 58 Rd3–d7+ Ke7–f8 59 Rd7–h7 h6–h5
60 Kf5–e5 h4–h3 61 f4–f5 Kf8–g8 62 Rh7xh5 a4–a3 63 Rh5xh3 a3–a2**
63 ... Rc4–a4 would not save the game: 64 e6–e7 Kg8–f7 65 Rh3–h7+ and
66 f5–f6 etc.

64 Rh3–a3 Rc4–c5+ 65 Ke5–f6 Black resigns.
A remarkable game. DEEP THOUGHT outplayed Karpov in the opening and
early middle game, and had more than one way to force an "easy draw" in the
endgame.

After this encounter can anyone really doubt that one day the likes of Karpov
and Kasparov will be taking lessons from IBM?

2

The Early Ideas

Babbage

It is not completely out of order to commence a historical survey of the early years of computer chess with Charles Babbage (1792–1871). Babbage's career was remarkable for both the sheer quantity and the originality of his ideas in mathematics, the mechanics of science, and various related fields. He was interested in chess as a rather weak player, and included in his biographical writings an account of some friendly games that he played while a student at Cambridge.

It was around the 1840s that Babbage became interested in the possibility of making a machine play a game of skill. In *The Life of a Philosopher* he wrote:

After much consideration I selected for my test the contrivance of a machine that should be able to play a game of purely intellectual skill successfully; such as tit-tat-to, drafts, chess, etc.

I endeavoured to ascertain the opinions of persons in every class of life and of all ages, whether they thought it required human reason to play games of skill. The almost constant answer was in the affirmative. Some supported this view of the case by observing, that if it were otherwise, then an automaton could play such games. A few of those who had considerable acquaintance with mathematical science allowed the possibility of machinery being capable of such work; but they most stoutly denied the possibility of contriving such machinery on account of the myriads of combinations which even the simplest games included.

On the first part of my inquiry I soon arrived at a demonstration that every game of skill is susceptible of being played by an automaton.

Further consideration showed that if *any position* of the men upon the board were assumed (whether that position were possible or impossible), then if the automaton could make the first move rightly, he must be able to win the game, always supposing that, under the given position of the men, that conclusion were possible.

Whatever move the automaton made, another move would be made by his adversary. Now this altered state of the board is *one* amongst the *many positions* of the men in which, by the previous paragraph, the automaton was supposed capable of acting.

Hence the question is reduced to that of making the best move under any possible combinations of positions of the men.

Now the several questions the automaton has to consider are of this nature:

1. Is the position of the men, as placed before him on the board, a possible position, that is, one which is consistent with the rules of the game?
2. If so, has the automaton himself already lost the game?
3. If not, then has the automaton won the game?
4. If not, can he win it at the next move? If so, make that move.
5. If not, could his adversary, if he had the move, win the game.
6. If so, the automaton must prevent him if possible.
7. If his adversary cannot win the game at his next move, the automaton must examine whether he can make such a move that, if he were allowed to have two moves in succession, he could at the second move have *two* different ways of winning the game; and each of these cases failing, the automaton must look forward to three or more successive moves.

Now I have already stated that in the Analytical Engine I had devised mechanical means equivalent to memory, also that I had provided other means equivalent to foresight, and that the Engine itself could act on this foresight.

In consequence of this the whole question of making an automaton play any game depended upon the possibility of the machine being able to represent all the myriads of combinations relating to it. Allowing one hundred moves on each side for the longest game of chess, I found that the combinations involved in the Analytical Engine enormously surpassed any required, even by the game of chess.

One could be tempted to believe that Babbage's estimate of the number of calculations required by his Analytical Engine to make a move in a game of chess was, of itself, within the bounds of reason. However, his comments on the subject do not suggest that he had considered how long it might take his engine to perform these calculations. But in a sense this is not important. What is clear is that Babbage had, in the mid-nineteenth century, formulated a scheme of look-ahead which could be used to automate the analytical process in a game of chess. Questions 1 through 6 above are equivalent to the statements: USE LOOK-AHEAD AND MINIMAX. Question 7 is equivalent to the statement: TRY TO MAKE A MOVE WHICH CREATES TWO THREATS SUCH THAT IT IS IMPOSSIBLE TO PREVENT BOTH OF THEM. Thus, a century before Shannon, Charles Babbage had sown the seeds of computer chess!

Zuse

The German pioneer of computer science, Konrad Zuse, first wrote about the possibility of creating a chess program in his book *Der Plankalkuel*, which was published in 1945. Zuse described how a legal move generator could be programmed, but he did not extend his work to consider evaluation or search techniques. He developed a computer, the Zuse-1, but so far as we know he did not attempt to program chess.

Shannon

On March 9th 1949 Claude E. Shannon, a research scientist at Bell Telephone Laboratories, Murray Hill, New Jersey, presented a paper at a New York convention. His paper was called "Programming a Computer for Playing Chess" and its enormous significance lies in that many of Shannon's original ideas can still be seen in today's programs. Shannon did not claim that computer chess was of any practical importance but he did realize that a satisfactory solution to the problem might result in progress being made in other areas of automated problem solving. In particular, he listed the possibility of "building machines" (that is, writing programs) that could design electronic circuits, handle complex telephone switching problems, translate from one language to another, make strategic decisions in simplified military operations, orchestrate a melody or handle problems of logical deduction.

Shannon proposed several features which might be included in a chess program's evaluation function:

1. Material advantage
2. Pawn formation:
    a. Backward, isolated and doubled pawns
    b. Relative control of the center (pawns at e4, d4, f4, c4 for White; e5, d5, f5, c5 for Black)
    c. Weakness of pawns near the king (e.g., an advanced g-pawn)
    d. Pawns on opposite colored squares from bishops (i.e., if you have only one bishop you should put your pawns on squares of the other color)
    e. Passed pawns

Figure 2.1. Claude Shannon at Edmonton, May 1989

3. Positions of pieces:
   a. Advanced knight (at e5, d5, f5, c5, e6, d6, f6, c6 for White) especially if protected by a pawn and free from attack by enemy pawns
   b. A rook on an open or semi-open file
   c. A rook on the seventh rank
   d. Doubled rooks
4. Commitments, attacks and options:
   a. Pieces which are required to guard other pieces and, therefore, commtted and with limited mobility
   b. Attacks on pieces which give one player the option of exchanging
   c. Attacks on squares adjacent to the enemy king
   d. Pins, where the pinned piece is of value not greater that the pinning piece, e.g., a knight pinned by a bishop
5. Mobility, measured by the number of legal moves available

Shannon described two different types of strategy for growing chess trees. The most primitive strategy, which Shannon referred to as a "type-A" strategy, is to grow the tree to a fixed depth along every branch and then to search for the best move by using the minimax algorithm. His "type-B" strategy introduced selective search whereby certain lines were searched more deeply than others.

There are three major disadvantages with Shannon's type-A strategy, all of which were pointed out by Shannon himself. In a typical middlegame position there are more than 30 moves to choose from. After just one move by each side there are roughly 1,000 terminal nodes to be evaluated. After three moves by each side there are 1,000,000,000 terminal nodes which means that at the rate of one evaluation every microsecond the program would take about 16 minutes to make each move. And even with an exhaustive search to a depth of six half-moves it would not be possible to play chess at a high standard because of the number of important variations that were more than six ply long.

A human chess master may examine some variations to a depth of only a few plies and others to a depth of 20 or more. One could argue that it is therefore vital that a chess program be given the facility to examine some variations in depth while rejecting others, but although the strongest chess programs do this to some extent their average breadth of search, known as the "branching factor," is much more than it is for humans. The relative inability to examine deep variations is the second disadvantage of the type-A strategy.

The third disadvantage can be shown by the example in Figure 2.2. If a

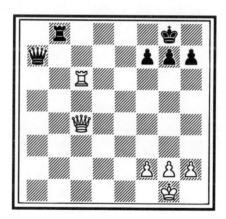

Figure 2.2 Position illustrating difficulty with Shannon's Type-A strategy

program with a fixed depth search of two ply were to analyze this position, part of its analysis would include the variations 1 Rc6–c8+ Rb8xc8. Here the program would terminate its look–ahead and assess the position. Seeing that it is a rook down it would proceed to analyze the other variations at its disposal and would eventually choose one of them. It would certainly not play 1 Rc6–c8+ because as far as it could "see" this variation loses a rook for nothing. Yet 1 Rc6–c8+ is a move that would be made by any human player with very little thought, because the human would see the merit in analyzing just a little further. It is obvious to the human player that it is not sensible to evaluate a position that arises in the middle of a sequence of captures, checks or direct threats — we can only evaluate positions that are "quiescent."

Shannon introduced the notion of quiescence (he called it "stability") into his second type of strategy. This type-B strategy had two distinct advantages over its predecessor:

1. It examined forcing variations as far as possible and evaluated only quasistable positions,
2. It selected the variations to be analyzed by some process that was intended to prevent the machine from wasting its time in totally pointless evaluation.

These two criteria, of course, could equally be applied to strong human players. The second criterion is effectively performed by the alpha-beta algorithm (see Chapter 9) which was first used by programs in the 1960s.

Shannon's admittedly crude interpretation of the concept of quiescence was somewhat inadequate for the purposes of writing a strong chess program, but it is interesting to note that many of today's chess programs are almost as deficient in the same area. Shannon's proposal was to call a position approximately stable if no pieces were en prise. This, if taken to include all checks (i.e., positions in which a king is en prise), is not sufficient to ensure good, or even satisfactory tactical play, since there are other, equally serious threats that one might be under even though one's pieces were all safely protected and free from attack. The position shown in Figure 2.3 is an example.

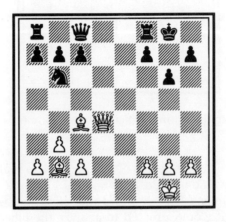

Figure 2.3 Black to move.

Figure 2.4. Shannon and Edward Lasker

Imagine that a computer program, playing Black, were to analyze a line of play in which White sacrificed material to reach the position in Figure 2.3, and that this position was a terminal node on the program's game tree. The program comes to evaluate the position and finds that none of Black's pieces is under threat. Furthermore, Black is not in check. The program therefore evaluates the position as highly advantageous for Black, who is well ahead on material. What the program fails to notice is that White is winning because he threatens an unstoppable mate (Qd4–g7 mate).

Turing and Hand Simulations

In 1951 Alan Turing wrote about the results of his work on computer chess at the University of Manchester. Turing was one of the outstanding pioneers during the early years of computer science and he was convinced that games constituted an ideal model in which studies of machine intelligence could be conducted. This view is widely held today by those who work in the field of artificial intelligence but in Turing's day his opinion was greeted with some scepticism.

Turing's earliest thoughts on computer chess date from 1944, when he discussed his ideas with various colleagues. Around 1947–1948 he and D.G. Champernowne devised a one move analyzer called the TUROCHAMP and at the same time Donald Michie and S. Wylie designed a rival analyzer named MACHIAVELLI. (Michie is the only pioneer in computer chess who is still actively involved today.) These analyzers permitted their creators to simulate the play of a computer that was searching to a depth of 1 ply. They simply hand-calculated the scores of all positions at a depth of 1 and then made the move leading to the one with the highest score. A match between the two was arranged but never completed. Thirteen years later, in 1961, MACHIAVELLI did play a game with another analyzer (SOMA) designed by Maynard Smith.

SOMA used an evaluation function in which three features were of paramount importance — material, mobility and *swap-off values*. For material calculations each pawn was worth 10 points, knights and bishops 30, rooks 50 and the queens were worth 90 if they were not on the back two ranks and the player had not castled, otherwise they were worth 100. This deterred moving the queen from the back two ranks before castling.

The mobility score was not a simple count of the number of moves that could be made by all pieces, but a weighted measure that placed a greater value on attacking squares. One point was scored for every square attacked. An extra 2 points were scored for every square attacked that was adjacent to the enemy king. For each attack on one of the four central squares an extra 1 point was credited. These "attacks" took into account pinned pieces by assuming that if a piece was pinned it did not actually attack any squares, and the feature also allowed for transparent attacks whereby, for example, if two rooks are on the same file they can both be considered to be attacking an enemy piece on that file because the attack by one of the rooks is being supported from behind by the other one. The squares attacked by each piece were enumerated separately and added, so that if a square was attacked by four white pieces this added four times the usual square attack value to White's score.

The most interesting feature of SOMA was the swap-off values. These values determined, in a very simple way, whether or not a particular exchanging sequence was likely to be profitable, without the necessity of performing any look-ahead whatsoever. By using swap-off values when evaluating terminal positions in which captures are feasible, it is quite possible to determine that a certain position offers an advantageous exchanging sequence without actually searching that part of the game tree in which the exchanges occur.

The three principal features of SOMA'S evaluation mechanism were weighted in the following way:

SCORE = [SQUARE ATTACK x 10] + MATERIAL + SWAP-OFF + r

where r represents a small residual score that took into account castling and other minor features. It took a human operator about 5 minutes to carry out the calculations for a single move. MACHIAVELLI worked similarly but it had more knowledge about chess strategy and rather less tactical insight.

White: **SOMA (Simulation)**
Black: **MACHIAVELLI (Simulation)**
Great Britain, 1961
Irregular Opening

1 e2–e3
This move increases the score for White's position by 8 points: 4 new squares
attacked by the bishop, 3 by the queen and 1 because the pawn now attacks a
center square and an ordinary square, whereas before it moved it attacked two
ordinary squares. Three other moves also increase SOMA's score by 8 points:
1 e2–e4, 1 Ng1–f3 and 1 Nb1–c3. In such cases where there is a tie, the move
to be played is chosen at random from those with the maximum score.

**1 ... e7–e5 2 d2–d4 Nb8–c6 3 Nb1–c3 d7–d5 4 Ng1–f3 e5–e4 5 Nf3–e5 Bf8–b4
6 Ne5xc6 b7xc6 7 Bc1–d2 Ng8–f6 8 a2–a4 Bb4–d6 9 h2–h4 Bc8–g4 10 Bf1–e2
Qd8–d7 11 O–O O–O–O 12 f2–f3 Bg4–f5 13 f3xe4 Bf5xe4 14 Be2–a6+ Kc8–b8
15 Nc3xe4 Nf6xe4 16 Qd1–e2**
SOMA is only a one move analyzer and so it does not see ... Ne4–g3 coming.

16 ... Qd7–e6
MACHIAVELLI's designers ascribe this tactical oversight to the fact that their
"program" prefers development to material gain.

17 Bd2–a5 Ne4–g3

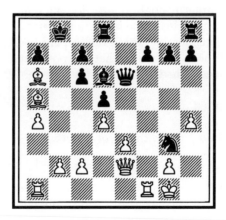

Figure 2.5 After 17 ... Ne4–g3

18 Qe2–f3
Obviously (to a human) White should play 18 Qe2–d3, and if 18 ... Ng3xf1
19 Qd3–b3+ Kb8–a8 20 Qb3–b7 mate.

18 ... Ng3xf1 19 Ra1xf1 f7–f6 20 Rf1–d1 Qe6–e4 21 Qf3xe4
SOMA does not know that a material advantage of 20 to 18 is much better than
one of 29 to 27.

21 ... d5xe4 22 d4–d5 c6xd5 23 Rd1xd5 Bd6–e5?
Black can win another exchange by 23 ... Bd6–h2+ 24 Kg1xh2 Rd8xd5. SOMA
would have found this combination because after 23 ... Bd6–h2+ there would
be two white pieces en prise: the king with a value of 100 and the rook with
a value of 5. The only black piece en prise would be the bishop (worth 3) and
so the swapoff value of the move would be +2 pawns.

**24 Rd5–b5+ Kb8–a8 25 Ba6–b7+ Ka8–b8 26 Bb7xe4+ Kb8–c8 27 Be4–f5+
Rd8–d7 28 Bf5xd7+ Kc8xd7 Draw agreed.**
Here the game was agreed drawn because neither program had been taught
anything about the endgame.

During the course of his research on computer chess Turing tried to program
both TUROCHAMP and MACHIAVELLI on the Ferranti Mark 1 computer at
Manchester, but he never completed the programming and so was unable to
play them against each other automatically.

The significance of Turing's work lay largely in that he was the first person
to design a program that could play chess. Admittedly the one recorded game
"played" by his "program" was really a tedious hand simulation, but if we
make the reasonable assumption that Turing's arithmetic was correct then we
have every reason to regard this game in the same vein as those played by real
live computers.

Turing used a simple evaluation function in which material was the
dominant factor. He grew his game tree to a uniform depth of two ply and
then examined all "considerable" moves at deeper plies, stopping a variation
when a "dead" position was reached (that is, a position from which there are
no considerable moves). He defined considerable moves as those that:

1. Capture undefended piece
2. Recapture a piece
3. Capture a defended piece with one of lower value
4. Give mate

To play a game by hand using such a scheme had the potential of taking a
great deal of time and patience. Before making a move Turing might have had
to consider as many as 1,000 terminal positions and perform evaluations for
many of them. Turing probably avoided scoring all of them by using a
variation of the alpha–beta algorithm, although he might not have done so
conscientiously. If the material evaluations were equal for two or more
positions at depth one, positional factors were used to break the tie. This
positional value did not take into account all the pieces on the board but only
those of the side on the move as well as his opponent's king. The features

employed in Turing's positional evaluation were:

1. Mobility: For the queen, rooks, bishops and knights, add the square roots of the number of moves that the piece can make, counting a capture as two moves. (For the sake of simplicity Turing approximated the square roots to one place of decimals.)
2. Piece safety: For the rooks, bishops and knights add 1 point if the piece is defended once, and 1.5 if it is defended at least twice.
3. King mobility: For the king use the same method of scoring as for the pieces, but do not count castling.
4. King safety: Deduct points for the king's vulnerability, defined as the number of moves that a queen could make were it on the square of the king.
5. Castling: Add 1 point if castling is still legally possible after this move (i.e., if neither the king nor the rook has yet moved). Add another point if castling is immediately possible or if the castling move has just been made.
6. Pawn credit: Score 0.2 points for each rank advanced and 0.3 points for each pawn defended by one or more non-pawns.
7. Checks and mate threats: Score 1 point for the threat of mate and 0.5 points for a check. The material values assigned to each of the pieces were:

$$\text{pawn} = 1, \text{knight} = 3, \text{bishop} = 3.5, \text{rook} = 5, \text{queen} = 10$$

The following game was played in Manchester in 1951 between Turing's hand simulation and a weak human opponent.

White: **Turing's Program (Simulation)**
Black: **Human**
1951
Vienna Game

1 e2–e4 e7–e5 2 Nb1–c3 Ng8–f6 3 d2–d4 Bf8–b4 4 Ng1–f3 d7–d6 5 Bc1–d2 Nb8–c6 6 d4–d5 Nc6–d4 7 h2–h4
Strangely enough, even though such moves would be almost unthinkable in a game between reasonable human players, they are not uncommon in computer games. The reason is not hard to find. The program's positional "judgment" is governed by its evaluation function which, in turn, is designed to incorporate various chess rules-of-thumb (called heuristics in computer jargon).

Two of the heuristics embodied in Turing's evaluation function, as well as in the evaluation functions of many more recent programs, are (1) Advance your pawns (exemplified by the bonus of 0.3 for each rank advanced); and (2) Increase your mobility (score the square root of the number of moves that a piece can make). The move 7 h2–h4 scores a bonus of 0.6 for advancing the pawn two ranks, and it increases the mobility of White's h1-rook from 2 (for which it scores 1.4) to 4 (for which it scores 2).

7 ... Bc8–g4 8 a2–a4
Thematic!

8 ... Nd4xf3+ 9 g2xf3 Bg4–h5 10 Bf1–b5+ c7–c6
Obviously 10 ... Nf6–d7 would be better.

11 d5xc6 O–O 12 c6xb7 Ra8–b8 13 Bb5–a6 Qd8–a5 14 Qd1–e2 Nf6–d7
Black can win back one pawn by 14 ... Bh5xf3 15 Qe2xf3 Qa5xa6.

15 Rh1–g1 Nd7–c5

Figure 2.6 After 15 ... Nd7–c5

16 Rg1–g5
Turing and others have commented that this move was made using the
"heads in the sand" approach. The program is faced with the loss of its
advanced b-pawn and it staves off this material loss for as long as possible.
 By playing 16 Rg1–g5 the program appears to be avoiding reality — it
simply pushes reality (in this case the loss of the b7-pawn) over its horizon.
Now, after Black moves his attacked bishop and White retreats his own
bishop, the capture of the b7-pawn has not been averted, but its capture will
occur at a depth too great for the program to see. This move demonstrates the
earliest example of what is known today as the "horizon effect."
 It is amusing that 16 Rg1–g5 is actually White's best move, but Turing and
many later commentators on this game have overlooked the reason.

16 ... Bh5–g6 17 Ba6–b5?
An aimless move. 17 Ba6–c4 was obviously the best choice since if Black were
then to capture the b7-pawn White could play 18 h4–h5, trapping the bishop

(*18 ... h7–h6 19 Rg5xg6*). If Black meets 17 Ba6–c4 with 17... Kg8–h8, avoiding the pin on the g8-a2 diagonal, White wins by 18 h4–h5. For example, 18... f7–f6 19 Rg5xg6 h7xg6 20 h5xg6, and it is impossible for Black to prevent White from mating him by Qe2–f1 followed by Qf1–h1, or f3–f4 followed by Qe2–h5.

17... Kg8–h8 18 h4–h5 h7–h6 is also no good because of 19 h5xg6 h6xg5 20 Qe2–f1 etc. It seems that Black must reply to 17 Ba6–c4 with 17... Nc5–e6 18 Bc4xe6 f7xe6, when White has an excellent position.

17 h4–h5 at once is not good enough because 17... Nc5–e6. So it would appear that in this position Turing's program had a clear advantage.

17 ... Nc5xb7 18 O–O–O?
18 Bb5–c4, threatening 19 h4–h5, probably gives White a won game. 18 h4–h5 h7–h6 19 h5xg6 h6xg5 20 Bb5–c4 is also very difficult to meet. The program, however, is more attracted by the bonus attached to castling.

18 ... Nb7–c5
Now it is too late for h4–h5 which can be met by 19 ... Nc5–e6, while 19 Bb5–c4 Nc5xa4 is also good for Black.

19 Bb5–c6 Rf8–c8?
19... Nc5–e6 was essential, for obvious reasons.

20 Bc6–d5 Bb4xc3 21 Bd2xc3 Qa5xa4 22 Kc1–d2?
22 h4–h5 wins for White.

22 ... Nc5–e6
At last, but it should be too late.

23 Rg5–g4?
23 Bd5xe6 was correct. Now Black's knight becomes a nuisance.

23 ... Ne6–d4?
23 ... Ne6–f4 followed by 24 ... Nf4xd5 would have put an end to White's kingside play.

24 Qe2–d3 Nd4–b5 25 Bd5–b3 Qa4–a6 26 Bb3–c4
26 Rd1–g1 gives White a winning attack.

26 ... Bg6–h5 27 Rg4–g3
Why not go back to g5?

27 ... Qa6–a4 28 Bc4xb5 Qa4xb5 29 Qd3xd6??
After 29 Qd3xb5 Rb8xb5 30 Rd1–g1 g7–g6 31 Kd2–e3 White could unravel his rooks and keep a big advantage because of the superiority of his own bishop over that of his opponent.

29 ... Rc8–d8 White resigns.
White had overlooked the strength of this "deep" move. The program only
looked to a depth of 2 ply and so when it considered 29 Qd3xd6 it was unable
to see as far as the position in which its queen was captured (which was at
depth 4).

Turing summed up the weakness of his "program" by describing it as a
caricature of his own play.

> It was in fact based on an introspective analysis of my thought processes when
> playing, with considerable simplifications. It makes oversights which are very
> similar to those which I make myself, and which may in both cases be ascribed
> to the considerable moves being inappropriately chosen.
>   This fact might be regarded as supporting the glib view which is often
> expressed, to the effect that one cannot program a machine to play a better game
> than one plays oneself.

Another interesting parallel that may be drawn between the play of this
program (and others) and weak human players is that members of both
groups often, through no fault of their own, find themselves in positions in
which a win can be forced through some relatively simple tactical idea, but
without realizing that such a tactical opportunity might be present they fail
to search for it and hence they fail to find it. Most club players, when faced
with the position at move 17 (and the similar ones that followed) would have
realized that White's a6 bishop belongs on the a2–g8 diagonal and that h4–h5
was likely to be very strong if it were played at the correct moment. The
concept of trapping and winning an immobile piece (Black's g6 bishop in this
case) and the idea of the attack on the weak f7 and h7 squares, are both simple
and common enough for them to occur to any reasonably experienced chess
player. It should merely be a question of working out in which order the
moves should be played and in calculating one or two variations. Since
computers are flawless in calculation the only problem would seem to be in
thinking of this plan, but planning is one area of problem-solving in which
computer programs, even today, are still in their infancy.

Prinz's Problem Solving Program

In November 1951 one of Turing's colleagues at Manchester University, D. G.
Prinz, wrote a program to solve simple mate-in-two problems. Since such
problems can be solved quite easily by conducting a 3-ply search, Prinz's
program was little more than an intellectual exercise. It contributed nothing
to the more general problems of computer chess.

The First Working Programs

The Los Alamos Program

The first documented account of a running program appeared in 1956, following the work of five scientists (James Kister, Paul Stein, Stanislaw Ulam, William Walden and Mark Wells) at the Los Alamos Scientific Laboratory in New Mexico, famous for its work on the Manhattan Project. The Los Alamos group mentioned a slightly earlier program, reported in an article in *Pravda* that had been written for a BESM computer in Moscow, but the *Pravda* article did not give a detailed account of the method by which the Soviet program had been written nor the results of its play, beyond the statement that a fair chess player was able to beat the machine.

The game played by the Los Alamos program was not really chess but a miniature version of it, played on a 6 x 6 board omitting the bishops. For its first move each pawn could advance only one square and castling was not permitted. The programming team found that although the game was much simpler than chess it nevertheless retained much of the flavor of the real game. The program ran on a MANIAC computer whose speed was 11,000 operations per second, and on average it was able to perform an exhaustive search to a depth of four ply in about 12 minutes. Since, in real chess, the number of legal moves at each stage would be almost twice as great, the time taken to make a move in the real game would have been in the region of three hours for an exhaustive 4-ply search.

The program employed an evaluation function using only two features: material and mobility. The first game played by MANIAC matched the program against itself. The programmers reported that "... like any game between beginners it contained weak moves, but in general we were very pleased with the quality of the play."

Several changes in the program were then made to correct the most obvious of the weaknesses. For example, the program seemed to have a mortal fear of checks, since its mobility after a check was almost nil, and it tended to sacrifice material to avoid being checked.

An improved version of the program was then matched against Martin Kruskal, a mathematician from Princeton who was also a strong chess player. Kruskal gave MANIAC odds of a queen. The game took many hours to play and attracted wide local interest. After about fifteen moves Kruskal had not recouped any material and had even started calling his opponent "he" instead of "it." As the game progressed it appeared that Dr. Kruskal might lose, but around move 19 the program chose a weak continuation and Kruskal was able to win its queen by threatening mate. After the program had been forced to give up its queen for a pawn it had no chance.

The program was then matched against a young woman member of the laboratory who had been taught to play chess one week earlier with the express intention of playing against MANIAC. She had been coached during the week in the principles of the game and in elementary combinations, and she had played several games against players of average strength. This is the way the game went (Note files are numbered from left to right as a, b, c, d, e and f, while ranks are numbered from bottom to top as 1, 2, 3, 4, 5 and 6.):

White: **Los Alamos Program**
Black: **Human**
Los Alamos, 1956

1 d2–d3 b5–b4 2 Ne1–f3
A good idea in 6 x 6 games — the knight is quite aggressively placed, attacking d4 and e5.

2 ... d5–d4 3 b2–b3 e5–e4 4 Nf3–e1 a5–a4 5 b3xa4?
A dreadful strategic error, giving Black's b6-knight its undeserved freedom and leaving White with an isolated a-pawn. Better would have been 5 Nb1–d2 intending 6 Nd2–c4+ Nb6xc4 7 b3xc4, with a good game.

5 ... Nb6xa4 6 Kd1–d2? Na4–c3 7 Nb1xc3 b4xc3+ 8 Kd2–d1 f5–f4 9 a2–a3 Ra6–b6 10 a3–a4
The program made these last two moves because they increase the mobility

of its a1-rook. The rule "advance your pawns" had not been programmed. This is a good example of a program playing the right move for the wrong reason.

10 ... Rb6–a6 11 a4–a5

Figure 3.1 After 11 a4–a5

11 ... Kd6–d5 12 Qc1–a3 Qc6–b5 13 Qa3–a2+ Kd5–e5 14 Ra1–b1? Ra6xa5 15 Rb1xb5 Ra5xa2 16 Rb5–b1
To prevent the back-rank mate!

16 ... Ra2–a5 17 f2–f3 Ra5–a4 18 f3xe4 c5–c4 19 Ne1–f3+ Ke5–d6 20 e4–e5+ Kd6–d5 21 e5xf6=Q Ne6–c5 22 Qf6xd4+ Kd5–c6 23 Nf3–e5 mate.

The Bernstein Program

> Chess is not only one of the most engaging but also one of the most sophisticated of human activities. The game is so old that we cannot say when or where it was invented; millions of games have been played and thousands of books have been written about it; yet the play is still fresh and forever new.

Thus began an article by Alex Bernstein and Michael de V. Roberts in the June 1958 issue of *Scientific American*, in which the authors described to the public a program that they had developed together with Timothy Arbuckle and Martin Belsky. It is true that Shannon had expressed his own ideas eight years earlier, but Shannon's paper was purely theoretical in nature whereas the Bernstein/Roberts article described a program that could play a reasonable game on a real live computer (in their case, an IBM 704).

The Bernstein/Roberts article had more than a dash of the 2001s about it. "You sit at the console of the machine with a chessboard in front of you and press the start button. Within four seconds a panel light labelled 'Program Stop' lights up on the console and now you make your choice of Black or White: to choose Black you flip a switch on the console; if you want White, you simply leave the switch as it is. Suppose you have picked Black. To begin the game you press the start button again. The machine now 'thinks' about its first move ... Some lights flash on the console but the computer is working so swiftly that it is impossible to say just what these flashes mean. After about eight minutes the computer prints out its move on a sheet of paper."

If the human made an illegal move the computer would print out "PLEASE CHECK LAST MOVE," and at the end of the game it printed the game score and the words "THANK YOU FOR AN INTERESTING GAME."

Their program's evaluation function used four features: (1) Mobility, (2) Area control, (3) King defence, and (4) Material. It searched to a depth of four ply. In order to ensure that its moves could be made within a reasonable period of time, instead of considering every move in a given position it chose the best seven moves as selected by a number of "decision routines." These decision routines examined a position to determine whether a certain state existed — if it did then certain moves were generated and added to a "plausible move table." The questions asked by the decision routines were:

1. Is the king in check?: If the answer is "yes" then the program looked to see if it was in check from more than one piece, in which case it would generate only king moves. If the king was only in check from a single piece then in addition the program generated interposing moves and moves that captured the checking piece. If the king is not in check, the program went to the next question.
2. Can material be (a) gained, (b) lost, or (c) exchanged? If the answer to question 2(a) was yes, the program listed those moves which gained material in the plausible move table; if 2(b) was yes, the program found which moves would put the attacked pieces in safety and entered them in the table; and if 2(c) was yes, it entered the exchanging moves in the table.

At the end of question 2, if the storage locations in the plausible move table were not yet full, the program went on to the following questions:

3. Is castling possible?
4. Can a minor piece be developed?
5. Can any pieces occupy the critical squares created by pawn chains? (These are the squares that are normally referred to in chess books as "weak" squares.
6. Can open files be occupied?
7. Can any pawn be moved?
8. Can any piece be moved?

This decision routine was stopped either if the plausible move table was filled or if the answer to question 3 was yes. The logic behind this second criterion is that castling is such an important element in bringing the king to safety that none of the less important routines should be questioned. The ordering of these routines was very important. At the beginning of the game questions 1, 2 and 3 did not apply and questions 4 and 7 were the only ones that generated moves. In the middlegame, questions 2, 5 and 6 generated the most moves. In the endgame it was questions 5, 6, 7 and 8 that were the most often used.

This decision routine resulted in the seven most plausible moves being stored in the table. The program performed a 4-ply search, considering, at each stage, the seven most plausible moves. It therefore examined 7 positions at a depth of one ply, 49 at depth two, 343 at depth three and 2401 at depth four: a total of 2800 position — quite manageable for a computer. The program played a passable amateur game at the rate of one move every eight minutes.

Here is a game that the program lost against a skillful opponent. The program's first four moves are not unreasonable but by the middlegame it had revealed its chief weakness: namely, a heavy bias towards moving attacked pieces rather than defending them. Since the program only searched to a depth of four plies it is obvious that a 5-ply (or in human terms, three move) combination would escape its notice. Since it was heavily materially biased it would always accept a sacrifice, but then so did Capablanca and some other outstanding players!

White: **Bernstein Program**
Black: **Human**
New York, 1958
Bishop's Opening

1 e2–e4 e7–e5 2 Bf1–c4 b7–b6 3 d2–d3 Ng8–f6 4 Bc1–g5 Bc8–b7 5 Bg5xf6 Qd8xf6 6 Ng1–f3 c7–c6 7 O–O d7–d5 8 e4xd5 c6xd5 9 Bc4–b5+ Nb8–c6 10 c2–c4?
White could win a pawn by 10 Nf3xe5 (*10 ... Qf6xe5 11 Rf1–e1*), but after Black's 11th move the material assessment of the (then current) situation would reveal that Black was a piece up for a pawn. The fact that Black was going to lose his queen on the next move was one ply too deep to be "seen" by the program.

10 ... d5xc4 11 Bb5xc6+ Qf6xc6 12 d3xc4
Better is 12 Rf1–e1.

12 ... e5–e4 13 Nf3–g5 Qc6–g6 14 Ng5–h3 e4–e3 15 f2–f3 Bf8–c5 16 Rf1–e1 O–O
After 16 ... e3–e2+ 17 Kg1–h1, the black e-pawn is pinned against his king so the white queen is immune from capture.

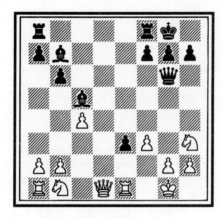

Figure 3.2 After 16 ... O–O

17 Nb1–c3??
This move shows up a deficiency in the decision routines — there was no routine that asked the question "Can I give check?" nor one that asked "Can I attack an enemy piece?" and so Black's next move would not be in the top seven.

17 ... e3–e2+ 18 Nh3–f2 Bb7xf3
Threatening mate next move on g2.

19 g2–g3 e2xd1=Q 20 Nc3xd1 Qg6–c2 21 b2–b3 Ra8–d8 22 h2–h4
Another deficiency in the system. The answers to questions 1-6 were all "no." Question 7 generated all six legal pawn moves and question 8 generated piece moves at random, but unfortunately for the program, the plausible move list was full after the first piece move was discovered. The program then went on to depth two where question 2(a) generated the move 22 ... Rd8xd1. All replies to 22 ... Rd8xd1 fail to save further material loss by White but the program had no mechanism for searching for alternative moves at depth zero. The program was then in the unfortunate situation of knowing that it was about to make a move that would lose material and that it was not allowed to add new moves to the plausible move list.

22 ... Rd8xd1 White resigns.

Early Soviet Programs

Although it was not very widely publicized in the West, there was almost as much research in computer chess in the Soviet Union during the mid-to-late 1950s as there was in the United States. As early as 1956 V. M. Kurochkin wrote a program to solve chess problems. His program ran on the Strela computer and it would find a two-move mate quicker than most human solvers (2 to 4 minutes) but three- and four-move-mates required ten to twelve minutes or even longer. Kurochkin pointed out that problem solving programs must conduct an exhaustive search and because of this they consider many moves that would be considered weak by human players.

A year or two later, V. D. Kukushkin wrote a program to play the ending of king and two bishops against king, but the first attempt at writing a program that could play a complete game was made by G. Sehlibs, whose program performed an exhaustive 3-ply search. No games played by Sehlibs's program were published and no mention was made of how strong or weak was its play.

The first well publicized chess program written in the Soviet Union made its debut in 1961. It was written at the Styeklov Mathematical Institute of the USSR Academy of Sciences by a team including Professor M. Shura-Bara, I. Zadykhailo, E. Lyubinsky and V. Smilga (a Soviet Candidate-Master). A description of their work was considered sufficiently important to be published in the 8th bulletin of the 1961 Tal—Botvinnik World Championship Match.

The Styeklov Program employed seven features in its evaluation function:

1. Material: pawn = 1; knight = bishop = 3.5; rook = 5; queen = 9.5; king = 1,000,000,000
2. Mobility: A special bonus was assigned to king mobility since "the more squares available to him, the less likely he is to be mated." Had the program used a deep lookahead this special bonus would probably have resulted in the king becoming too exposed!
3. Defence of pieces: Attacks on enemy pieces were considered less important than the loss of the program's own men, even though the attacked piece might be much more valuable than the piece lost. This heuristic, to some extent, preserved the program from gross blunders.
4. Pawn structure: Advanced pawns were given a bonus while backward and isolated ones were assigned a penalty.
5. Center control: The program was encouraged to occupy the center with pawns and to support the center with pieces.
6. Pins: Special consideration was given to pieces pinned against the king.
7. King protection: The pawns nearest the king were discouraged from moving, with the exception of the d-pawn and e-pawn.

The program performed no look-ahead and so its play was rather limited. It took between 30 and 58 seconds to make each move. The following game was played by the same program against a more experienced opponent.

White: **Styeklov Program**
Black: **Amateur**
USSR, 1961
Center Game

1 e2–e4 e7–e5 2 d2–d4
The programmers had made a slight adjustment to the program after
2 Qd1–h5 was played in the previous game.

**2 ... e5xd4 3 Qd1xd4 Nb8–c6 4 Qd4–d5 Ng8–f6 5 Qd5–f5 Nc6–d4 6 Qf5–e5+
Nd4–e6 7 Bc1–e3 Nf6–g4 8 Qe5–h5 Ng4xe3 9 f2xe3 Bf8–c5 10 Ke1–d2**
This move satisfies two criteria. It guards the e3-pawn and gives the king
more free squares (thereby "reducing" the chance of mate). It should also be
mentioned that the program had not been taught to castle, and therefore
found nothing wrong in moving its king.

10 ... Qd8–f6 11 Nb1–c3
Guarding against the threats 11 ... Qf6xb2 and 11 ... Qf6xf1, but overlooking
a third threat because of its lack of look-ahead.

11 ... Qf6–f2+ 12 Qh5–e2 Bc5xe3+ 13 Kd2–d3
Again looking for freedom. On d1 the king would have no moves.

13 ... Ne6–f4+ 14 Kd3–c4 Nf4xe2 15 Ng1xe2 d7–d6 16 Nc3–d1 Qf2–f6
16 ... Qf2–e1 keeps the bishop.

17 Nd1xe3 Qf6xb2 18 Ra1–d1 Qb2xa2+
And the programmers soon resigned.

Newell, Shaw, and Simon

Alan Newell, John Shaw and Herbert Simon began their work on computer
chess in 1955 at Carnegie Institute of Technology (now Carnegie Mellon
University) in Pittsburgh. Simon, a distinguished scientist on his own, was
awarded the Nobel Prize in Economics in 1978. Their progress on computer
chess was slow because their major interest lay in developing programs that
discovered proofs for theorems in logic. This area of artificial intelligence is
not, in fact, far removed from computer chess, since proving theorems and
playing chess involve the same problem: reasoning with heuristics that select
fruitful paths of exploration in a fast growing tree of possibilities.

    The NSS Program was constructed from a basic set of modules, each module
being associated with a particular goal in chess. Typical goals are king safety,
material balance, center control, development, attack against the king and
pawn promotion. Each goal had associated with it a collection of processes:

a move generator, a static evaluation function and an analysis generator.

The move generator associated with each goal proposed various moves relevant to that goal. They carried the burden of finding positive reasons for doing things. Thus, only the center-control generator would propose e2–e4 as a good move in the opening and only the material balance generator would propose moving out of danger a piece that was en prise.

Each move proposed by a move generator was assigned a value by an analysis procedure whose job it was to decide on the acceptability of a move once it had been generated. The value assigned to a move was obtained from a series of evaluations, one for each goal, so that each goal took the place of the features referred to in our earlier discussions. (In fact goals and features are conceptually equivalent.) The score associated with a given position was made up of a number of components, each component corresponding to one goal (or feature). Each component expressed the acceptabililty or otherwise of a position from the viewpoint of the goal corresponding to that component.

An example of the goals used is center control. This goal always operated unless there were no more center pawns to be moved to the fourth rank. The move generator for center control attempted to make moves as follows:

1. Move e2–e4, d2–d4 (called primary moves — the corresponding moves for Black were ... e7–e5 and ... d7–d5).
2. Prevent your opponent from making his primary moves.
3. Prepare your own primary moves by:
   a. Adding a defender to your e4 or d4 square (or, if Black, to e5 and d5);
   b. Eliminating a block to moving the e-pawn or d-pawn.

The static evaluation for center control simply counted the number of blocks that prevented making the primary moves. The move generator for center control is concerned only with the two primary moves e2–e4 and d2–d4 (or the equivalent black moves). It would propose these moves if they were legal and it was the responsibility of the analysis procedures for all the goals to reject the moves if there was anything wrong with them, for example if they put a pawn en prise. Thus, after 1 d2–d4 d7–d5, the center control move generator would propose 2 e2–e4 but the evaluation routine of the material balance goal would reject this move because 2 ... d5xe4 results in a of the loss of material.

If the primary moves could not be made, the center control generator had two choices: to prepare them or to prevent the opponent from making his own primary moves. If the program was written so that it preferred prevention to preparation then it would generally play more aggressively in the opening.

The move generator approached the subgoal of preventing the opponent's primary moves (whenever this subgoal was evoked) in the following way. It first determined whether the opponent could make one of these moves by trying the move and then obtaining an evaluation of it from the opponent's viewpoint. If one or both of the primary moves was not rejected, then prevention would serve some useful purpose. Under these circumstances the center-control move generator would generate preventative moves by finding moves that brought another attacker to bear on the opponent's central squares (e4, d4 for White; e5, d5 for Black) or that pinned a defender of one of these squares. Among the moves that this generator would normally propose were Ng1–f3, Nb1–c3, f2–f4 and c2–c4 (and the corresponding moves for Black).

The move generator prepared its own primary moves by first determining why the moves could not be made without preparation, i.e., whether the pawn was blocked by one of its own pieces, or whether the fourth rank square was unsafe for the pawn. In the first case the move generator proposed moves for the blockading piece, in the second case it found moves that added support to the fourth rank square, drove away or pinned attackers, and so on. The task of the evaluation routine for center control was essentially that of the devil's advocate — to ensure that move proposed by some other goal would not be made if they jeopardized control of the center.

When the program began to "think" about making its move, a preliminary analysis was carried out to establish that some particular chess situation or "state" existed. This state evoked a set of goals appropriate to it and the goals were put onto a list with the most crucial ones first. This list then controlled the remainder of the move-making procedure. What kind of game the program would play clearly depended on what goals were available to it and chosen by it for any particular move. One purpose of this modular construction was to provide flexibility throughout the course of the game in the way the program expended its efforts. For example, the goal of denying stalemate to the opponent would only be invoked in certain endgame situations where the opponent was on the defensive and his king was in a constrained position.

The importance of considering the most crucial goals first lay in the use of the alpha-beta algorithm, whose first use in game playing programs was in the NSS Program. This method of tree searching guarantees finding the minimax solution to a tree search (i.e., it will always make the move that would be chosen by a minimax search) but it does so very much faster by eliminating from its consideration whole sections of the tree. The alpha-beta algorithm is explained in more detail in Chapter 9.

The following game was played by Simon against the NSS Program which was running on the RAND JOHNNIAC computer. This computer operated at about half the speed of the IBM 704 used by Bernstein and his colleagues and the program's moves took from 2 to 50 minutes. The program had three goals: material balance, center control and development.

White: **NSS Program**
Black: **Simon**
Carnegie Institute of Technology, 1960
Queen's Pawn Game

1 d2–d4 Ng8–f6 2 Nb1–c3 d7–d5 3 Qd1–d3?
Chess programs can often be seen to move their queens at a very early stage of the game. The usual reason is that the development feature (or in this case

the development goal) does not give more credit for developing minor pieces than it does for developing major ones. In this instance the move might also have been promoted by the center control goal, since White's move adds a protector to the e4-square.

3 ... b7–b6 4 e2–e4 Bc8–b7 5 e4xd5 Nf6xd5 6 Ng1–f3 e7–e6 7 Bf1–e2 Bf8–e7 8 Bc1–e3 O–O 9 O–O Nb8–d7 10 Rf1–e1 c7–c5 11 Ra1–d1 Qd8–c7 12 Nc3xd5 Bb7xd5 13 a2–a4?

To a human, 13 c2–c4 is obviously best. The move generator for the material balance goal would have generated the moves 13 c2–c4, 13 a2–a3 and 13 a2–a4. Moves such as 13 Rd1–a1 are not generated because the rook has another function — adding support to White's control of the center.

There is nothing in the programmers' description of their move generators to explain why the program preferred the weakest of the three moves but it is clear that their center control mechanism should have been designed to give a bonus for attacking d5 even though there is no black pawn on d7 or d6.

13 ... Ra8–c8 14 Qd3–c3 Be7–f6 15 Be2–b5

Black was threatening 15 ... c5xd4 16 Qc3xc7 Rc8xc7 17 Nf3xd4 Bf6xd4 18 Be3xd4 Rc7xc2, so by attacking the knight White saves his pawn.

But did White make this move for the right reason? It seems more likely that the program feared 15 ... Bd5xf3 16 Be2xf3 e6–e5 (this is one of the primary moves) and that its 15 Be2–b5 was aimed at attacking a piece that adds support to one of the primary moves. Once its center control move generator had proposed the move 15 Be2–b5, the program would have examined the exchanging sequences beginning with 15 ... c5xd4 and found that they did not win material for Black.

Other 15th moves proposed by the program's move generators would be seen to lose a pawn and so 15 Be2–b5 would be the only acceptable move. But what a strange way to find it!

15 ... Bd5xf3 16 g2xf3 Rf8–d8 17 Bb5xd7?

Aimless. White could have held the pawn by moving the queen — after 17 ... c5xd4 18 Be3xd4 Bf6xd4 19 Rd1xd4, Black cannot capture the c-pawn because his knight would be lost.

17 ... Qc7xd7

Attacking the a-pawn as well.

18 b2–b3 c5xd4 19 Qc3–d2 Qd7–c6 20 Be3–f4 Qc6xc2 21 Qd2xc2 Rc8xc2 22 Rd1–c1 Rd8–c8 23 Rc1–d1 Rc8–c3 24 b3–b4 Rc3xf3 25 Bf4–g3 d4–d3 26 Rd1–c1

The program does not know about forks.

26 ... Bf6–g5

Nor does its opponent: 26 ... d3–d2 27 Rc1xc2 d2xe1=Q+ 28 Kg1–g2 Qe1–d1 wins at once.

27 Rc1xc2 d3xc2 28 Bg3–e5 c2–c1=Q 29 Re1xc1 Bg5xc1 White resigns.

The Anderson/Cody Program

In 1959 a Canadian program was demonstrated at the University of Toronto. It was written by Frank Anderson, an international master, and Bob Cody, and it ran on an IBM 605 computer. The program dealt only with simple pawn endings (the most complex was king and two pawns versus king and pawn). The programmers devised a unique strategy that reportedly enabled their program to play these endings perfectly. Their first version could cope with more than 180,000 different positions, a figure that was increased in later versions of the program.   When the program was demonstrated at the Canadian Conference of Scientists it played against more than 50 different opponents, each of whom was allowed to choose his own starting position, given the small number of pawns. In each case the program apparently played perfectly. Unfortunately, the strategy that enabled these endings to be programmed successfully was never documented, and Anderson even confessed to me in the early 1970s that he couldn't explain why they worked!

The Kotok/McCarthy Program

In 1961 Alan Kotok wrote a chess program for his bachelor's dissertation at the Massachusets Institute of Technology. His program was written under the guidance of John McCarthy, one of the leading figures in the world of Artificial Intelligence, who was then a professor at MIT. Among McCarthy's accomplishments was the creation of the programming language LISP, which is still widely used by programmers working in the field of artificial intelligence.

Kotok's program performed a variable depth search. It looked ahead until a stable position had been reached or until its depth of search reached an arbitrary maximum. In order to avoid growing enormous trees the program examined fewer and fewer successor positions as the depth of search increased. Moves were proposed by a plausible move generator whose job it was to find moves that fulfilled various goals. In this respect Kotok's work was similar to that of Newell, Shaw and Simon. The plausible move generator supplied 4 moves at the root of the tree, 3 at the next level, then 2, 2, 1, 1, 1, 1, 0, 0, ... etc. In addition to the plausible moves considered at each level, the program examined captures and checks.

Kotok's evaluation function used four features: Material, Pawn Structure, Center Control and Development. Looking at the board from the side of the player about to move, Kotok weighted the 16 center squares as follows:

```
4  4  8  8
4  8  8  4
2  4  4  2
1  1  1  1
```

These weightings give more credit for attacking squares in the opponent's half of the board, and for attacking squares near his king (the weights 4, 4, 8, 8, for the squares on the sixth rank were adjusted to 8, 8, 4, 4, if the opponent had castled on the left-hand side of the board).

Each center square point was worth one-sixtieth of a pawn at the beginning of the game. After 20 moves center control became less important and after move 30 the feature was discarded. The program assigned points for each developed piece: 1 for a pawn, rising to 3 or 4 for the other pieces. Each development point was worth one-fifteenth of a pawn at the start of the game but this value too was diminished as the game progressed.

Pawn structure points were each worth one-twentieth of a pawn: For each pawn on a semi-open file the program scored 8 pawn structure points; for each isolated pawn -1; for a backward pawn -5; for a doubled pawn -3 and for a passed pawn 10.

Kotok's work began in the Spring of 1961. By the time that he presented his thesis in 1962 his program had played four long game fragments, calculating for between five and 20 minutes per move. It played rather poor chess (even for a program) and in one of the four game fragments it made an illegal move, advancing a pawn two squares when the intervening square was occupied.

After graduating from MIT Kotok's interest in computer chess died but his program remained alive. When McCarthy left MIT to take charge of the Artificial Intelligence Laboratory at Stanford University he took Kotok's program with him and improved its tree searching routine. At the end of 1966 a four game match began between the Kotok/McCarthy Program, running on Stanford's IBM 7090 computer, and a program developed on a Soviet M20 computer at the Institute of Theoretical and Experimental Physics (ITEP) in Moscow. The ITEP Program was written by Vladimir Arlazarov, George Adelson-Velsky, Alexander Bitman (a Soviet Master), Alexander Ushkov and Alexander Zhivotovsky. It used an evaluation function with four features:

1. Pawn structure: Four aspects of pawn-structure were considered:
   a. Central pawns: For White the central squares are e4, d4, e5, d5, e6 and d6. Each pawn on a central square receives a bonus of 10 points.
   b. The pawn phalanx: Two pawns on the same rank and on neighbouring files are called a phalanx. N pawns on the same rank and on neighbouring files are counted as N–1 phalanxes. For each phalanx a bonus of 4 points was scored.
   c. Isolated and doubled pawns: Doubled pawns are only penalized if they are also isolated, and isolated pawns that are not doubled are only penalized if they are on a semi-open file. For each such pawn there is a penalty of 12 points.

   d. Passed pawns: For each passed pawn score a bonus of $32 - 4xS$ where
      S is the number of ranks separating the pawn from the queening square.
2. Mobility: For each square attacked by a piece, a bonus is scored according
   to the piece that is attacking. For the king this bonus is 0, for the queen
   1, for a rook 2, for a knight or bishop 5 and for a pawn 0. This method
   of scoring encourages minor pieces to be developed before major ones.
3. Castling: When a player castles he scores a bonus of 11 points, but if
   he forfeits the right to castle he suffers a penalty of 11.
4. Material: The ratios of the values of the pieces are:

      pawn = 1; bishop = knight = 3.5; rook = 5; queen = 10

   The ITEP Program used Shannon's type-A strategy. In two of its games, it
carried out a 3-ply search, while in the other two it seached to a depth of five
ply. The American program, using Shannon's type-B strategy, emplyed a four
ply search in all four games. The ITEP Program won two games and the other
two were agreed drawn on move 40. This agreement, made before the match
started, was prompted by the abysmal endgame play of both programs. In
the two unfinished games the ITEP Program had advantages which would
certainly have proved decisive in human Master play.
   The annotations to these four games and the three paragraphs that follow
are taken from an article written by Arlazarov and Bitman which appeared in
the February 1968 issue of the leading Soviet chess magazine, *Shakhmaty v
CCCP.*

Game 1
White: **ITEP Program (3 half-moves)**
Black: **Kotok/McCarthy Program**
Stanford—Moscow, 1966–1967
Four Knights' Game

1 e2–e4 e7–e5 2 Nb1–c3 Nb8–c6 3 Ng1–f3 Bf8–c5 4 Bf1–c4
In this position, which occurred in the 3rd game as well, the program found
the stronger line 4 Nf3xe5 when playing five half-moves.

4 ... Ng8–f6 5 O–O O–O 6 d2–d3 d7–d6 7 Bc1–e3 Bc8–g4 8 h2–h3 Bg4–h5
9 Bc4–d5
The developing moves have finished and the program does not know what to
do. Here a human being might have played 9 Nc3–a4 followed by 10 c2–c3,
livening the pawns up in the center. It seems though that 3 half-moves are just
not sufficient for seeing the advantages of the resulting position.

9 ... Bc5–d4
It appears that the American program suffers from the same difficulties.

10 g2–g4
In this the program had a "human" idea. It thinks that this move forces an advantageous exchange.

10... Bd4xc3 11 b2xc3 Bh5–g6 12 Be3–g5 Rf8–e8 13 Ra1–b1 Ra8–b8 14 Qd1–e2
In the variation 14 Rb1xb7 Rb8xb7 15 Bd5xc6, the 3 half-moves have run out and White is still short of material. A computer playing 4(5-DNLL) half-moves would have played 14 Rb1xb7.

14 ... Kg8–h8 15 d3–d4 Kh8–g8
It might appear that in playing 14 ... Kg8–h8 Black was preparing to reply to 15 d3–d4 with 15 ... e5xd4, to be followed by 16 c3xd4 Bg6xe4 17 Bd5xe4 d6–d5, winning a pawn, since White cannot play 18 Be4xh7+. In fact, however, neither of the machines saw this line.

16 Qe2–c4
It is curious that White "thought" five times as long over this bad move as over most other moves.

16 ... Nc6–a5

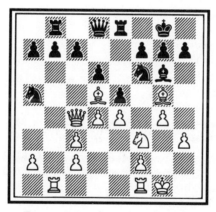

Figure 3.3 After 16 ... Nc6–a5

17 Bg5xf6
Feeling that something is wrong the program makes an intermediate exchange. After 17 Bg5xf6 Qd8xf6 18 Qc4–d3, its counting has finished and it thinks all is well.

17 ... Qd8xf6 18 Qc4–d3 c7–c6 19 d4xe5 d6xe5
Our program considered the move 19 ... Qf6–f4 to be best for Black, thinking that after 20 Bd5–b3 d6xe5, Black wins back the pawn. And if 20 ... Bg6xe4, then it had a pretty variation in reserve: 21 Bb3xf7+ Kg8xf7 22 Qd3xe4 Qf4xe4 23 Nf3–g5+ and 24 Ng5xe4.

This is an example of the complex combinations the computer can carry out without even noticing the simple intermediate exchange 20 ... Na5xb3, because after 21 a2xb3 Bg6xe4 it considered its position satisfactory.

20 Bd5–b3 Rb8–d8 21 Qd3–e3 b7–b6 22 Rf1–d1 Rd8–d6 23 g4–g5 Qf6–e7 24 Rd1–d3 Rd6xd3 25 c2xd3 Re8–d8 26 Rb1–a1
White thinks that Black should play 26 ... Na5xb3, and therefore occupies the open file in advance.

26 ... Qe7–d6 27 d3–d4 e5xd4 28 c3xd4 Na5xb3 29 a2xb3 a7–a5 30 Ra1–a4 Qd6–e6 31 Nf3–e5 Qe6–e8 32 f2–f4 Rd8–d6 33 f4–f5
Our program did not see that this move won a pawn, but made the move out of positional considerations.

33 ... Bg6–h5 34 Ne5–c4
Now it can see.

34 ... Rd6–d8 35 Nc4xb6 Rd8–b8 36 Nb6–c4 Bh4–d1 37 Ra4–a3 Bd1–c2
Because game two had reached the 40th move it was decided to call a halt to the match and agree a draw in this game.

Game 2
White: **Kotok/McCarthy Program**
Black: **ITEP Program (3 half-moves)**
Stanford—Moscow, 1966–1967
Alekhine's Defense

1 e2–e4 Ng8–f6 2 e4–e5 Nf6–d5 3 Ng1–f3 e7–e6 4 Bf1–b5 a7–a6 5 Bb5–a4 b7–b5 6 Ba4–b3 Bf8–b4
This is a typical case of a positional mistake due to an insufficient depth of calculation. Black develops a piece and prevents 7 d2–d4, not noticing that after 6 ... Bf8–b4 7 c2–c3 Bb4–c5 (three half-moves have come to an end!) White can nevertheless play 8 d2–d4.

7 Nb1–c3 Nd5–f4 8 O–O Bc8–b7 9 d2–d4 Bb4xc3 10 b2xc3 Nf4–d5 11 Bb3xd5 Bb7xd5 12 Bc1–a3 d7–d6 13 e5xd6
Our program considered the move 13 e5xd6 to be very weak. Its assessment of the position changed sharply in its own favor.

13 ... c7xd6 14 Rf1–e1 Nb8–c6 15 Re1–e3 O–O 16 Qd1–e2 Bd5–c4 17 Qe2–e1 Qd8–c7 18 Ba3–b4 a6–a5 19 Bb4–a3 Kg8–h8
However strange it may seem this is not just for "something to do." Black is intending to play 20 ... f7–f5, which it cannot do immediately because of the answer 20 Re3xe6 (and if 20 ... Bc4xe6 21 Qe1xe6+ Kg8–h8 22 Ba3xd6 – DL).

**20 Nf3–g5 h7–h6 21 Ng5–e4 Rf8–d8 22 Ne4xd6 Rd8xd6 23 Ba3xd6 Qc7xd6
24 a2–a3 Nc6–e7 25 Re3–e5 Ne7–c6**
Now if 26 Re5–e3 the game would be drawn by repetition.

26 Re5–c5 e6–e5 27 Qe1–e4 Ra8–a6
It is only now that the computer can see that 27 ... Ra8–c8 can be followed by
28 a3–a4. According to assessments printed out by our computer its position
is worsening very fast.

   Here we have an example of a position in which the strategy of a deep
analysis of a small number of moves does better than a short but comprehensive
analysis. White's moves Re5–c5, Qe1–e4 and a3–a4 are essential to any
reasonable line of play, while Black cannot interfere with his opponent's plan
even by means of the most exotic variations.

28 Ra1–d1 g7–g6 29 Rd1–d2 g6–g5
Defending against the threat of Qe4–e3, winning a pawn.

30 Rd2–d1
White can no longer find any move to improve his position.

30 ... a5–a4 31 Rd1–d2 f7–f6
To strengthen such a position is difficult even for a human being. In any case

Figure 3.4 John McCarthy, AI pioneer, at Edmonton, 1989

it would need a subtle plan lasting a number of moves. This, of course, is beyond the computer's capacity while it has such a shallow depth of calculation.

Having no plan Black makes a very weak move. It saw, of course, the reply 32 Qe4–g6 but considered that after 32 ... Qd6–f8 it was quite safe. A chess player would never have ended the analysis of a variation in such a position, except perhaps to conclude that it was acceptable.

32 Qe4–e3 e5xd4 33 c3xd4 Nc6–e7 34 Qe3–g3 Qd6xg3 35 h2xg3
Against 35 f2xg3 the program was going to play 35 ... Ra6–e6, when the best variation for both sides would be: 36 g3–g4 f6–f5 37 g4xf5 Ne7xf5, getting rid of the weak pawn, since 38 Rc5xf5 is not possible because of 38 ... Re6–e1+ 39 Kg1–f2 Re1–f1+ and 40 ... Rf1xf5.

35 ... Ne7–d5 36 Rc5–c8+ Kh8–h7 37 Rc8–f8 b5–b4 38 a3xb4 Nd5xb4 39 c2–c3 Nb4–d5 40 Rf8–c8 Draw agreed.
From a chess player's point of view, of course, this position is easily won for Black, but both computers showed such a total lack of comprehension of the game that there was no point in examining it further.

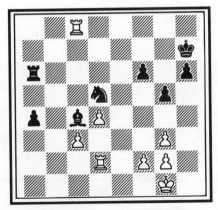

Figure 3.5 After 40 Rf8–c8

Game 3
White: **ITEP Program (5 half-moves)**
Black: **Kotok/McCarthy Program**
Stanford—Moscow, 1966–1967
Three Knights' Game

1 e2–e4 e7–e5 2 Ng1–f3 Nb8–c6 3 Nb1–c3 Bf8–c5 4 Nf3xe5!
This move was quite a surprise for us, since the computer attaches a high value to the right to castle. Nevertheless, the positional advantages secured seem to have pushed the scale in favor of 4 Nf3xe5 (as against *4 Bf1–c4*). Our program gave as the best variation for both sides: 4 ... Bc5xf2+ 5 Ke1xf2 Nc6xe5 6 d2–d4.

4 ... Nc6xe5 5 d2–d4 Bc5–d6 6 d4xe5 Bd6xe5 7 f2–f4
With this move White "issued" the following optimal sequence: 7 ... Be5xc3+
8 b2xc3 Ng8–f6 9 Qd1–d4.

7 ... Be5xc3+ 8 b2xc3 Ng8–f6 9 e4–e5
As in games between human beings plans can change during the play: in its
preliminary calculations our program intended to play 9 Qd1–d4, but now
it can see new possibilities. It is interesting that the line 9 Bf1–c4 was rejected
by the program because of 9 ... Nf6xe4 10 Bc4xf7+ Ke8–f8!?, when Black wins
a pawn because of the threat on c3 and a queen check on h4.

9 ... Nf6–e4 10 Qd1–d3
The variation given by the program was this: 10 ... d7–d5 11 e5xd6 Ne4xd6
12 Bc1–a3. Note however, that in calculating 5 half-moves ahead the program
did not find the strongest move in the position: 10 Qd1–d5!
     Why did that happen? Evidently because in the line 10 ... Ne4xc3 11 Qd5–c4
Qd8–h4+ 12 g2–g3, Black is obliged to make a 6th half-move, after which
White enters a forcing variation which wins a knight. Thinking only 5 half-
moves ahead, in the position after 12 g2–g3, it appears that Black wins a pawn
and so the move 10 Qd1–d5 is rejected.

10 ... Ne4–c5 11 Qd3–d5 Nc5–e6 12 f4–f5 Ne6–g5
In making its 12th move our program expected 12 ... c7–c6 13 Qd5–d3 Ne6–c5
14 Qd3–d6.

13 h2–h4 f7–f6 14 h4xg5 f6xg5

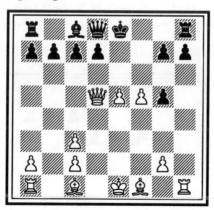

Figure 3.6 After 14 ... f6xg5

15 Rh1xh7!
This simple tactical coup would have been found even with a calculation for
one half-move.

15 ... Rh8–f8 16 Rh7xg7 c7–c6 17 Qd5–d6

After the program made this move it "announced" that Black's only salvation from mate was the variation beginning with the moves 17 ... Qd8–f6 18 e5xf6 Ke8–d8.

17 ... Rf8xf5 18 Rg7–g8+ Rf5–f8 19 Qd6xf8 mate.

Game 4
White: **Kotok/McCarthy Program**
Black: **ITEP Program (5 half-moves)**
Stanford—Moscow, 1966–1967
Alekhine's Defense

1 e2–e4 Ng8–f6 2 e4–e5 Nf6–d5 3 Ng1–f3 Nd5–b4

This looks senseless. The program is really trying to play 4 ... d7–d5 and the interpolation of 4 c2–c3 Nb4–c6 will not, in the program's opinion, improve White's position.

4 Bf1–b5 c7–c6 5 Bb5–a4 d7–d6 6 d2–d4 Qd8–a5 7 c2–c4

A bad blunder which our program did not expect when it played 6 ... Qd8–a5.

7 ... Nb4–c2++ 8 Ke1–f1 Nc2xa1 9 Nb1–c3 Qa5–b4

The program can see that in quiet continuations White wins the knight on a1. Now it manages to keep the extra rook (at least for the present).

**10 Qd1–e2 d6xe5 11 d4xe5 Bc8–e6 12 Qe2–d1 Be6xc4+ 13 Nc3–e2 b7–b5
14 Ba4–c2 Na1xc2 15 Qd1xc2 Bc4xa2 16 Ne2–d4 Qb4–c4+ 17 Kf1–g1 c6–c5
18 Qc2–d2 c5xd4 19 Nf3xd4 e7–e6 20 Nd4–f3 Nb8–c6 21 Qd2–g5 Ra8–d8
22 Bc1–d2**

Figure 3.7 After 22 Bc1–d2

22 ... Qc4–c1+
The computer is not looking for "beauty" : it is simply winning a pawn.

23 Bd2–e1 Qc1xb2 24 Qg5–f4 Ba2–d5 25 Qf4–g3 Qb2–e2 26 Be1–c3 b5–b4
27 Bc3–e1 Bd5xf3 28 g2xf3 Qe2xe1+ 29 Kg1–g2 Qe1xe5 30 Qg3–h4 a7–a5
31 Rh1–c1 Nc6–d4 32 Rc1–f1 Nd4xf3!
The program did not find this move in its earlier analysis. If now 33 Kg2xf3,
then 33 ... Rd8–d4! wins the queen.

33 Qh4–h3 Rd8–d3 34 Qh3–g3 Nf3–e1+ 35 Rf1xe1 Rd3xg3+ 36 Kg2–f1
Qe5–b5+
Here the program had been intending to play 36 ... Rg3–g1+ but then found
a more lucrative continuation.

37 Re1–e2 Rg3–a3 38 Kf1–e1 Ra3–a1+ 39 Ke1–d2
After this the Soviet program can see that it is mating.

39 ... Qb5–d5+ 40 Kd2–e3 Ra1–a3+ 41 Ke3–f4 Qd5–f5 mate.

The problem of creating a chess computer belongs to a young branch of
cybernetics — heuristic programming. There is one task facing this discipline,
the solution of which would have practical applications: to work out methods
of orienting in a continuously changing situation depending on a large
number of factors which cannot be subjected to a complete mechanical
analysis. Chess is an excellent model of such a situation.

In the course of work on chess programs some very valuable heuristic
methods have been found which shorten the analysis many times over.
Remembering the best moves in deep analyses, the use of forced variations
and certain a priori evaluations of moves and positions are among these
techniques. The heuristic methods discovered in the course of creating chess
programs have already found application in the study of networks, finding
the minimum of functions of several variables and also in working out the
results of some physical experiments.

And as far as the eternal question (which excites all chess players) is
concerned of whether the computer will defeat man, the authors of this article
are bold enough to claim that it will happen in the next ten to fifteen years.

The Stanford—Moscow match did much for the development of computer
chess by creating the stimulus for further work in the United States. Even as
the match was taking place, a new program was being developed at MIT, and
the next eight years saw an explosion of interest in the subject. Computer
competitions became more and more frequent and some scientists believed
that a master standard chess program was not far away.

CHAPTER

4

The Formative Years

I think that the problem can be solved only by chess specialists using their creative experience.

Mikhail Botvinnik

The Greenblatt Program

Beginning in mid-November 1966, a chess program was developed on a PDP-6 computer at the Artificial Intelligence Laboratory at MIT. The program was written primarily by Richard Greenblatt, then an undergraduate student, with the assistance of Donald E. Eastlake III. The program was written quickly — by February 1967 it was ready to play in a local tournament where it lost four games and drew one to achieve a USCF rating of 1243. In March 1967 it played in another tournament, winning one game and losing four. Its performance rating for that event was 1360 and its overall rating went up to 1330. One month later in yet another tournament it scored two wins and two losses for a performance rating of 1640. The program was named MACHACK VI and it was made an honorary member of both the United States Chess Federation and the Massachusetts Chess Association.

Greenblatt's program contained several powerful interactive aids for locating errors in the program and for improving its performance. These aids included facilities to look, on a screen, at the evaluation of any selected node of the search tree, to examine all the factors that caused a move to be considered plausible, to look at the main variation of the program's analysis from each position at the first ply that was analyzed, and to examine statistics on how long the computation took and how many plausible moves were generated at any point. By using these facilities and by playing hundreds of games against the program within a few months, Greenblatt was able to produce a program that was efficient, fast, and relatively free of bugs.

Greenblatt's plausible move generator had three basic functions. It selected the moves that it considered plausible, put them into their order of merit so as to optimize the advantage of using the alpha-beta algorithm, and calculated certain positional and "developmental" values that would decide the program's move if several moves led to the same static value. The major reason for the quality of the program's play was that considerable chess knowledge was included. In fact there were about fifty chess heuristics used in computing the plausibility of moves, though many of the fifty were only applicable in special cases or at certain stages of the game.

Each square was assigned a value during each plausible move computation, corresponding roughly to the estimated worth of having another piece bearing on the square or the cost of moving away a piece presently attacking the square. The principal criteria used for assigning these values included the closeness of the square to the center of the board, its proximity to the opponent's king, and its occupation by one of the program's own pieces which was en prise. Small values were given for occupation of the square by one of the program's pieces and for its closeness to the opponent's side of the board.

The developmental value of a piece was the sum of the values of the squares it attacked, plus values accumulated for actual attacks on enemy pieces. When a move was being considered for plausibility the new development value of the piece was calculated assuming the piece to be on its new proposed location. The difference between the new and old developmental values was used as a factor in assessing plausibility, encouraging developing moves and discouraging antipositional ones. Gains or losses in development resulting from blocking or unblocking the opponent's or the program's pieces were also considered in the developmental value. Other factors were added to encourage attacking the opponent's pieces, his weak pawns, his pinned pieces and pieces defending other pieces, and so on.

Greenblatt noticed that sometimes his program would give a high plausibility value to an antipositional move because it attacked an enemy piece. If the attack led to material gain, all was well and good; but if the opponent could simply move the attacked piece away then the move was a pointless waste of time. Moves were therefore scored separately on their positional merit and if this proved bad then the move would be rejected if there was a better positional move leading to the same terminal score.

The evaluation function used five features: Material balance, piece ratio, pawn structure, king safety and center control. The piece ratio term was aimed at promoting exchanges when the program was ahead in material and avoiding them when behind. Greenblatt's pawn structure feature was slightly more reliable than those used in earlier programs because it made allowances for backward pawns as well as for doubled and isolated ones.

The program's tree search was conducted along the lines of Shannon's type-B strategy, with variable widths of search at different levels of the tree. At the root of the tree the fifteen most plausible moves were chosen and ordered. For each of these the fifteen most plausible reply moves were chosen and ordered. Then the nine most plausible replies to these, then nine replies to them and seven moves at depth five. These are the basic settings that were used when the program played tournament games. The only way that the program could fail to consider the indicated number of moves was if the requisite number of moves simply did not exist or if the alpha-beta algorithm produced a cutoff before all these moves at any node had been examined. Just as efficient tree searching was sometimes responsible for the basic settings not being reached, so it was often the case that the basic width had to be increased in order to allow for safe checks to be considered, as well as captures (at the first and second ply) and at least some of the moves of a reasonable number of pieces. The logic behind this last heuristic is quite sound. If all the moves of a single piece are highly plausible (e.g., those of a queen because it is en prise) then the rest of the board might not be looked at because the number of plausible moves might have reached the basic setting. But by examining the moves of a few other pieces it might be possible to find a clever tactical blow that succeeds even though the queen is left en prise.

The program kept a record of each position considered during its search for a move, together with information concerning the value of that position. If the position arose again during the search, either on part of the same tree (by transposition) or as part of a different tree (for example, when the program was considering a later move) then the position could be looked up in the table and its value retrieved. This, technique, known as "hash tables" often avoided the necessity of evaluating the same position twice, and it also helped to detect draws by threefold repetition. Hash tables are discussed more fully in Chapter 9.

If two moves were found by the search to lead to the same static evaluation, the move with the higher plausibility value was preferred. However, in some situations this move was not the most desirable one to make. In order to take such cases into account two types of modification were made to the values found at the lower levels of the tree. The first modification subtracted a few points if the current move being investigated was marked as being developmentally poor by the plausible move generator. The second modification subtracted small amounts for moving pieces that had already moved higher up in the tree. This had the effect of avoiding moving pieces twice in the opening, avoiding making moves that result in the moved piece being attacked and forced to retreat, and avoiding making a two move maneuvre when the maneuvre was possible in one move.

The program's performance was improved by introducing a secondary search whenever the normal tree search resulted in a new candidate for the best move at the top level. What was done was to descend the principal variation for that move as far as the variation was computed by the plausible move generator, and then to conduct an additional search, usually limited to two plies although captures and checks could increase this number. The value obtained by the secondary search was then used in place of the value found for the principle variation if it was worse for the side to move.

Another feature that was new to chess programs was the use of a small library of opening variations. This "book" was compiled by two MIT students, Larry Kaufmann, who represented the United States in Student Chess Olympiads, and Alan Baisley, an expert on the USCF scale. Almost two decades later Kaufmann remains one of the human chess world's most interested observers in the activities of the computer fraternity.

The following game was played by MACHACK VI when it was only two months old, and is the first tournament game ever played by a computer. The program's opponent was rated 2190 on the USCF scale — almost a master.

White: **Human**
Black: **MACHACK VI**
1967
Irregular Opening

1 g2–g3 e7–e5 2 Ng1–f3 e5–e4 3 Nf3–d4 Bf8–c5 4 Nd4–b3 Bc5–b6 5 Bf1–g2 Ng8–f6 6 c2–c4 d7–d6 7 Nb1–c3 Bc8–e6 8 d2–d3 e4xd3 9 Bg2xb7 Nb8–d7 10 e2xd3 Ra8–b8 11 Bb7–g2 O–O 12 O–O Be6–g4 13 Qd1–c2 Rf8–e8 14 d3–d4 c7–c5 15 Bc1–e3 c5xd4 16 Nb3xd4 Nd7–e5 17 h2–h3 Bg4–d7 18 b2–b3 Bb6–c5 19 Ra1–d1 Qd8–c8 20 Kg1–h2 Ne5–g6 21 Be3–g5 Re8–e5 22 Bg5xf6 g7xf6 23 Nc3–e4 f6–f5 24 Ne4–f6+ Kg8–g7 25 Nf6xd7 Qc8xd7 26 Nd4–c6 Rb8–e8 27 Nc6xe5 Re8xe5 28 Qc2–c3 f7–f6 29 Rd1–d3 Re5–e2 30 Rd3–d2 Re2xd2 31 Qc3xd2 Ng6–e5 32 Rf1–d1 Qd7–c7 33 Bg2–d5 Kg7–g6 34 b3–b4 Bc5–b6 35 Qd2–c2 Ne5–c6 36 Bd5–e6 Nc6–d4 37 Rd1xd4 Bb6xd4 38 Qc2xf5+ Kg6–g7 39 Qf5–g4+ Kg7–h6 40 Qg4xd4 Qc7–e7 41 Qd4–h4+ Kh6–g6 42 Be6–f5+ Kg6–g7 43 Qh4xh7+ Kg7–f8 44 Qh7–h8+ Kf8–f7 45 Qh8–a8 Qe7–c7 46 Qa8–d5+ Kf7–g7 47 Kh2–g2 Qc7–e7 48 h3–h4 Kg7–h6 49 g3–g4 Kh6–g7 50 h4–h5 Qe7–e2 51 h5–h6+ Kg7–f8 52 h6–h7 Qe2xf2+ 53 Kg2xf2 Kf8–e7 54 h7–h8=Q a7–a6 55 Qd5–e6 mate.

The next game is the first ever won by a computer program in tournament play. It was played in the second round of the Massachusetts State Championship, March 1967.

White: **MACHACK VI**
Black: **Human (rated 1510)**
Massachusetts State Championship, 1967
Sicilian Defense

1 e2–e4 c7–c5 2 d2–d4 c5xd4 3 Qd1xd4 Nb8–c6 4 Qd4–d3 Ng8–f6 5 Nb1–c3
g7–g6 6 Ng1–f3 d7–d6 7 Bc1–f4 e7–e5 8 Bf4–g3 a7–a6 9 O–O–O b7–b5
10 a2–a4 Bf8–h6+ 11 Kc1–b1 b5–b4 12 Qd3xd6! Bc8–d7
If 12 ... Qd8xd6 13 Rd1xd6 b4xc3 14 Rd6xc6 Bc8–d7 15 Nf3xe5, and White is
two pawns up. Presumably Human overlooked the fork of the two knights
by White's rook.

13 Bg3–h4 Bh6–g7 14 Nc3–d5 Nf6xe4 15 Nd5–c7+ Qd8xc7 16 Qd6xc7 Ne4–c5
17 Qc7–d6 Bg7–f8 18 Qd6–d5 Ra8–c8 19 Nf3xe5 Bd7–e6 20 Qd5xc6+ Rc8xc6
21 Rd1–d8 mate.

By the time that MACHACK VI had played in one or two tournaments it had
attracted considerable public attention, and it acquired an even higher profile
when in one of its games it discovered a nice, 9-ply combination that was
reputedly missed by some of the U. S. masters who were shown the same
position.

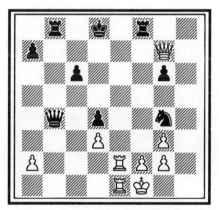

Figure 4.1 MACHACK VI finds mate in five

Here MACHACK VI found:

1 ... **Rf8xf2+ 2 Kf1–g1**
If 2 Re2xf2 Ng4–h2+ 3 Kf1–e2 (or *3 Kf1–g1 Qb4xe1+ 4 Kg1xh2 Qe1xe2* and Black
is a rook ahead) 3 ... Qb4–b2+ 4 Ke2–d1 Qb2–b1+ 5 Kd1–e2 Rb8–b2 mate.

2 ... **Rf2xe2 3 Qg7–h8+ Kd8–c7 4 Qh8–f6 Re2xe1+ White resigns.**

MACHACK VI certainly started a resurgance of interest in computer chess. It was on show in Edinburgh during the 1968 congress of the International Federation for Information Processing (IFIP) where it took on all comers and scored about 50 percent — not a bad result in view of the fact that many computer scientists are also stronger than average chess players.

Botvinnik's Research

Mikhail Botvinnik was World Chess Champion for twelve years. He first won the title in 1948 and finally relinquished it, to Petrosian, in 1963. Apart from two spells, each of a year, when Smyslov (1957–58) and Tal (1960–61) held the crown, Botvinnik was invincible.

As well as being an outstanding chess player Botvinnik was also an electrical engineer, and channelled his interest in computers into the problem of automating his own thought processes. His ideas were highly original and led to many stimulating publications on computer chess.

Figure 4.2 Mikhail Botvinnik in Moscow, 1988

Botvinnik devised an algorithm for enabling a computer to search the game tree in the same kind of way as he himself would do. His most often quoted example was the position shown in Figure 4.3. White wins with 1 g5–g6 Kf5–f6 2 g6–g7 Bc2–h7! 3 e3–e4 Ne1–f3 4 e4–e5+ Nf3xe5 5 Kh8xh7 Ne5–f7 6 g7–g8=Q Nf7–g5+ 7 Qg8xg5+ Kf6xg5 8 h5–h6 c5–c4 9 Kh7–g7 c4–c3 10 h6–h7 c3–c2 11 h7–h8=Q c2–c1=Q 12 Qh8–h6+! and White wins. His publications described how his program PIONEER was able to solve such positions while examining only a very small number of positions in the game tree. In this particular case, only 200 positions were examined.

Unfortunately Botvinnik's most active period as a reasercher into computer chess coincided with the era when access to computer time in the Soviet Union was severely limited. Had he been given access to virtually unlimited amounts of time on powerful computers, there is no telling how much he and his programmers could have achieved.

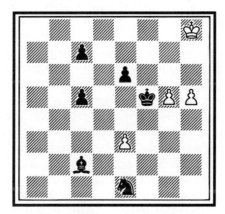

Figure 4.3 Position solved by Botvinnik's program: White to play

The Origins of the "Levy Bet"

Immediately after the 1968 IFIP Congress, the Department of Machine Intelligence and Perception at Edinburgh University held one of its annual "Machine Intelligence Workshops." These meetings brought together many of the most prominent workers in the field of Artificial Intelligence and the Proceedings of the workshops have been published as a well-known series of books: "Machine Intelligence 1," ... etc). The Machine Intelligence Workshops were hosted by Donald Michie, head of the Edinburgh University department, and during each workshop it was traditional for him to arrange a number of cocktail parties and other social events. It was during one of these parties that my now famous bet was born. I was talking to John McCarthy, Professor of Artificial Intelligence at Stanford University and one of the world's leading authorities on the subject. After losing a game of chess to me McCarthy expressed the opinion that within ten years there would be a program strong enough to beat me. I was Scottish Champion at the time, and was extremely skeptical of his statement. Both McCarthy and Michie were sure I was wrong and within a couple of minutes I offered to bet each of them 250 £ that I was right, i.e., that no program would be able to beat me in a match by the end of August 1978. They both accepted the bet with confidence and my only regret is that I did not make it for a much larger sum, but in those days I was earning less than 1,000 £ per annum and 500 £ sounded like a lot of money.

The following year I was asked to present a paper at the Machine Intelligence Workshop and during the course of my presentation I was heckled by Professor Seymour Papert who worked at the Artificial Intelligence Laboratory at MIT. Papert was so skeptical at some of my assertions that I asked him whether he would like to come in on my bet and increase it by 250 £. He said that he was quite sure that within five years, not ten, I would be beaten by a computer program, but I felt that it would have been unfair of me to bet with him on such a short time span. So we agreed that he would become a third member of the consortium, with 1978 remaining the key date.

In 1970 the Association for Computing Machinery (ACM) held the first chess tournament in the world in which all of the participants were computer programs. The 1970 tournament was held in the New York Hilton as part of the ACM's annual convention and it attracted six entries and widespread publicity. The winner of the tournament was a program called CHESS 3.0 which was written at Northwestern University, Evanston, Illinois.

The ACM tournament in 1970 was such a success that it was decided to repeat it the following year, and since then it has become a regular event and it usually proves to be the most popular attraction at the ACM conventions. I was invited to be the tournament director at the 1971 competition in Chicago where the number of contestants was increased from six to eight. As well as being concerned with the rules of the competition and ensuring fair play, my job was to give a running commentary to the audience so that the spectators could understand what was happening in the games. The playing styles and weaknesses of the programs made these events more entertaining for the audience than watching most Grandmaster tournaments.

During the 1971 competition I was talking to some of the programmers about my bet. Professor Ed Kozdrowicki, then working at the Bell Telephone Laboratories at Murray Hill, New Jersey, felt sure that I was going to lose and he even offered to increase the bet by $1,000 (about 400 £). I was still an unprosperous programming assistant and I was afraid to take on such a "big" commitment so I agreed to take 250 £ of his action and Professor Ben Mittman took the remainder of the bet. Mittman was one of the organizers of the 1971 tournament and director of the Vogelback Computing Center at Northwestern, where CHESS 3.0 was born.

A few hours after Kozdrowicki came in on the bet his program, COKO III, reached the following position in its game against GENIE, which had been programmed by Herbert Raymond at the Fleet Computer Center in San Diego.

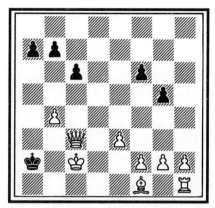

Figure 4.4 White: COKO III Black: GENIE, White to move

It would appear here that White held some advantage. He had at his disposal two different mates-in-one (38 Bf1–c4 and 38 Qc3–b2) as well as various mates-in-two, -three, -four or indeed almost any number of moves. But because of a defect in the program this plethora of mating continuations led to COKO III's tragedy. Had there been only one forced mate in this position COKO III would have played it, but because there was more than one mate and because COKO III's scoring function did not distinguish between the values of a mate-in-one and a mate-in-two, -three or -four, it had no incentive to choose the quickest mate.

38 Kc2–c1
This was just as good, from the program's point of view, as giving mate-on-the-move, since mate still cannot be prevented.

38 ... f6–f5 39 Kc1–c2
And this was just as good as giving mate-on-the-move ...

39 ... f5–f4 40 Kc2–c1 g5–g4 41 Kc1–c2 f4–f3 42 Kc2–c1 f3xg2 43 Kc1–c2 g2xh1=Q
Now White had one last chance to end the game with a single blow.

44 Kc2–c1??
Inexplicable! COKO III's programers were so distraught now that they could not even speculate as to why COKO III had missed this final chance to mate.

44 ... Qh1xf1+ 45 Kc1–d2 Qf1xf2+ 46 Kd2–c1 Qf2–g1+ 47 Kc1–c2 Qg1xh2+ 48 Kc2–c1 Qh2–h1+ 49 Kc1–c2 Qh1–b1+ 50 Kc2–d2 g4–g3 51 Qc3–c4+ Qb1–b3 52 Qc4xb3+ Ka2xb3 53 e3–e4 Kb3xb4 54 e4–e5 g3–g2
COKO III's programmers had seen enough and they resigned on behalf of their program. Ed Kozdrowicki was heard to be muttering something about a bad bet as he left the playing hall.

So by August 1971 my bet had grown to 1,000 £. By this time I had become an international master but the standard of the best chess programs had improved little, if at all, since I made the first bet three years earlier. As time went on I became more and more confident and I was therefore delighted in the Autumn of 1974 when Donald Michie offered to up the stakes. He wanted to increase his stake in the original bet to 500 £, thereby increasing the total wager to 1,250 £ (roughly $2,900 at that time), and to add a rider that if I did lose this bet then the program that beat me would have been written by him or under his direction. Since, at that time, the world's strongest chess program was KAISSA, written in Moscow, and since I expected that KAISSA'S success in the 1st World Computer Championship in Stockholm (August 1974) would mean more financial support and programming effort for the Moscow group, I felt that in the unlikely event that anything did turn sour on me it would be from the East that my conqueror would come, and not from the West. I therefore accepted both parts of Michie's new wager but I turned down his "offer" to extend the period of the bet from August to December 1978. After all, by August 1978 the value of my winnings would already have been severely eroded by inflation.

Soviet Research

Between the time of the Moscow—Stanford match in 1967 and the birth of the KAISSA program in 1971 only one Soviet chess program was heard of. It played very weakly and was annihilated in a game played against the readers of the newspaper *The Ural Worker* (Uralsky Rabochy). Each week the program's move would be published in the newspaper and the readers were invited to send in their suggestion for reply moves. The move that received the most votes was played.

The game was published in *Shakhmaty v USSR*, August 1968, with notes by International GM Lev Polugayevsky. No details were revealed concerning the computer or its programmers, perhaps because of the poor play of the program. Here is the game with Polugayevsky's annotations. Presumably this is the first mass contest against a computer in history.

White: **Readers of *The Ural Worker***
Black: **Soviet Program**
1968
Nimzowitsch Defense

1 e2–e4 Nb8–c6
A move suggested by Nimzowitsch. It is not very popular and has almost vanished from tournaments, but the computer has its own "theoretical taste," which does not coincide with the conclusions of contemporary chess theory.

2 d2–d4 d7–d5 3 Nb1–c3 d5xe4

The computer prefers to take the pawn.   More cautious is 3 ... e7–e6.

4 d4–d5 Nc6–e5 5 Bc1–f4

White is quite right in not hurrying to recapture the pawn. By chasing the knight White tries to make the development of Black's kingside more difficult.

5 ... Ne5–g6 6 Bf4–g3 f7–f5?

It seems that a computer also has human weaknesses — it can be just as greedy as a human being. The computer does not want to part with the extra pawn, and moreover it threatens 7 ... f5–f4.

However, the move 6 ... f7–f5 is obviously antipositional. It weakens the king and opens the a2–g8 diagonal. Furthermore, the computer appears to have forgotten one of the most important principles in chess — the principle of development. 6 ... a7–a6 would have been a better solution and if 7 Nc3xe4, then 7 ... Ng8–f6 8 Ne4xf6+ (*8 Qd1–d4 e7–e5! 9 Bg3xe5 Nf6xe4 10 Qd4xe4 Qd8–e7*) 8 ... e7xf6. White's position is better but Black will succeed in completing his development. Instead of 7 Nc3xe4, 7 Qd1–d4 is stronger. After 7 ... Ng8–f6 8 O–O–O, White still has pressure.

7 Bf1–b5+ Bc8–d7 8 Ng1–h3!

The readers have correctly determined the weak points in their opponent's camp. The white knight is aiming at e6.

8 ... c7–c6!

A natural move, but since it was made by the computer it deserves an exclamation mark. This move bears witness to the great possibilities of the electronic chess player. Evidently the computer is able to assess the position correctly. Black's Achilles' Heel is the square e6 and the computer correctly decides not to allow the exchange of his light-squared bishop, which is the only piece defending that square.

9 Bb5–c4 Qd8–b6

White's main threat of 10 Nh3–g5 followed by 11 d5xc6 and 12 Bc4–f7 mate is noticed by the computer, which prepares to castle queenside to remove the king from the danger zone. However, it does not manage to realize this plan.

Black's position was compromised by his 6th move, but he should have tried as an emergency measure to neutralize his main enemy — the bishop on c4. The computer should have "paid attention" to 9 ... b7–b5. For example: 10 d5xc6 b5xc4 11 c6xd7+ Qd8xd7, or 10 Bc4–b3 c6–c5 11 a2–a4 c5–c4 12 Bb3–a2 a7–a6, when in spite of the strong move 13 f2–f3 for White, Black can still put up a fight.

10 Qd1–d2 Qb6–c5

The computer is alert. It avoids the trap prepared by the humans: 10 ... O–O–O 11 Nc3–a4, when the queen has nowhere to go. The computer also refuses the

"Greek gift" — the pawn on b2: 10 ... Qb6xb2 11 Ra1–b1 Qb2–a3 12 Rb1xb7, with an overwhelming advantage for White. Who could say after this move that the computer thinks in a primitive way?

11 d5xc6
In order to profit from his advantage in development White must open up the game.

11 ... Bd7xc6
As will transpire, later 11 ... b7xc6 12 O–O–O Ng8–f6 is correct.

Figure 4.5   After 11 ... Bd7xc6

12 Bc4–e6!
Well played! Now Black's kingside is frozen and White can calmly prepare for the decisive attack.

12 ... Ng8–h6
What would a chess player have played in this position? He would have chosen the lesser evil: 12 ... Ra8–d8 13 Be6–f7+ Ke8xf7 14 Qd2xd8 h7–h6, but the computer cannot part with the exchange. We should note however that the computer's combinative ability is not too bad: it saw the piquant variation: 12 ... h7–h6 13 O–O–O Ng8–f6 14 Bg3–c7, and then 15 Qd2–d8+.

13 O–O–O Ng6–e5
How else can he defend against 14 Bg3–c7? If 13 ... Qc5–a5 then 14 Nh3–g5 Ra8–d8 15 Qd2xd8+ Qa5xd8 16 Rd1xd8+ Ke8xd8 17 Rh1–d1+ Kd8–e8 18 Bg3–c7 wins.

14 Nh3–g5 Nh6–g4
Otherwise 15 Bg3xe5 follows.

15 f2–f3 g7–g6
It has to give up the knight, so the fight is over but the computer (like some chess players) does not like resigning on time.

16 f3xg4 Bf8–g7 17 Bg3xe5 Qc5xe5
This leads to an attractive finish. The computer "did not like" 17 ... Bg7xe5 18 Be6–f7+, followed by 19 Ng5–e6+ and Black loses his queen. Could the computer have seen the final combination? Perhaps, but even a computer is entitled to count on his opponent's mistakes ...

18 Qd2–d8+! Ra8xd8 19 Be6–f7+
and the computer resigned. The electronic chess player will undoubtedly try to take revenge on the readers in a fresh match. The future will show whether he can succeed.

The Northwestern University Chess Program

The program written at Northwestern University won the first four ACM tournaments (1970 through 1973). It finished second, behind KAISSA, at the 1st World Computer Championship in Stockholm (1974) and was second, behind RIBBIT, at the 5th ACM tournament (San Diego 1974). It regained its ACM title at Minneapolis in 1975. The original program was written by Larry Atkin, Keith Gorlen and David Slate while they were students at Northwestern University, and it was improved a little each year, even after its programmers graduated. When Gorlen left Northwestern University Slate and Atkin continued to work on the program.

The version of the Northwestern program that first appeared in the ACM tournaments was called CHESS 3.0. As the program grew in age and strength so its name was amended. The first digit changed when Slate and Atkin created a new generation program, while the digit after the point referred to a version number within a particular generation. Here is a brief description of how CHESS 4.4 decided on its moves.

The program performed a depth-first tree search using the alpha-beta algorithm. The way in which the program grew the tree is interesting — there was a special routine whose job it was to choose the next move to be searched or to decide not to search any more moves from some particular position. To choose a move this routine invoked one of fifteen selector modules, each of which was a different move selection algorithm. A module could select a move and/or it could determine which module is to be used the next time the selection routine was called into operation for the same position. Here is a list of the modules and their functions:

START: This module initialized a position. It called GENMOV to generate and evaluate the legal moves.

LIBRARY: The program had a library of positions that had been "learned" and this library was searched for a move applicable to the current position. When a position was added to the library a suggested move was also added, this move being either the book move, in the case of a stored opening variation, or the move actually played in that position, in the case of a position already encountered.

ENDPOINT: was invoked to terminate the search of a move by returning a final evaluation for that move.

CHPRUNE: tried to find a checking move whose score suggested that it was worth looking at for reasons other than the check.

LMBLAS: looked at the best variation of the previous move tree to see the program's expected response, at that time, if the opponent made the move predicted by that tree. A human analyzes in much the same way — if his opponent makes an expected move a human master will first consider the move that he had planned to make when thinking about his previous move.

ISTBST: chose the move having the best score from the evaluation function, that is, the apparently best move.

BSTLAS: chose the move which turned out best at the last position examined at the same ply level. This is another human approach — if a particular move is strong in reply to one of our opponent's moves, then maybe the same move will be strong in reply to another of his moves.

MORBST: selected up to L best valued moves, where L was a pre-set limit. The limits were usually different for different levels in the tree, though at any one level the limit was the same. It was this limit parameter that determined the width of search and hence, to a great extent, the time taken to make a move. COMBO: selected a number of the most promising moves as determined by a "combination potential" score.

FLEX: selected moves in almost the same way as MORBST but with the difference that it only tried to find moves that defended against a threat not met by previously searched moves.

BANANA SUPER BEYOND: selected moves at the first ply whose scores were not high enough to justify a full depth search by previous modules. SUPER BEYOND moves were searched to a depth of three ply and, if their score looked good, to full depth by the EXPAND module. The purpose of SUPER BEYOND was to solve such problems as the difficulty of transferring a piece from one square to a better one by passing through a worse one. For example, a human player as White would not normally put his knight on, say, h3 unless he intended to move it to a good square such as f4. But since such an operation takes 3 plies it is a good idea to examine a number of moves to that depth.

BEYOND: selected all moves that were not chosen by SUPER BEYOND and examined them to a depth of 2 plies. This module was a computationally cheap way to catch certain kinds of moves that would be missed otherwise.

EXPAND: re-searched moves that passed the tests set by BEYOND and SUPER BEYOND. This expansion took the search to full depth.

QUIESCE: varied the depth of search according to the degree of quiescence of the position.

CHESS 3.0 and its descendants had an impressive record against other chess programs. In the first three ACM tournaments it played ten games and won them all. In the 4th ACM tournament it scored 3.5 out of 4. It was not until the 1st World Championship tournament in 1974 that CHESS 4.0 (as it was then called) lost a "serious" game to another program. Later that same year CHESS 4.0 lost another game to a computer program, this time to RIBBIT from the University of Waterloo, which thereby became the first program to stop the Northwestern University program from winning the ACM event.

CHESS 4.0 was not only successful against other computer programs. It competed in a tournament with 50 humans at Northwestern University during the winter of 1973–1974 and finished in a tie for third place with a score of 4.5 out of 6. The average rating of its opponents was 1537 and its performance rating for the tournament was 1736 which placed it in the middle of class B on the USCF scale.

TECH

The "Technology" chess program was written by James Gillogly while he was a graduate student at Carnegie Mellon University. Its name, TECH, is derived from the basic philosophy that underlines Gillogly's work — he wanted to write a program that relied almost entirely on technology (fast computers) and hardly at all on chess heuristics. The aim was simply to generate all legal moves to a fixed depth, then evaluate the terminal positions only with respect to material. Such an approach can never lead to a program that plays perfect chess, but Gillogly's idea was not to create a grandmaster program but rather to produce a standard of play against which other programs could be measured. In order to justify the effort of developing a more complex program it would be necessary that the more complex program could defeat TECH. Since TECH's performance would improve with an increase in computer speeds it could always be used as a "bench-mark" program.

Gillogly's first experiments showed that this ultra-primitive approach did not result in a useful program, since the standard of play was low for any observed depth of search. The program often reached a position that was strategically hopeless before it was able to achieve anything by tactics, and it even made tactical blunders through evaluating non-quiescent positions. Gillogly therefore decided to devote a small proportion of the program's computation time to chess heuristics.

TECH's move generator consisted of two main parts: positional and tactical analysis. The positional analysis routine sorted the moves at the top level of the tree so that the moves with the best superficial positional scores were examined first. This helped to get the most out of the alpha-beta algorithm. No tactical considerations were included in the positional analysis. The tactical analyzer was a "brute-force" tree search which investigated all moves to a fixed depth and evaluated terminal positions provided that they conformed to a simple quiescence criteria. The alpha-beta algorithm would select the move at ply one that was seen to be materially the best. If there were two or more moves of equal material merit then the first of these was chosen since that was the one whose superficial positional score was the highest. One feature of TECH that was unique among its rival chess programs at that time (1975) was that it used its opponent's thinking time for its own analysis. While its opponent was thinking it predicted its opponent's move and then began to compute its reply. If the opponent made the predicted move then TECH's clock time would be small. In many cases TECH was able to reply immediately because it completed its search to the predicted opponent's move long before its opponent had himself finished his own search.

The most important part of the program (in terms of playing ability) was the tactical analysis component (i.e., the brute-force search). All moves were searched to a fixed depth, usually five plies, and then all captures were examined and all captures in reply to these captures, and so on until there were no more captures. Even though the alpha-beta algorithm was used, this search strategy resulted in as many as 500,000 terminal positions being examined when the program was choosing its move in a tournament game. This was only made possible by the simplicity of the evaluation function (material being the only feature considered) and the efficiency of the move generator. Captures were recognized and sorted during move generation with the highest valued captures being put first on the list. This helped speed up the tree search since the refutation of a weak move is often a capture.

The positional pre-sorting routine discriminated between moves of equal material value. When used in conjunction with the tactical search routine it could often achieve a satisfactory position from the opening, even though it knew no opening theory. The program distinguished between five phases of the game and for each phase it employed different heuristics for the positional pre-sort at the top of the tree. Among heuristics that were used throughout the game were one to encourage exchanges when TECH was ahead in material and one to adjust the basic maximum depth for the tactical analysis on the basis of how much time, on average, TECH had for each move before the next time control. If the program had significantly more time available per move than it used (on average) on its previous nine moves, then its depth of search was increased. If it used more time on its previous moves then the depth was decreased.

TECH considered the opening to be the first eight moves. The most important heuristic in the opening evaluation was occupation of the center. Each square on the board was weighted with a desirability value ranging from 0 points for the corners to 8 points for the center. Each move represented a gain or loss of center control, for example the move 1 Ng1–f3 would yield a gain of 5 points for center control. This was multiplied by a priority factor for the piece that moved: pawn = 1, queen = 1, rook = 2, bishop = 3, knight = 4, and king = –1. These weightings encouraged the development of knights before bishops, of minor pieces before major pieces (bringing out the queen was discouraged during the opening) and it encouraged castling by giving the king a negative priority value so that it scored the greatest number of center control points when it was in a corner.

Each move in the opening was given a final positional score of the center control term plus the value of whichever of the following heuristics applied to the move (they are defined here from White's side):

> Pawn from e2 to e4: 30 points, from e3 to e4: 2 points
> Pawn from d2 to d4: 20 points, from d3 to d4: 2 points
> Kingside castling: 30
> Queenside castling: 10
> Nb1–a3 or Ng1–h3: –15
> Putting a piece on e3 or d3 where it blocks a pawn: –50
> Moving a kingside piece: 2
> Playing the Petroff Defence: –50
> Pawn captures towards (away from) the center: 5 (-5)
> Pawn captures leading to doubled isolated pawns: –10
> Advancing a rook's pawn: –10
> Capturing an undefended (defended) center pawn: 50 (-15)

The best way to show the effectiveness of these heuristics is to give some examples of TECH's opening play. Remember that TECH is playing purely from first principles — it has no "book" knowledge whatsoever.

White: **TECH**
Black: **DAVID**
2nd ACM Championship, Chicago 1971
French Defense

1 e2–e4 e7–e6 2 d2–d4 Qd8–h4 3 Nb1–c3 Nb8–c6 4 Ng1–f3 Qh4–h5 5 Bf1–d3 Qh5–g4 6 O–O f7–f6 7 Bc1–e3 a7–a6 8 Qd1–e2 g7–g5

White: **TECH**
Black: **CHESS 3.5**
2nd ACM Championship, Chicago 1971
Sicilian Defense

1 e2–e4 c7–c5 2 Ng1–f3 Nb8–c6 3 d2–d4 c5xd4 4 Nf3xd4 Ng8–f6 5 Nb1–c3
d7–d6 6 Bf1–c4
Bobby Fischer's favorite move in this position! So even in 1971 a program that
knew no opening theory could play the first six moves as well as Fischer!

6 ... e7–e6 7 O–O a7–a6 8 Bc1–e3 Nc6–e5

White: **SCHACH**
Black: **TECH**
3rd ACM Championship, Boston 1982
Queen's Gambit Accepted

1 d2–d4 d7–d5 2 c2–c4 d5xc4 3 Ng1–f3 Nb8–c6 4 e2–e4 b7–b5 5 d4–d5 Nc6–b4
6 Bc1–g5 Ng8–f6 7 Bg5xf6 e7xf6 8 Bf1–e2 Bf8–c5

White: **TECH**
Black: **USC Program**
3rd ACM Championship, Boston 1972
Sicilian Defense

1 e2–e4 c7–c5 2 Ng1–f3 Nb8–c6 3 d2–d4 c5xd4 4 Nf3xd4 Ng8–f6 5 Nb1–c3
d7–d6 6 Bf1–c4 e7–e5 7 Nd4–f3 Bc8–e6 8 Qd1–d3 Nc6–b4

White: **CHESS 3.6**
Black: **TECH**
3rd ACM Championship, Boston 1972
Ruy Lopez

1 e2–e4 e7–e5 2 Ng1–f3 Nb8–c6 3 Bf1–b5 Ng8–f6 4 O–O Bf8–c5 5 Nb1–c3
d7–d6 6 Bb5xc6+ b7xc6 7 d2–d4 e5xd4 8 Nf3xd4 O–O

White: **OSTRICH**
Black: **TECH**
Play-off for 2nd place, 3rd ACM Championship, Boston 1972
English Opening

1 c2–c4 e7–e5 2 Nb1–c3 Nb8–c6 3 e2–e4 Ng8–f6 4 d2–d3 Bf8–c5 5 Bc1–g5 O–O
6 Ng1–f3 d7–d6 7 Bf1–e2 Bc8–e6 8 O–O Nc6–d4

White: **TECH**
Black: **COKO III**
Play-off for 2nd place, 3rd ACM Championship, Boston 1972
Petroff Defense

**1 e2–e4 e7–e5 2 Ng1–f3 Ng8–f6 3 d2–d4 Bf8–b4+ 4 Bc1–d2 Bb4xd2+
5 Nb1xd2 e5xd4 6 Nf3xd4 O–O 7 Bf1–c4 Nf6xe4 8 Nd2xe4 d7–d5**

These examples should be sufficient to convince the reader that it is quite
possible for a computer to get reasonable positions in the opening without
having any book knowledge.

TECH considered the middle game to begin with move nine and to continue
until one side had less than 1950 points worth of material (in the initial
position each side had 4420 on TECH's scale). The center control heuristic was
still used in the middlegame but the priority factors were slightly altered:
pawn = 3, knight = 4, bishop = 3, rook = 2, queen = 1 and king = 1. Since the
pieces have usually found good squares by the middlegame, this factor had
less influence than in the opening. Each move was credited with a mobility
term which was, as usual, the number of potentially legal moves available
after the move was made. Movement of a piece into the area near the
opponent's king was rewarded in the same way as the center control heuristic,
and the net improvement was again multiplied by the priority value for that
piece. The pawn heuristics were the same as in the opening except that
advances of wing pawns scored –5 instead of –10. If TECH was ahead in
material piece captures scored a 10 point bonus. Moving a piece which
blocked an f-pawn or c-pawn scored 5.

The third, fourth and fifth phases were devoted to three different types of
endgame: endgame with pawns, general endgames and endgames with only
pieces. The most important goals in pawn endgames are advancing one's
own passed pawns and blocking those of one's opponent, so each move was
credited with the net gain in the realm of passed pawns and this allowed
TECH to escort its own pawns towards promotion and to block the advance
of its opponent's pawns.

Pawn moves were weighted by the rank of their destination and by whether
they were opposed:

Rank	Opposed	Unopposed
3	2	3
4	1	5
5	3	10
6	4	13
7	-	27
8	-	80

If TECH had more than one pawn on a file only the first was given this
bonus; the other pawns on the same file lost 10 points.

As in the pawn endgame, TECH's main goal in the general endgame was to promote. The pawns were given the same weights for advancing as in the previous paragraph. The material value of a pawn was raised by 20 percent but if TECH had two pawns or less then their material value was increased by 90 percent. This would mean, for example, that if TECH had a knight and two pawns against a bishop and one pawn it would not allow its opponent to sacrifice the bishop in return for the two pawns. A move which placed a rook behind a passed pawn of either color was rewarded with 15 points. The center control term used priorities of: pawn = 0, knight = 4, bishop = 3, rook = 1, queen = 1 and king = 4. This encouraged centralization of the king.

Unlike the other forms of endgame, TECH's goal in the endgame with pieces was to drive its opponent's king to the edge in order to deliver mate. This was achieved by doing a small (two-ply) search and using a special evaluation function that was largely invented by the Northwestern University programming team.

TECH was always one of the stronger programs of its generation. At the 2nd ACM Championship in Chicago 1971, it finished in a tie for second place from a field of eight programs and subsequently won the play-off. At the 3rd ACM Championship in Boston the following year, TECH again tied for second place but this time it was defeated in the play-off by OSTRICH. In 1974, when there were twelve competing programs in the 4th ACM Championship at Atlanta, TECH tied for fifth place. The program that finished second in Atlanta was TECH II, a reworked version of TECH, developed at MIT by Alan Baisley, Stan Kugell and James Cooper. (Baisley was one of the people instrumental in adding the opening library to Greenblatt's program in 1967).

One of the refinements of TECH was its storage of all positions evaluated during the tree search. If a position occurred again later in the same search (by transposition) or during the search for the next move, it was retrieved from storage and the score associated with it was used instead of being recomputed.

While TECH was active it competed in a number of human tournaments as well as three of the annual ACM events. Between May 1971 and March 1972 it particpated in seven human tournaments scoring 12 points from 31 games. By July 1975 it had reached a USCF rating of 1243.

To end this "biography" of TECH, here is one of the best games of its career.

White: **COKO III**
Black: **TECH**
2nd ACM Championship, Chicago 1971
Two Knights' Defense

**1 e2–e4 e7–e5 2 Ng1–f3 Nb8–c6 3 Bf1–c4 Ng8–f6 4 d2–d3 d7–d5 5 Bc4xd5
Nf6xd5 6 e4xd5 Qd8xd5 7 Nb1–c3 Bf8–b4 8 O–O Bb4xc3 9 b2xc3 O–O**
Black has achieved a perfectly satisfactory game from the opening.

10 Nf3–g5 Bc8–f5 11 Ra1–b1 f7–f6 12 c3–c4

A normal computer move, attacking the opponent's queen, but Black soon takes advantage of the weakness at d4.

12 ... Qd5–c5 13 Ng5–h3? Bf5xh3 14 Bc1–e3 Nc6–d4 15 g2xh3 Qc5–c6 16 c2–c3? Nd4–f3+ 17 Kg1–h1 Nf3–d2+ 18 f2–f3 Nd2xf1 19 Qd1xf1 f6–f5 20 Rb1–b5 f5–f4
20 ... e5–e4 would open up White's king.

21 Rb5–c5 Qc6–e6 22 Be3–c1 c7–c6
Threatening 23 ... b7–b6.

23 d3–d4 Ra8–e8?
This move was due to a bug in the program. 23 ... e5xd4 is obvious and correct. Now Black loses a pawn.

24 Rc5xe5 Qe6–g6 25 Re5xe8 Qg6xe8 26 Qf1–f2 Qe8–e6 27 Qf2–f1 Rf8–f5 28 h3–h4 c6–c5! 29 d4–d5 Qe6–d6 30 Qf1–h3 Qd6–e5 31 Qh3–f1 Qe5xc3 32 d5–d6 Qc3–d4 33 Qf1–e2 Qd4xd6 34 Qe2–e8+ Rf5–f8 35 Qe8–a4 Rf8–f5 36 Qa4–e8+ Rf5–f8 37 Qe8–a4 Qd6–e6
TECH knew that it was ahead and so avoided a draw by threefold repetition of position.

38 Qa4–b3 Qe6–e2! 39 h2–h3 Rf8–d8
Forcing the win of the queen.

40 Bc1xf4 Rd8–d1+
And here COKO III's programmers resigned.

KAISSA

In 1971 a group of programmers at the Institute of Control Science began to rewrite the ITEP program that had been used in the 1967 match with Stanford, and by the following year it was ready, in its new form, to play a two game match against the readers of the newspaper *Komsomolskaya Pravda* conducted in the same way as the game played against *The Ural Worker* (see pages 70–73). On most Sundays throughout 1972 the newspaper published KAISSA's moves in each of the two games and the readers sent in their suggested replies. In every case the move suggested by the majority of the readers was chosen and KAISSA's reply was published the following week. KAISSA drew one game and lost the other. The previous year Spassky had played two games against the readers of the same newspaper and scored one win and one draw. Obviously the combined force of the readership of *Komsomolskaya Pravda* produces rather strong chess and the program's result was quite creditable.

KAISSA's basic look-ahead was set at seven ply, with further analysis along variations that involved captures and other forcing moves.

Game 1
White: **KAISSA**
Black: **Readers of** *Komsomolskaya Pravda*
1972
Sicilian Defense

1 e2–e4 c7–c5 2 Nb1–c3
KAISSA was playing without any openings book. This move took 40 minutes'
computation.

**2 ... Nb8–c6 3 Ng1–f3 d7–d6 4 Bf1–b5 Bc8–d7 5 O–O g7–g6 6 d2–d4 c5xd4
7 Bb5xc6 d4xc3 8 Bc6xb7 Ra8–b8 9 Bb7–d5 Bf8–g7**
Not 9 ... c3xb2 10 Bc1xb2 Rb8xb2 11 Qd1–d4, forking the two rooks.

**10 b2–b3 Ng8–f6 11 Bc1–e3 Qd8–c7 12 Qd1–d4 a7–a5 13 Bd5–c4 O–O
14 Ra1–e1 Bd7–c6 15 e4–e5 Bc6xf3 16 e5xd6 e7xd6 17 g2xf3 Nf6–h5
18 Qd4–d3 Bg7–e5 19 Be3–d4 Kg8–g7 20 Re1–e3 f7–f6 21 Rf1–e1 Nh5–f4
22 Qd3xc3 Rb8–c8 23 a2–a4 Qc7–d7 24 Bd4xe5 f6xe5 25 Kg1–h1 Qd7–h3
26 Re1–g1 Nf4–d5 27 Qc3xa5 Rc8–c5 28 Qa4–a7+ Rc5–c7 29 Qa7–a5 Rc7–c5
30 Qa5–a7+ Rf8–f7 31 Qa7xc5 d6xc5 32 Bc4xd5 Rf7–f4 33 Re3xe5 Rf4xf3
34 Bd5xf3 Qh3xf3+ 35 Rg1–g2 Drawn.**

Game 2
White: **Readers of** *Komsomolskaya Pravda*
Black: **KAISSA**
1972
Larsen's Opening

1 b2–b3
This move was chosen by the chess correspondent of the newspaper.

**1 ... e7–e5 2 Bc1–b2 Nb8–c6 3 c2–c4 f7–f6 4 Nb1–c3 Bf8–b4 5 Nc3–d5 Ng8–e7
6 a2–a3 Bb4–d6 7 g2–g3 O–O 8 Bf1–g2 Ne7–g6 9 e2–e3 f6–f5 10 Ng1–e2
Rf8–e8 11 Qd1–c2 e5–e4 12 d2–d3 e4xd3 13 Qc2xd3 Re8–f8 14 f2–f4 Bd6–e7
15 h2–h4 h7–h6 16 h4–h5 Ng6–h8 17 e3–e4 d7–d6 18 O–O–O Rf8–f7
19 Nd5xe7+ Qd8xe7 20 Ne2–c3 Bc8–e6 21 Nc3–d5 Qe7–d7 22 Nd5–e3 f5xe4
23 Bg2xe4 Nc6–e7 24 Be4xb7 Ra8–b8 25 Bb7–e4 Ne7–f5 26 Ne3–d5 a7–a5
27 g3–g4 Nf5–e7 28 Nd5xe7+ Rf7xe7 29 g4–g5 h6xg5 30 f4–f5 Nh8–f7 31 f5xe6
Qd7xe6 32 Be4–d5 Qe6–e3+ 33 Qd3xe3 Re7xe3 34 Rd1–f1 Black resigns.**

Thus KAISSA made its public debut. When the newspaper games ended the
programming team continued to work on the program. Altogether about ten
people were involved, including most of the group that created the ITEP
program plus Mikhail Donskoy, who had just graduated from Moscow State
University and who assumed the leading role in KAISSA's creation.

KAISSA used a complex evaluation function involving many features. In fact it was so complex that when I first asked Donskoy about it he replied "... I don't even remember what is in it." The program used the familiar method of searching all moves to a specified depth and then considering only captures, checks, other forcing moves and moves that were replies to checks. An upper bound of 30 plies was put on the depth of these forcing variations but this depth was reached very seldom during the tree search.

KAISSA used a slight modification to the alpha-beta algorithm so that before the search for a move began the values of alpha and beta were not set to minus infinity and plus infinity (as was usually the case in those days) but to rather narrower limits between which the value of the current position was expected to lie. In this way the search was reduced still further. This technique is known as windowing and is discussed in more detail in Chapter 9.

An improvement in the performance of the alpha-beta search was obtained by using what the programmers called the "best move service." They point out that in chess the number of possible moves (less than 10,000) is far smaller than the number of possible positions and that a classification of moves is therefore much easier than a classification of positions. The underlying principle of the best move service is that a move which was the best in many similar positions would most likely be plausible in the current position.

For each ply, ten moves were stored. These were the moves that were most frequently the best ones in other positions at the same depth. When ordering the moves from a particular position these "best moves" were put at the head of the list and hence they were considered earlier. The application of the best

Figure 4.6 Part of the KAISSA programming team: Vladimir Arlazarov, Alexander Ushkov, and Mikhail Donskoy

84   Chapter 4

move service produced a ten-fold reduction in the time taken to search trees whose basic depth was five plies. This use of best moves, which soon became known as killer moves, is described more fully in Chapter 9.

Another innovation was the idea of introducing a dummy move at certain points in the game tree. If it is White's turn to move and Black makes a "blank" move then it is White's turn to move once again. If White can now gain a material advantage then the previous White move must have carried this threat. Under some circumstances a threat can be used to create a cut-off in the search process and this technique can therefore lead to a further reduction in the search time. Another use of the discovery of threats was that they can be included in the list of moves that need to be examined.

KAISSA was able to reduce its search still further by being able to recognize positions that were analagous to positions that had already been examined. If a move is absurd in a particular position then it is likely to be absurd in similar positions and it can therefore be excluded from the search until such time as circumstances appear that change the variation arising after the absurd move. A simple example of this strategy can be shown by considering the following position.

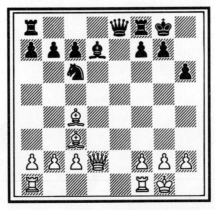

Figure 4.7 Position illustrating KAISSA's method of analogies

Under normal circumstances a chess program would always consider the moves Qd2–d4 and Qd2–g5 when making a move from this position, and KAISSA's use of the blank move would normally result in these two moves being considered because they are threats. But in the present position both moves are absurd because they put the white queen en prise. Let us assume that White plays 1 a2–a3 and that Black replies 1 ... a7–a5. Now most programs would once again consider 2 Qd2–d4 and 2 Qd2–g5, even though both moves are still absurd for the same reasons, but KAISSA has a list of all the squares attacked by each of Black's pieces and it would not consider Qd2–g5 until Black's h-pawn had advanced, nor would it examine Qd2–d4 until the black knight had moved. This is how a human plays chess and KAISSA's programmers pointed out that the standard of a human's play increases with the accuracy with which he determines when a move rejected earlier as absurd should be re-examined. (KAISSA defined absurd moves as those that lead to the immediate loss of material.)

The only problem in implementing this "method of analogies" was in deciding when the position had changed sufficiently to warrant re-examining a move that was rejected earlier. KAISSA's programmers made some progress in solving this problem but their research is beyond the scope of this book.

KAISSA's first appearance outside the Soviet Union came in August 1974 when it participated in the 1st World Computer Championships in Stockholm. It won two of its games very convincingly, it was temporarily in trouble in a third and totally lost for much of the game in the vital last round. But in the end KAISSA won all four games and the title of World Champion.

The Mid-1970s

Following their unsuccessful attempt to win the 1st World Computer Championship in Stockholm, the Northwestern University team had another disappointment. At the 1974 ACM tournament in San Diego, three months later, CHESS 4.0 finished behind the Canadian program RIBBIT. The computer chess cognoscenti still felt that Slate and Atkin had the strongest program but it had been "off form" during the two most important events of the year.

In 1975 computer chess activity in Europe became more co-ordinated with the 1st German Computer Chess Championship. This tournament was held in Dortmund in October and did much to encourage the German programmers. Their efforts were not up to the standard of KAISSA or the leading North American programs but there were some interesting aspects to the tournament. The program ORWELL III, which finished in 4th place (out of 8), was written by a mathematician and artist called Thomas Nitsche. A few years later Nitsche created the first of the MEPHISTO programs which started the Munich company Hegener & Glaser on their road to fame and fortune.

The most interesting game of the tournament was the following massacre. Its significance lies in the fact that the SCHACH MV 5.6 program had no look-ahead whatsoever — its aggression was purely the result of its king attack heuristics. But playing over this game one gets the impression that White had a plan from the very beginning and carried it out in a methodical fashion. In fact nothing could be further from the truth.

White: **SCHACH MV 5.6**
Black: **Fischer / Schneider Program**
1975 German Computer Chess Championship
Irregular Opening

1 Nb1–c3 d7–d5 2 d2–d4 Bc8–g4 3 f2–f3 Bg4–f5 4 e2–e4 d5xe4 5 f3xe4 Bf5–d7
6 Ng1–f3 Nb8–c6 7 e4–e5 e7–e6 8 Bc1–g5 Bf8–e7 9 Qd1–d2 g7–g6 10 Bf1–d3

Pointing towards the black king.

10 ... b7–b6 11 Bg5xe7 Ng8xe7 12 O–O–O O–O 13 Qd2–h6
Increasing the pressure against the black king.

13 ... Ne7–f5 14 Bd3xf5 g6xf5 15 Nf3–g5
Threatening mate, although White was unaware of the threat! The move was
made because it gave additional fire power to White's attack.

15 ... Qd8xg5+ 16 Qh6xg5+ Kg8–h8 17 g2–g4
Opening up another line of attack against Black's king. It is remarkable how
logical White's play appears to be, especially given the program's lack of look-
ahead.
17... f5xg4 18 Qg5xg4 f7–f5 19 Qg4–h4 f5–f4 20 Nc3–e4
Here comes the other knight, rekindling the attack.

**20 ... f4–f3 21 Ne4–g5 Rf8–f7 22 Ng5xf7+ Kh8–g8 23 Qh4–f6 f3–f2 24 Nf7–h6
mate.**

The first occasion that large numbers of human chess players began to take
programs at all seriously was the 1976 Paul Masson Chess Classic, held at
Sarasota, California. The 756 human players enjoyed the experience of open
air chess amidst the Paul Masson Vineyards, not suspecting that they were
about to witness a little piece of chess history. In the Class "B" section, for
players whose USCF ratings were in the 1600–1800 range, CHESS 4.5 achieved
a runaway victory with a 100 percent score. In its five games it played
opponents rated 1693, 1704, 1751, 1742 and 1784, and its performance rating
for the event was in the region of 1950. So the latest version of the Nortwestern
University program, combined with Control Data Corporation's most
advanced Cyber 176 computer, created a good "A" class player. CHESS 4.5
also won the 1976 ACM tournament in Houston and had clearly
re-established its reputation as the world's strongest program, despite
the fact that KAISSA still held the World Championship title.

The interest created by CHESS 4.5's performance in the California tournament
made it easier to gain credence for the idea that computer programs
should compete regularly in human chess tournaments. There has always
been some opposition to this concept, for various reasons, but the idea has
steadily grown in acceptance since the mid-1970s. While the Paul Masson
result was something of a surprise, the chess world was rocked by a new
sensation in February 1977 when CHESS 4.5 won the Minnesota Open
Championship. This was a six round, Swiss system tournament, in which the
program scored 5 out of 6, losing only to a player with a high expert rating
(2175).

This victory entitled the Northwestern program to participate in the state's
"closed" championship the following weekend, in which only the very
strongest players in Minnesota were permitted to take part. The human

players took the matter very seriously, and for the first time in the history of chess the previous games played by a program were studied as part of the humans' pre-tournament preparation. CHESS 4.5 scored "only" one win and one draw from its five games in the championship, but it had made its mark on human chess. It was no surprise to anyone that when the 2nd World Computer Championship took place in August 1977 in Toronto, CHESS 4.6 took the title. (KAISSA finished in a tie for second place.) One of the spectators at the tournament was former World Champion Mikhail Botvinnik, whose presence prompted Monty Newborn to make the following prophecy:

> Chess masters used to come to computer chess tournaments to laugh. Now they come to watch. Soon they will come to learn.

The Challenges for the Levy Bet

The Toronto World Championship tournament was only one year away from the final year of my long standing bet. Until 1977 there seemed to be no point in my playing a formal challenge match against any chess program because none of them were good enough. But when CHESS 4.5 began doing well in human events (winning the 1977 Minnesota Open Championship, for example), it was time for me to face up to my responsibilities and to defend the human race against the coming invasion.

My first challenge was against CHESS 4.6 in April 1977. I accepted an invitation to play it a two-game match at Carnegie Mellon University, but I won the first game and so the second game became moot. Then, at the end of 1977, I played KAISSA at McGill University in Montreal and beat it rather easily. But the tension was beginning to mount. The bet had only another eight months to run and Slate was devoting half of his working year to a new program, a complete rewrite that would be named CHESS 5.0.

I had decided some time earlier that I wanted to play my final match at the end of August 1978 in a blaze of publicity. I tried to persuade the Canadian National Exhibition to sponsor the event in Toronto and after various difficulties the match was finally scheduled to be held there.

About three weeks before leaving England for Toronto I received a most unexpected challenge from Richard Greenblatt of MIT. Greenblatt, it will be recalled, was the author of the program MACHACK VI. Although very little news about chess had been emanating from MIT's Artificial Intelligence labs during the previous decade, scientists there were known to be working on a piece of hardware designed to do nothing but generate and evaluate chess positions at the rate of 150,000 per second, an awesome number in 1978. This machine, called CHEOPS, ran an improved version of the Greenblatt program in the following way: whenever the main program reached a position it considered strategically satisfactory, CHEOPS would take a look at the further tactical possibilities. This enabled the program to avoid numerous traps. CHEOPS is described in more detail in Chapter 10.

I agreed to a two-game match against Greenblatt's MACHACK/CHEOPS program. Since I had wagered that I would not lose a match I needed to score only one point in the two games. The rate of play for all my challenge matches had been agreed at 40 moves in two hours followed by 20 moves per hour. Under these conditions the following game was played in Cambridge, Massachusetts, on August 23, 1978.

Game 1
White: **MACHACK/CHEOPS**
Black: **Levy**
MIT, August 23, 1978
Sicilian Defense

1 e2–e4 c7–c5
Since I knew nothing about this program's style or openings repertoire, I thought it best to play something with which I was reasonably familiar rather than try to confuse the program from the outset. I had played the Sicilian throughout my career.

2 Ng1–f3 d7–d6 3 d2–d4 c5xd4 4 Nf3xd4 Ng8–f6 5 Nb1–c3 g7–g6
The Dragon Variation, my favorite line and one on which I had written a detailed book.

6 f2–f4
I began to smell a rat. I knew that International Masters Ken Rogoff and Norman Weinstein had visited MIT a few days earlier and I was worried that one of them might have busted a line in my book on the Dragon Variation of the Sicilian Defense. But now it was too late to turn back.

6 ... Bf8–g7!
This move, which used to be considered a grave error, is probably Black's best reply.

7 e4–e5 Nf6–h5 8 Bf1–b5+
Not 8 g2–g4?? Nh5xf4! 9 Bc1xf4 d6xe5, winning a pawn.

8 ... Bc8–d7 9 e5–e6 f7xe6 10 Nd4xe6 Bg7xc3+ 11 b2xc3
Thus far both sides have been following a well-known path which used to be
thought very good for White.

11 ... Qd8–c8!
A relatively new idea at the time, maintaining threats against c3, b5, and e6,
which seems to rehabilitate the move 6 ... Bf8–g7. During the game, however,
I could not help worrying that the program was about to unleash a crushing
innovation, courtesy of Rogoff or Weinstein. All of MACHACK/CHEOPS'
moves thus far had been played without hesitation. But now it "thought" for
a couple of minutes, so I knew that my earlier fears were unfounded. I learned
later that the opening book had been prepared by Ken Church, one of
Greenblatt's research students, and he had not even used my Dragon book!

12 Qd1–d4 Nh5–f6 13 Qd4–c4 Nb8–c6 14 Ne6–d4 Nc6xd4
Exchanging into a slightly favorable endgame for Black.

15 c3xd4
If 15 Bb5xd7+ Qc8xd7 16 c3xd4 (or *16 Qc4xd4 Qd7–e6+*, when White's king
is the more exposed) 16 ... Ra8–c8, with a good game for Black.

15 ... Qc8xc4 16 Bb5xc4 Bd7–f5!
Better than 16 ... Ra8–c8, when it is not clear that Black has any advantage.

17 Bc4–b5+
To stop me from castling; not that I would want to.

17 ... Ke8–f7 18 Bb5–c4+ d6–d5

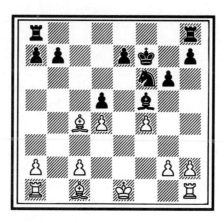

Figure 5.1 After 18 ... d6–d5

19 Bc4–d3!
Excellent judgment. After 19 Bc4–b3 the bishop would be badly placed and
Black would pile up on the c-pawn without worrying about counterplay
along the b-file. Black can capture on d3 at once, saddling White with doubled,
isolated pawns, but Black's knight would be left without a really good square.

19 ... Rh8–c8 20 O–O
I was told after the game that the strategic part of the program wanted to trade
bishops on f5, but MACHACK/CHEOPS realized that this would leave the
c-pawns indefensible. When the program castled, the audience, who had
been following this thought process, let out a cheer. I was happy because the
text move shows that the program did not understand what was going to
happen. The king is needed in the center to protect the c2/d3 structure.

20 ... Rc8–c7 21 Ra1–b1 Ra8–c8 22 Bc1–e3?! Nf6–e4 23 Rf1–f3
Hereabouts White's play is rather aimless.

23 ... Ne4–d6 24 Rb1–b2 b7–b6 25 a2–a4 Bf5xd3
Now that my pieces are on their best squares and the b-pawn is protected, it
is time to cash in on the weakness of White's pawn structure.

**26 c2xd3 Rc7–c3 27 Rf3–h3 h7–h5 28 Be3–d2 Rc3–c2 29 Rb2xc2 Rc8xc2
30 Bd2–e1 Nd6–f5 31 a4–a5 b6xa5 32 Be1xa5 Nf5xd4 33 Rh3–e3 Rc2–a2
34 Ba5–c7 a7–a5**
Outside passed pawns seem awfully strong against chess programs.

**35 Re3–e1 a5–a4 36 Bc7–e5 Nd4–c6 37 Be5–h8 a4–a3 38 Re1–d1 Ra2–c2
39 Bh8–a1 a3–a2 40 h2–h3 Nc6–a5 41 d3–d4 Na5–b3 42 f4–f5 Rc2–c1
43 Rd1xc1**
Greenblatt resigned for his program because of 43 ... Nb3xc1 followed by
44 ... Nc1–b3, etc.

By winning this game I had rendered the second game of the match academic,
but Richard Greenblatt asked me to play it at a 30–30 speed and I agreed. It
was a dull game, in which I outplayed the program in a rook ending only to
reach a position in which my extra pawn might not have been enough to win
against best play, but MACHACK/CHEOPS, after very cleverly seeing a
number of tricks, went completely wrong and lost.

The Main Event

The final match to decide the bet began on August 26th 1978 at the Canadian
National Exhibition in Toronto. CHESS 5.0 was not ready in time so I played
its predecessor, CHESS 4.7. I was seated in an almost soundproof booth,
wearing a tuxedo. The program was represented by David Slate (Larry Atkin

was vacationing in England), along with two representatives of Control Data Corporation: David Cahlander and John Douglas. Cahlander had built a special chessboard with a switch beneath each square to enable the program to detect its opponent's moves by sensing magnets in the bases of the chess pieces. This board also indicated the program's moves by illuminating the "from" and "to" squares as well as the other squares along the path of the moving piece.

The Toronto match was scheduled for six games. Since I had wagered that I would not lose a match to a computer program I needed three points to collect my wager; my opponent needed three and a half to make me famous. The first game of the match produced a horrible shock for me.

Game 1
White: **Levy**
Black: **CHESS 4.7**
Canadian National Exhibition, Toronto, August 1978
Reversed Pirc

1 g2–g3 d7–d5 2 Bf1–g2 e7–e5 3 d2–d3 Ng8–f6 4 Ng1–f3 Nb8–c6 5 O–O Bc8–d7 6 b2–b3 Bf8–c5 7 Bc1–b2 Qd8–e7 8 a2–a3 e5–e4 9 Nf3–e1 O–O 10 d3–d4 Bc5–d6 11 e2–e3
When faced with a strong computer program I try to play the opponent, not the position. It was my plan to create a situation in which nothing was happening, and then to expand gradually on the queenside. Unfortunately, the program had learned how to attack on the kingside.

11 ... Nf6–g4! 12 h2–h3??
12 c2–c4 must be played, but even then 12 ... Qe7–g5 is strong. I completely overlooked Black's 13th move.

Figure 5.2 After 12 h2–h3

12 ... Ng4xe3!!
The program replied instantly, indicating that it had expected 12 h2–h3 and had already worked out its reply while I was thinking!

13 f2xe3 Qe7–g5 15 g3–g4
Realising that I was completely busted, I thought my only hope was to sacrifice the exchange in order to trade off the queens.

14 ... Qg5xe3+ 15 Rf1–f2 Bd6–g3 16 Qd1–e2 Qe3xf2+
Of course it would be crushing to take with the bishop and keep the queens on so that my king would die of exposure, but the program knows that it should trade down when materially ahead.

17 Qe2xf2 Bg3xf2+ 18 Kg1xf2 f7–f5! 19 g4xf5 Nc6–e7 20 c2–c4 Rf8xf5+ 21 Kf2–g1 c7–c6 22 Nb1–c3 Rf5–h5 23 Kg1–h2 Ra8–f8 24 Nc3–d1 Ne7–g6 25 Ra1–c1 Bd7xh3!
I had seen this coming but was powerless to prevent it.

26 Bg2xh3 Rf8–f1 27 Ne1–g2 Rf1–f3 28 c4xd5 Rh5xh3+ 29 Kh2–g1 c6xd5 30 Rc1–c8+ Ng6–f8? 31 Bb2–c3 Rf3–d3 32 Nd1–e3 Rh3xe3 33 Ng2xe3 Rd3xe3 34 Bc3–b4
My first threat of the game, but I was not too happy about being three pawns down.

34 ... Re3–f3 35 Rc8–d8 h7–h6
The program no doubt saw that 35 ... Rf3–f5 36 Bb4xf8 Rf5xf8 37 Rd8xd5 would be followed by the win of the e-pawn or the b-pawn and probably did not analyze past this point.

36 Rd8xd5 Rf3xb3 37 Rd5–d8 Rb3–f3 38 Rd8–a8 g7–g5 39 d4–d5 h6–h5 40 d5–d6 Kg8–g7 41 Ra8xa7 Rf3–f7 42 Ra7–a5
Suddenly the position is no longer *totally* hopeless — it is merely *rather* hopeless.

42 ... Kg7–f6 43 Bb4–c3+ Kf6–g6 44 Ra5–e5 Rf7–f3 45 Bc3–b4 Rf3–f4 46 Re5–e7 Rf4–f7 47 Re7xe4 Rf7–d7 48 Re4–e7 h5–h4 49 Kg1–g2 g5–g4 50 Kg2–h2?!
50 Bb4–c5 would have prevented 50 ... b7–b6.

50 ... b7–b6 51 Kh2–g2 Rd7–d8
Help! Black is beginning to untangle its pieces.

52 a3–a4 Nf8–d7 53 a4–a5 Nd7–f6
I was expecting 53 ... b6xa5 54 Bb4xa5 Rd8–a8, and hoping that 55 Ba5–c3 might hold.

54 a5xb6!
Material equality at last. Now I thought I had a draw, and if my opponent made one more mistake, then maybe ...

54 ... Nf6–d5 55 b6–b7!
At this point in the proceedings the computer got sick and the doctors were called. Twenty-five minutes later, with the program still having plenty of time of its clock, it played

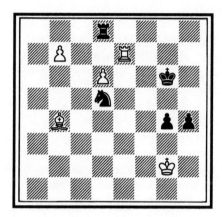

Figure 5.3 After 55 b6–b7

55 ... Nd5xe7!
A brilliant decision. 55 ... Nd5xb4 does nothing for Black, if only because of something like 56 Re7–e4 Nb4–c6 57 Re4xg4+ Kg6–h5 58 Rg4–c4. Also 55 ... Nd5–f4+ 56 Kg2–h1 looks good for White. CHESS 4.7 had probably found the only way for Black to draw!

56 d6xe7 Rd8–h8!
On 56 ... Rd8–e8, 57 Bb4–a5 wins.

57 Bb4–d6 Kg6–f6 58 b7–b8=Q Rh8xb8 59 Bd6xb8 Kf6xe7 60 Bb8–f4 Ke7–f6 61 Bf4–d2 Kf6–g6 62 Bd2–e1 Kg6–g5 63 Be1–f2 Kg5–h5 64 Bf2–e1
And David Slate offered me a draw on behalf of his program. This was a remarkable game, and the first time a computer program had ever drawn with an international master under tournament conditions. Before the match David Slate had some doubts as to whether his program was ready to play me, but this game removed them.

   The next day saw Game 2 of the match, in which the program was faced with more difficult problems from an early stage.

Game 2
White: **CHESS 4.7**
Black: **Levy**
Canadian National Exhibition, Toronto, August 1978
Sicilian Defense

1 Nb1–c3 c7–c5 2 e2–e4 Nb8–c6 3 f2–f4 a7–a6
To take the program out of its openings book. I played this system as White
several times in international events and would not feel comfortable on the
other side.

4 Ng1–f3 g7–g6 5 d2–d4 c5xd4 6 Nf3xd4 Bf8–g7 7 Bc1–e3 d7–d6 8 Nd4xc6?
This move is a strategic mistake because it strengthens Black's control of the
center (the pawn on c6 attacks the d5-square) and it gives Black the possibility
of play along the b-file. Many programs like making this exchange because
it saddles Black with an isolated a-pawn, though in this type of position the
isolated pawn is usually of little consequence.

After making this strategic error against my Sicilian Defense in a game
played the previous year, the Northwestern program had been altered in an
attempt to prevent it from exchanging in similar situations. Some of the
factors causing this exchange were eradicated, but apparently not enough of
them.

8 ... b7xc6 9 Bf1–e2 Ra8–b8 10 Qd1–c1 Qd8–a5 11 Be3–d2 Qa5–b6 12 Nc3–a4
Qb6–a7 13 Na4–c3 Bg7–d4 14 Nc3–d1 Ng8–f6 15 c2–c3 Bd4–b6 16 Qc1–c2
Nf6–g4 17 Qc2–a4 O–O 18 Be2xg4
If 18 Qa4xc6 Ng4–f2, exchanging knights and then bishops after which
White's exposed king must cost him the game.

18 ... Bc8xg4 19 Qa4xc6 Bg4xd1 20 Ke1xd1
20 Ra1xd1 Bb6–e3 is equally horrible for White.

20 ... Bb6–e3 21 b2–b3 Be3xd2 22 Kd1xd2 Rb8–c8 23 Qc6–a4 Qa7–f2+
24 Kd2–d3 Qf2xg2 25 Qa4–d4 Qg2–f3+ 26 Kd3–c2 Qf3–e2+ 27 Kc2–c1 e7–e5
28 f4xe5 d6xe5 29 Qd4xe5 Rf8–e8 30 Qe5–g3 Re8xe4 31 Qg3–h3 Rc8–d8
32 Qh3–f1 Qe2–d2+ 33 Kc1–b1 Re4–e2 34 Qf1xe2 Qd2xe2 35 Rh1–e1!
Otherwise it is mate in 4.

35 ... Qe2xe1+ 36 Kb1–b2 Rd8–d2+ 37 Kb2–a3 Qe1xa1
The remaining 17 moves are of no real interest. In all fairness to the program,
I should say that it occasionally saw ways I could have forced mate which I
myself did not see.

After the second game there was a 5-day break before hostilities resumed.
In Game 3 my do-nothing-but-do-it-well strategy scored another convincing
victory.

Game 3
White: **Levy**
Black: **CHESS 4.7**
Canadian National Exhibition, Toronto, August 1978
English Opening

1 c2–c4 Ng8–f6 2 a2–a3
Out of book again!

2 ... Nb8–c6 3 Nb1–c3 d7–d5 4 c4xd5 Nf6xd5 5 d2–d3
Played so as to encourage the program to play ...

5 ... Nd5xc3
and thereby make exactly the same strategic error as it had on move 8 in
Game 2.

**6 b2xc3 e7–e5 7 g2–g3 Bf8–e7 8 Bf1–g2 Qd8–d6 9 Ng1–f3 Bc8–e6 10 O–O
O–O 11 Qd1–a4**
Intending to put pressure on b7 with Rf1–b1.

11 ... Qd6–c5 12 Bc1–d2 b7–b5?
A typical program failing. It weakens its pawn structure without sufficient
provocation.

13 Qa4–c2 f7–f6 14 Rf1–b1 Ra8–d8 15 Qc2–b2
Not 15 Bd2–e3 Nc6–d4! 16 Qc2–b2 Qc5xc3! 17 Qb2xc3 Nd4xe2+.

15 ... Rd8–b8 16 Bd2–e3 Qc5–d6 17 Nf3–d2
Intending Nd2–b3 or Nd2–e4, followed by putting the knight or bishop on c5.

17 ... Be6–d5 18 Bg2xd5+ Qd6xd5 19 Qb2–b3
Programs can analyze far more deeply in the ending than in the middlegame
because there are fewer pieces on the board and fewer possible moves. For
this reason I usually try to avoid the endgame until the program has
compromised its position, which it had done here — I felt that Black's poor
pawn structure would soon prove fatal.

19 ... Qd5xb3 20 Nd2xb3 f6–f5 21 Be3–c5 Be7–d6!
The exchange on c5 would permit White's knight to enter the game with great
effect.

22 Rb1–b2 Kg8–h8
When they do not know what else to do many programs put their king "into
safety." They are aware that the king should be nearer the corner in the
middlegame and centralized in the endgame. In the case of CHESS 4.7 (and
many other programs) the threshold between middlegame and endgame was

not sufficiently defined, and here the program thought that it was still in the middlegame.

23 Ra1–b1 a7–a6 24 Bc5xd6 c7xd6 25 Nb3–d2 f5–f4 26 Kg1–g2 f4xg3 27 h2xg3 Rb8–d8 28 a3–a4! Nc6–a7!
Perceiving that 28 ... b5xa4 29 Rb2–b6 would be extremely unpleasant for Black.

29 Nd2–e4 b5xa4 30 Rb2–b6 d6–d5 31 Ne4–c5 Na7–b5 32 Nc5xa4 Rd8–a8 33 c3–c4
Remember what I said about passed pawns when playing against computer programs!

33 ... d5xc4 34 d3xc4 Nb5–d4 35 e2–e3 Nd4–f3 36 c4–c5 Nf3–g5
Or 36 ... Nf3–d2 37 Rb1–b4, when the black knight has nothing to do.

37 c5–c6 Ng5–e4 38 c6–c7 Rf8xf2+
With this move the program warned "Be careful!" (but I was not told of this until after the game). In fact Black has no defense to the threat of 39 Rb6–b8+ in conjunction with Na4–b6.

39 Kg2–g1 Rf2–f8 40 Rb6–b8 h7–h5 41 Rb8xa8 Rf8xa8 42 Rb1–b8+
David Slate resigned for his program.

I now had a lead of 2.5 – 0.5 and needed only one draw in the last three games to win my bet. I had demonstrated to everyone's satisfaction that my do-nothing strategy worked to perfection, so I considered it worthwhile to experiment in Game 4 by attempting to beat the program at its own game, playing sharp, tactical chess and endeavouring to outanalyze the program. This was the result.

Game 4
White: **CHESS 4.7**
Black: **Levy**
Canadian National Exhibition, Toronto, August 1978
Latvian Gambit

1 e2–e4 e7–e5 2 Ng1–f3 f7–f5 3 e4xf5 e5–e4 4 Nf3–e5 Ng8–f6 5 Ne5–g4 d7–d5 6 Ng4xf6+ Qd8xf6 7 Qd1–h5+
The program is a pawn up and is thus quite willing to trade queens.

7 ... Qf6–f7 8 Qh5xf7+ Ke8xf7 9 Nb1–c3 c7–c6 10 d2–d3 e4xd3 11 Bf1xd3 Nb8–d7 12 Bc1–f4 Nd7–c5 13 g2–g4 Nc5xd3+ 14 c2xd3 Bf8–c5
Preventing O–O–O and therefore encouraging O–O. The program likes to castle when its pieces have been developed.

15 O–O h7–h5 16 Nc3–a4 Bc5–d4 17 Bf4–e3 Bd4–e5 18 d3–d4 Be5–d6
19 h2–h3 b7–b6 20 Rf1–e1 Bc8–d7 21 Na4–c3 h5xg4 22 h3xg4 Rh8–h4
23 f2–f3 Ra8–h8 24 Kg1–f1!

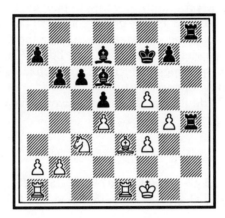

Figure 5.4 After 24 Kg1–f1

24 ... Bd6–g3?
The immediate 24 ... Bd7–c8 is better, and if 25 Kf1–e2 (even worse for White
is *25 Nc3–e2 Bc8–a6*) 25 ... Rh4–h2+ 26 Ke2–d1 (not *26 Be3–f2?? Bd6–g3
27 Re1–f1 Rh8–e8+* winning a piece) 26 ... Rh2xb2, with an overwhelming
position.

**25 Re1–e2 Bd7–c8 26 Kf1–g2 Bg3–d6 27 Be3–g1 Rh4–h3 28 Ra1–e1 Rh3–g3+
29 Kg2–f2 Rh8–h3 30 Re2–e3 Bc8–a6**
If 30 ... Bd6–f4 31 Re3–e7+ Kf7–f6 32 Re1–e3!, with Nc3–e2 to follow. Had I
noticed these defensive resources earlier I would have played 24 ... Bd7–c8.

31 Nc3–e2 Ba6xe2 32 Re1xe2 c6–c5 33 f3–f4!
I had overlooked this move.

33 ... Rg3xe3 34 Re2xe3 Rh3–h4
34 ... Rh3xe3 35 Kf2xe3 c5xd4+ 36 Ke3–d3! gives White a won bishop ending.

35 Kf2–g3 Rh4–h1 36 Bg1–f2 Rh1–d1! 37 Re3–a3 c5xd4 38 Ra3xa7+ Kf7–f8??
38 ... Kf7–e8 39 Ra7xg7 d4–d3 40 Kg3–f3 Rd1–b1 would probably have been
sufficient to win.

39 Ra7–d7 Rd1–d3+??
An idea that fails because of White's 48th move. Correct is 39 ... Bd6–c5
40 Rd7xd5 d4–d3 41 Bf2xc5+ b6xc5, when CHESS 4.7 would almost certainly
not have been able to win; it may even have lost because of the passed d-pawn.

**40 Kg3–g2 Bd6–c5 41 Rd7xd5 Rd3–d2 42 b2–b4 Bc5xb4 43 Rd5–d8+ Kf8–f7
44 Rd8–d7+ Kf7–f8   45 Rd7xd4 Rd2–b2 46 Kg2–f3 Bb4–c5 47 Rd4–d8+
Kf8–e7??**

The final blunder by the computer. I had still not noticed White's next move
and assumed that the program was going to play 48 Bf2xc5+, when either
48 ... b6xc5 or 48 ... Ke7xd8 49 Bc5–d4 (of course *49 Bc5xb6* is also possible,
but the program would be expected to go after the g-pawn in order to
add to its passed pawns) 49 ... Rb2xa2   50 Bd4xg7, would produce the
unbalanced type of endgame at which the program fares less well due to its
inferior understanding of passed pawns.

   After 47 ... Kf8–f7 I doubt that the program would have won.

48 Bf2–h4+!

The end:

**48 ... Ke7–f7 49 g4–g5 g7–g6 50 Rd8–d7+ Kf7–f8 51 f5xg6 Rb2xa2 52 f4–f5
Ra2–a3+ 53 Kf3–g4 Ra3–a4+ 54 Kg4–h5 Ra4–d4 55 Rd7–c7 Bc5–e7 Black
resigns.**

So the experiment failed, but computer persons all over the world had
something to rejoice about. For Game 5, I returned to my no-nonsense
approach.

Game 5
White: **Levy**
Black: **CHESS 4.7**
Canadian National Exhibition, Toronto, August 1978
English Opening

1 c2–c4 Ng8–f6 2 a2–a3 c7–c6

Slate added this move to the program's openings library after Game 3.

3 d2–d3 d7–d5 4 Qd1–c2

No, I was not going mad, there was a perfectly valid reason for these moves.
In a blitz game between CHESS 4.6 and Grandmaster Michael Stean in
London the previous year, the program opened 1 e2–e4 b7–b6 2 d2–d4 Bc8–b7
3 Nb1–c3 c7–c5 4 d4xc5. If the program likes to exchange center pawns for
wing pawns, who am I to stop it?

4 ... d5xc4 5 Qc2xc4 e7–e5

So now I had my favorite Sicilian pawn structure!

**6 Ng1–f3 Bf8–d6 7 g2–g3 Bc8–e6 8 Qc4–c2 Nb8–d7 9 Bf1–g2 O–O 10 O–O
Qd8–b6 11 Nb1–d2 Qb6–c5 12 Qc2–b1**

I wanted to keep the queens on as long as I could to force the program to examine as many moves as possible at each ply, thereby restricting its search depth.

12 ... h7–h6 13 b2–b4 Qc5–b5 14 Qb1–c2 Nd7–b6 15 Bc1–b2 a7–a5 16 a3–a4 Qb5–a6 17 b4xa5 Qa6xa5

The game had become sharper than I had intended, but with Black's queen offside I was very happy with the situation.

18 Bb2–c3 Qa5–c5 19 Rf1–c1 Nb6–d7

The threat was simply 20 Bc3xe5.

20 a4–a5 Qc5–a7 21 Qc2–b2 Nf6–g4 22 Nd2–e4 Bd6–c7

22 ... f7–f5 23 Ne4xd6 Qa7xf2+ 24 Kg1–h1 leaves Black with insufficient compensation for the piece.

23 h2–h3 f7–f5 24 h3xg4 f5xe4 25 d3xe4 Be6xg4 26 Bc3–e1

Unnecessary overprotection. The immediate 26 Rc1–b1 is stronger, but in any event Black cannot easily prevent White's plan.

26 ... Nd7–c5 27 Rc1–b1

At this point the computer became indisposed and required 25 minutes' consultation with its medical team. When it recovered only 20 minutes remained for the 13 moves to the time control, but CHESS 4.7 managed to find the best defensive moves that I could see in the position.

27 ... Ra8–e8 28 Be1–d2

The point. White will put pressure on the black knight defending b7.

28 ... Rf8–f7

If 28 ... Nc5xe4 29 Bd2–e3 Qa7–a6 (29 ... Ne4–c5 30 Rb1–cl Bc7–d6 31 Qb2–c2) 30 Qb2xb7 Qa6xe2 31 Qb7xc7 Rf8–f7 32 Qc7xc6 forking rook and knight.

29 Bd2–e3 Bc7–d6 30 Qb2–c2 Bg4xf3 31 Bg2xf3 Re8–a8 32 Rb1–c1 b7–b6 33 Kg1–g2

If 33 a5xb6 Qa7xa1 34 Rc1xa1 Ra8xa1+ 35 Kg1–g2 Ra1–a5 it is not immediately clear that White can win.

33 ... Qa7–b7 34 a5xb6 Ra8xa1 35 Rc1xa1 Nc5–e6 36 Ra1–a7 Qb7–c8 37 Qc2–a2 Rf7–f6 38 Ra7–a8 Bd6–b8 39 Bf3–g4 Kg8–f7 40 Qa2–a7+ Bb8xa7 41 Ra8xc8 Ba7xb6 42 Bg4xe6+ Rf6xe6 43 Be3xb6

Once again the computer failed and David Slate decided to resign the game and the match.

After I returned to England I soon received cheques from Professors McCarthy, Michie and Pappert. McCarthy commented that he was glad I had not lost to a brute force program — in making the bet he had assumed that my defeat would come as the result of genuine "intelligence" in the winning program. To the time of writing this book (1990) I am still awaiting my 250 £, plus 11 years' compound interest from Kozdrowicki!

Having won this famous bet I felt that it would be rather a pity to remove the goal that chess programmers everywhere had been aiming for. At the suggestion of Christopher Evans, who was one of the original consulting editors for *Omni* magazine, *Omni* and I offered a prize, without time limit, of $5,000 for the first program that did win a match against me. One thousand dollars would come from me and the other $4,000 from *Omni*. At about the same time I was challenged to make another bet. I was afraid of making it for a ten year period because I had been so surprised at the progress made by Slate and Atkin during the previous few years, and so I agreed to a five year, $1,000 bet with Dan McCracken, a former president of the ACM and famous for his many books on FORTRAN. The five years was due to expire at the end of 1983.

My new bet was made during the 1978 ACM tournament in Washington. As if to show that it was casting doubt on my optimism a newcomer to the tournament, called BELLE, played the most beautiful combination created by a computer program to date.

White: **BLITZ 6.5**
Black: **BELLE**
ACM NACCC, Washington, October 1978
Four Knights' Game

1 e2–e4 e7–e5 2 Ng1–f3 Nb8–c6 3 Nb1–c3 Ng8–f6 4 Bf1–b5 Nc6–d4 5 Bb5–c4 Bf8–c5 6 Nf3xe5 Qd8–e7 7 Bc4xf7+ Ke8–f8
Only now does BLITZ 6.5 realise that it must lose material.

8 Ne5–g6+ h7xg6 9 Bf7–c4 Nf6xe4 10 O–O

Figure 5.5 After 10 O–O

10 ... Rh8xh2!!
A beautiful combination. However White plays there is no defense.

11 Kg1xh2 Qe7–h4+ 12 Kh2–g1 Ne4–g3 13 Qd1–h5
Delaying the end without changing the result.

13 ... g6xh5 14 f2xg3+ Nd4–f3 mate.
With this game the world of computer chess witnessed the start of a new era.

The Computer Becomes a Master

It is quite remarkable that in the fast flowing river of computer chess there should be almost total domination of the field by one team for so long a period as a decade. Yet David Slate and Larry Atkin, assisted in the "early days" by Keith Gorlen, did dominate the world of computer chess throughout the 1970s. It is true that they failed to win the 1st World Championship (Stockholm 1974), and that they did not win every one of the ACM tournaments which started in 1970, but the performance record of the various generations of the CHESS program was outstanding.

ACM 1970 (New York)	1st (3 out of 3)
ACM 1971 (Chicago)	1st (3 out of 3)
ACM 1972 (Boston)	1st (3 out of 3)
ACM 1973 (Atlanta)	1st (3.5 out of 4)
World Championship 1974 (Stockholm)	2nd (3 out of 4*)
ACM 1974 (San Diego)	2nd= (3 out of 4)
ACM 1975 (Minneapolis)	1st (4 out of 4)

* There was a tie for second place on 3 out of 4 and CHESS 4.0 won the play-off game to take clear second.

ACM 1976 (Houston)	1st (4 out of 4)
World Championship 1977 (Toronto)	1st (4 out of 4)
ACM 1977 (Seattle)	1st= (3.5 out of 4)
ACM 1978 (Washington)	2nd (3 out of 4)
ACM 1979 (Detroit)	1st (3.5 out of 4)

So from 46 games (including the 1974 play-off game) in the 12 most important computer chess tournaments of the decade, the Northwestern University program scored 40 wins, 3 draws and 3 losses (90.22 percent).

Slate and Atkin were most fortunate in their choice of university. At a time when many aspiring chess programmers were finding it extremely difficult, if not impossible, to get adequate access to a computer, they were working in an ideal environment. The Vogelback Computing Center at Northwestern University in Evanston, Illinois, was under the direction of Ben Mittman, a professor of computer science, who gave his charges every opportunity to develop their program. Mittman's center used mainframes manufactured by Control Data Corporation — initially a CDC 6400 and later a 6600.

When the chess program became well known, CDC itself, through David Cahlander, offered more and more powerful computers whenever there was an important chess event. Slate and Atkin were among the first people outside CDC to be able to run their programs on the CYBER range of computers, which superceded the 6600, and if their computing time on CDC hardware had been paid for with real money they would have needed to have been millionaires to afford it.

By the end of the 1970s the Northwestern team had peaked. Their contribution to the field had been enormous, not only in terms of pushing forward the frontiers of knowledge but also in the great P. R. which their successes had brought to computer chess. When they started work in the late 1960s the only program to have received any kind of credence in the chess world was Greenblatt's MACHACK VI, whose best performance rating in a human tournament had been 1640 on the USCF scale. By the time Slate and Atkin emerged from the seventies they had created an expert-rated program, but then the time had come for others to show new directions in computer chess. Slate and Atkin went their seperate ways, Atkin concentrating on writing games programs for microcomputers. Slate wrote a new mainframe program called NUCHESS, which finished 2nd at ACM 1981 (behind BELLE); 1st= at ACM 1982; 4th= in the 1983 World Championship; and 6th= (scoring 50 percent) at ACM 1984. Although he was still in the big league, Slate was being eclipsed by BELLE and others.

Ken Thompson and Joe Condon's BELLE first came to prominence at the ACM Championship in Washington, DC in 1978, where it swept the board to take first place. The previous chapter ended with one of its most decisive victories. Thompson had taken part in previous years with conventional chess programs, but had failed to demonstrate superiority over the Northwestern team. He and Condon later wrote that in their early days (1973-74) it was "... painfully clear that computer chess belonged to the fastest computer." The conclusion they came to was that special-purpose chess hardware should be designed to replace some of the computationally intensive tasks normally performed by chess software.

No one who was familiar with Thompson's other work in the computing field was particularly surprised at their success in Washington. They had taken part the previous year in the Toronto World Championship with a small

Figure 6.1 Ken Thompson, David Slate and Feng-hsiung Hsu, 1989

machine that contained 25 chips, finishing in a tie for 4th place with two wins, a draw and a loss from four games. In Washington they had new, larger hardware, with 325 chips. Their exciting defeat of CHESS 4.7 follows, and marked the end of the latter's dominance in the field.

White: **BELLE**
Black: **CHESS 4.7**
9th ACM NACCC, Washington, 1978
French Defense

**1 e2–e4 Nb8–c6 2 d2–d4 d7–d5 3 Nb1–c3 e7–e6 4 Ng1–f3 Bf8–b4 5 e4–e5
Ng8–e7 6 Bc1–d2 Ne7–f5 7 Nc3–e2 Bb4–e7 8 c2–c3 O–O 9 Ne2–f4 f7–f6
10 Bf1–d3 f6xe5 11 d4xe5 g7–g5!?**
Typical computer play, but maybe the idea is sound. Black's idea is that after the knight moves from f4, Black can advance with 12 ... g5–g4 driving away the f3-knight and thereby winning the pawn on e5. Being a materialist Black was willing to weaken its kingside in order to win this pawn — certainly a double-edged proposition. But White is also a materialist and therefore found a way to avoid losing the e5-pawn, also at the cost of weakening its kingside!

12 g2–g4 Nf5–g7 13 Nf4–g2 b7–b6?
Berliner suggested 13 ... Rf8xf3! 14 Qd1xf3 Nc6xe5 15 Qf3–e2 Ne5xd3+ 16 Qe2xd3 e6–e5 with a strong pawn center and active pieces to compensate for the modest material sacrifice. In 1978 it would be almost unthinkable for a computer to make a positional sacrifice of this nature, even though it is probably sound. The only example we had seen at that time was in the CHAOS—CHESS 4.0 game at the 1st World Championship. (See page 110.)

14 Qd1–e2 Bc8–b7 15 Rh1–g1
It is high time for White to castle queenside. Black still has the opportunity to sacrifice the exchange on f3, but being a materialist CHESS 4.7 did not like the idea.

15 ... a7–a5 16 a2–a4 Kg8–h8 17 h2–h3 Kh8–g8
Black exhibits the well-known syndrome: All my pieces are on their best squares. Since it cannot see any way to improve the position of any of its pieces, Black moves the king back and forth until something happens.

18 Rg1–h1 h7–h6 19 h3–h4 d5–d4?
Black tries to side-step the tension on the kingside by creating counterplay in the center, but the best way to do this would still have been Berliner's idea 19 ... Rf8xf3. The move, 19 ... d5–d4, gives White an opportunity to unleash a tremendous attack with 20 Qe2–e4! Rf8xf3 21 Qe4–h7+ Kg8–f8 22 Bd3–g6. BELLE did not see deeply enough to realize that this variation wins for White and instead decided to continue the attack in a more mundane fashion.

20 h4xg5?

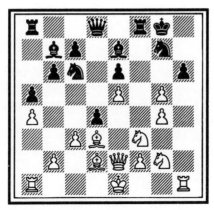

Figure 6.2 After 20 h4xg5

20 ... Nc6–b4!!

An astounding move leading to wild complications, after which Berliner's analysis suggests that the game should be drawn: 21 c3xb4 Bb7xf3 22 Bd3–h7+! Kg8–h8! (not *22 ... Kg8xh7 23 Rh1xh6+! Kh7–g8 24 Qe2–d3 Bf3xg2* and Black's attack peters out) 23 Rh1xh6! Bf3xe2 24 Bh7–b1+ Kh8–g8 25 Bb1–h7+ Kg8–f7 26 Bh7–g6+ Kf7–g8 etc.

21 g5xh6??

White's chances lay on the h-file and so closing the file in this way is illogical.

21 ... Nb4xd3+??

Returning the compliment. Black could have won with 21 ... d4xc3, when there are threats of 22 ... Bb7xf3, 22 ... c3xd2+ and 22 ... Nb4xd3+ (or *22 ... Qd8xd3*). If 22 Bd3–h7+ Kg8xh7 23 h6xg7+ Kh7xg7 24 Bd2–h6+ Kg7–g8 25 Ra1–d1 Bb7xf3 26 Rd1xd8 Ra8xd8 27 Bh6xf8 Bf3xe2 and Black wins. Nowadays DEEP THOUGHT would take this variation in its stride.

22 Qe2xd3 d4xc3 23 Qd3–g6! c3xd2+ 24 Nf3xd2 Rf8–f7 25 h6xg7 Rf7xg7 26 Qg6xe6+ Rg7–f7 27 Qe6–h6 Rf7–g7 28 Qh6–h8+ Kg8–f7 29 e5–e6+ Kf7xe6
Or 29 ... Kf7–f6 30 Rh1–h6+ etc.

30 Qh8xg7 Bb7xg2 31 Rh1–h6+ Ke6–d7 32 O–O–O
At last.

32 ... Bg2–d5 33 Nd2–e4 Kd7–c8 34 Rh6–h8 Bd5xe4 35 Rd1xd8+ Be7xd8 36 Qg7–e7 Kc8–b7 37 Qe7xe4+ Kb7–a7 38 Rh8–g8 Ra8–b8 39 g4–g5 Bd8–e7
This is not a simple blunder — Black cannot prevent the loss of the bishop. White's threat was Qe4–e6 followed by Qe6–d7 and the bishop is dead.

40 Rg8xb8 Be7xg5+ 41 f2–f4 Bg5xf4+ 42 Qe4xf4 Ka7xb8 43 Kc1–d2 Kb8–b7 44 Kd2–d3 Kb7–c8 45 b2–b4 a5xb4 46 Qf4xb4 Kc8–d7 47 Qb4–b5+ Kd7–d8 48 Kd3–e4 Black resigns.

By the time of the 3rd World Computer Championship, in Linz, Austria, in 1980, BELLE had grown to a 1700 chip machine, and it took the World Championship title though not without the need for a play-off game against CHAOS. Slate's NUCHESS won a dramatic game against CHAOS but was unable to finish near the top.

White: **CHAOS**
Black: **NUCHESS**
3rd World Computer Chess Championship, Linz 1980
Queen's Gambit Accepted

1 d2–d4 d7–d5 2 c2–c4 d5xc4 3 Ng1–f3 Ng8–f6 4 e2–e3 e7–e6 5 Bf1xc4 c7–c5 6 Qd1–e2 a7–a6 7 O–O b7–b5 8 Bc4–b3 Bc8–b7 9 Rf1–d1 Nb8–d7 10 Nb1–c3 Bf8–d6 11 e3–e4 c5xd4 12 Nf3xd4 Qd8–b8 13 g2–g3 b5–b4 14 Nc3–a4 Bb7xe4
This pawn grab looks risky but it is probably quite safe.

15 f2–f3 Be4–b7?
Deja vu! This position had already arisin in the game CHAOS—CHESS 4.0, 1st World Computer Championship, Stockholm 1974. NUCHESS was David Slate's new program, written after he and Larry Atkin finally ended a decade of collaboration. NUCHESS inherited the openings book used by the CHESS 4.x generation of programs, but after Stockholm, Slate had forgotten to correct Black's last move in the openings book, which is clearly inferior to 15 ... e6–e5! 16 Nd4–e6 f7xe6 17 f3xe4 Bd6–c5+ 18 Na4xc5 Nd7xc5 19 Qe2–c4 Qb8–b5 when Black is a safe pawn ahead. Now NUCHESS is bashed flat in the same way that its parent was destroyed six years earlier.

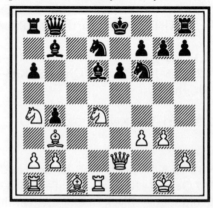

Figure 6.3 After 15 ... Be4–b7

16 Nd4xe6!!
Sacrificing material for positional compensation. When this move was played in the 1974 game it was the first time we had seen a positional sacrifice by a computer program.

16 ... f7xe6 17 Qe2xe6+ Ke8–d8
In Stockholm, CHESS 4.0 had tried 17 ... Bd6–e7, but after 18 Rd1–e1 Qb8–d8 19 Bc1–f4 Ke8–f8 20 Ra1–d1 White's position was overwhelming.

**18 Rd1xd6 Qb8–c7 19 Bc1–e3 Rh8–e8 20 Be3–b6 Re8xe6 21 Bb3xe6 Bb7xf3
22 Ra1–c1 Ra8–a7 23 Rc1xc7 Ra7xc7 24 Bb6xc7+ Kd8xc7 25 Rd6xa6 Bf3–c6
26 Ra6–a7+ Kc7–b8 27 Ra7–a5 Kb8–c7 28 b2–b3 Kc7–d6 29 Be6xd7 Bc6xd7
30 Na4–b6 Kd6–c6 31 Nb6xd7 Nf6xd7 32 Kg1–f2 Nd7–c5 33 Kf2–e3 Kc6–b6
34 Ra5–a8 Nc5–e6 35 Ke3–e4 Kb6–c5 36 Ra8–a5+ Kc5–b6 37 Ra5–e5 Ne6–c5+
38 Ke4–d4 Nc5–b7 39 Re5–e7 Nb7–d6 40 Kd4–e5 Nd6–b5 41 Re7xg7 h7–h5
42 Rg7–f7 Nb5–c3 43 Rf7–f2 Kb6–c5 44 Rf2–d2 Nc3–b5 Black resigns.**

White: **BELLE**
Black: **CHAOS**
Play-Off Game, 3rd World Computer Chess Championship, Linz 1980
Alekhine's Defense

**1 e2–e4 Ng8–f6 2 e4–e5 Nf6–d5 3 d2–d4 d7–d6 4 Ng1–f3 d6xe5 5 Nf3xe5
g7–g6 6 g2–g3**
More usual is 6 Bf1–c4.

6 ... Bc8–f5 7 c2–c4 Nd5–b4
Black must be careful. If 7... Bf5–e4, White wins a piece with 8 f2–f3.

8 Qd1–a4+ Nb4–c6?!
Probably correct is 8 ... Nb8–c6, and if 9 Ne5xc6 Nb4xc6 10 d4–d5 Bf5–d7 11 d5xc6 Bd7xc6 forking White's queen and rook.

9 d4–d5 Bf5–c2 10 Qa4–b5 Qd8–d6?
In view of Black's difficulties it would probably have been better to try 10 ... a7–a6 11 Qb5xb7 Nc6xe5 12 Qb7xa8 Ne5–f3+ 13 Ke1–e2 Nf3–d4+ when it is not clear who stands better.

11 Ne5xc6 Nb8xc6 12 Nb1–c3
White cannot yet capture on c6 because of mate on d1.

**12 ... Bf8–g7 13 Qb5xb7 O–O 14 Qb7xc6 Qd6–b4 15 Ke1–d2 Bc2–e4
16 Rh1–g1 Rf8–b8 17 Bf1–h3 Bg7–h6+ 18 f2–f4**
Now that Black's threats have all been repulsed White can play to consolidate its material advantage.

**18 ...   Qb4–a5 19 Rg1–e1 f7–f5 20 Qc6–e6+ Kg8–f8 21 b2–b3 Bh6–g7
22 Bc1–b2 Bg7–d4 23 g3–g4 Rb8–b6 24 Qe6–d7 Rb6–d6 25 Qd7–a4 Qa5–b6
26 Bb2–a3 Bd4xc3+ 27 Kd2xc3 Rd6–d8 28 Ra1–d1 Qb6–f2**

Although White is a piece ahead, its task is not that easy. The exposed king
gives rise to all sorts of tactical possibilities.

**29 g4xf5 Qf2–c2+ 30 Kc3–d4 g6xf5 31 Qa4–c6 Qc2–f2+ 32 Kd4–e5 Kf8–g8
33 Re1–g1+ Kg8–h8 34 Ba3xe7**

With this move BELLE announced that it had found a forced mate. The
immediate threat is 35 Be7–f6 or 35 Qc6–f6.

**34 ... Qf2–g2 35 Qc6–f6+ Kh8–g8 36 Bh3xg2 Rd8xd5+ 37 Ke5–e6 h7–h6
38 Qf6xh6 Rd5–e5+ 39 f4xe5 Ra8–f8 40 Bg2–f3 mate.**

BELLE pointed the way for the strides in computer chess that came in the late
1980s. The fast hardware brigade of Thompson, Scherzer, Berliner, Hsu and
others believe that it is only a matter of a few more ply of search depth before
Kasparov can retire to his dacha. Berliner, understanding much more than the
others about the game, contends that to play as well as a human World
Champion a chess program must also be endowed with a considerable
amount of chess knowledge, a view which is reflected in his own program
HITECH.

Following its sucess in the 1980 World Championship, BELLE also took first
prize in the next three ACM tournaments: Nashville (1980), Los Angeles
(1981) and Dallas (1982), but in Dallas, Thompson had to be content with a
four way tie for first place with CRAY BLITZ, CHAOS and David Slate's
NUCHESS. Thompson and Condon's machine continued to improve, and in
1983 BELLE became the first program to reach an important milestone in the
history of computer chess. Based exculsively on its results in human chess
tournaments its rating on the U.S. Chess Federation scale had risen to 2203,
thereby qualifying the program for the title of U.S. Master. The Fredkin
Foundation presented BELLE's creators with a prize of $5,000 which had been
stipulated for the first program to be awarded the U.S. master title. Ironically,
the cheque was presented to Thompson and Condon during the 1983 World
Computer Championship in New York, which was won by CRAY BLITZ.

Robert Hyatt's BLITZ program first appeared on the scene in 1976, at the
ACM tournament in Houston, where it tied for second place. Its performance
ratings in its first few ACM tournaments were: 1319 (in 1976), 1535 (in 1977),
1724 (in 1978) and 1516 (in 1979). In 1980 the program's name was changed
to CRAY BLITZ to reflect the more powerful hardware which had been placed
at the program's disposal, and its performances improved steadily: from 1791
at Nashville in 1980 to over the 2000 mark from 1981 onwards. In 1981 CRAY
BLITZ became the second program to win a state championship, when it took
the Mississippi title. Here is a game from that event.

White: **Human (U.S. Master, rated 2262)**
Black: **CRAY BLITZ**
Mississippi State Championship, 1981
Slav Defense

1 c2–c4 Ng8–f6 2 Nb1–c3 c7–c6 3 Ng1–f3 d7–d5 4 c4xd5 c6xd5 5 d2–d4
Nb8–c6 6 g2–g3 Nf6–e4 7 Bf1–g2 Ne4xc3 8 b2xc3 e7–e6 9 O–O Bf8–d6
10 Qd1–c2 O–O 11 Nf3–g5 f7–f5 12 f2–f4 Nc6–a5 13 Qc2–d3 Qd8–d7
14 Bc1–d2 Na5–c4 15 Bd2–c1 Qd7–a4 16 g3–g4 h7–h6 17 g4xf5 h6xg5
18 f4xg5 Bd6–a3 19 g5–g6 Ba3xc1 20 Ra1xc1 Nc4–d6 21 Qd3–h3 Rf8xf5
22 Qh3–h7+ Kg8–f8 23 Qh7–h8+ Kf8–e7 24 Qh8xg7+ Ke7–d8 25 Rf1xf5
Nd6xf5 26 Qg7–f6+ Nf5–e7 27 g6–g7 Qa4–e8 28 Bg2–f3 Kd8–d7 29 Rc1–f1
Ne7–g8 30 Bf3–g2 Qe8–e7 31 Qf6–g6 Kd7–d6 32 e2–e4 d5xe4 33 Bg2xe4
Qe7–h4 34 Qg6–g3+ Qh4xg3+ 35 h2xg3 Bc8–d7 36 Rf1–f8 Ra8–c8 37 Be4–h7
Rc8xc3 38 Rf8xg8 Rc3xg3+ 39 Kg1–f2 Rg3–g5 40 Bh7–e4 b7–b6 41 Kf2–e3
e6–e5 42 Rg8–a8 Rg5–g3+ 43 Ke3–f2 Rg3xg7 44 d4xe5+ Kd6xe5 45 Be4–f3
Bd7–e6 46 a2–a4 Rg7–f7 47 Kf2–e3?? Rf7xf3+ 48 Ke3xf3 Be6–d5+ 49 Kf3–e3
Bd5xa8 50 a4–a5 Ba8–e4 51 Ke3–d2 Ke5–d4 52 Kd2–c1 b6–b5 53 Kc1–b2
Kd4–c4 54 a5–a6 b5–b4 55 Kb2–a2 Kc4–c3 and CRAY BLITZ announced
mate in 6 moves: 56 Ka2–a1 Be4–c2 57 Ka1–a2 b4–b3+ 58 Ka2–a3 b3–b2
59 Ka3–a2 b2–b1=Q+ 60 Ka2–a3 Qb1–b2 mate.

Whereas the 1970s were marked by the domination of a single programming
team, the next decade produced a struggle between CRAY BLITZ and
three "chess engines" — BELLE, HITECH and DEEP THOUGHT (which
originally went under the name CHIPTEST). These four captured all the
major titles during the 1980s, but following closely on their heels was a
number of other programs including the microprocessor based CHESS
CHALLENGER and MEPHISTO chess computers.

Why this sudden burst forward in the strength of the best chess programs
and in the number of programs able to perform at a respectable level? There
appear to be four principal reasons. Firstly, commercially available hardware
continued to grow in computing power. Whereas CRAY BLITZ started life on
a single Cray-1 computer, by the time of the 1989 World Championship in
Edmonton it was running on a four-processor Cray-XMP. Combined with
this increase in raw hardware speed there came a dramatic reduction in the
cost of fabricating small quantities of application specific integrated circuits,
so that deigning a chip which did nothing but play chess was suddenly a
realistic prospect. This enabled former World Correspondence Chess
Champion Hans Berliner to design a 64 processor system called HITECH,
which achieved some outstanding performances against human opponents.
Working in the same department at Carnegie Mellon University, Pittsburgh,
a graduate student called Feng-hsiung Hsu produced an even more powerful
chip than Berliner's, and the resulting program (CHIPTEST) quickly overtook
HITECH.

The third reason for the explosion in computer chess strength in the 1980s is simply the fact that more was known about how to write good chess programs. The literature abounds with papers, theses, magazine articles and books on the subject, and anyone who wishes to write a program can choose his source material from several hundred publications.

But perhaps the single most significant change between the 1970s and the 1980s is the fact that whereas Slate and Atkin were lucky to be given so much computer time on a "powerful" CDC 6400 or 6600 computer in the early 1970s, nowadays almost anyone who wishes to do so can walk into their local store and for a few hundred dollars leave with more computing power than a 6400 tucked underneath their arm. This cheap availability of computing resources means that today chess programming is within the reach of literally millions of people. It is perhaps not a good analogy to say that if a million monkeys are each given a typewriter one of them will one day write a Shakespeare sonnet, but it is true to say that if a million intelligent people who know how to program are each given a personal computer, some of them will produce fairly powerful chess programs.

The rise of CRAY BLITZ to world championship caliber occurred in 1983. The annual ACM computer chess tournament was scheduled for New York, and since North America was, by tradition, the chosen continent for the1983 World Championship, it was decided to merge the two events. Thus the 1983

Figure 6.4   Levy, Botvinnik, Newborn and Mittman at the 1983 World Championship in New York

ACM conference played host to the 4th World Championship, to which Mikhail Botvinnik was invited as an honoured guest. The tournament was a 5 round, Swiss system event with 22 participants. CRAY BLITZ scored 4.5 points, finishing half a point clear of Tony Scherzer's BEBE and Tony Marsland's AWIT. CRAY BLITZ' performance was crowned by a last round win over the previous World Champion BELLE.

White: **BELLE**
Black: **CRAY BLITZ**
4th World Computer Chess Championship, New York, 1983
Sicilian Defense

1 e2–e4 c7–c5 2 c2–c3
Many chess programs employ this move against the ever popular Sicilian Defense, and with good reason. The positions arising after 2 Ng1–f3 and 3 d2–d4 are generally easier for a computer to play as Black than as White. The move 2 c2–c3 gives nothing away and leaves White with a more flexible position.

2 ... d7–d5 3 e4xd5 Qd8xd5 4 Ng1–f3 e7–e6 5 d2–d4 Ng8–f6 6 Bf1–d3 Nb8–c6

Figure 6.5 The CRAY BLITZ team: Harry Nelson, Robert Hyatt, and Bert Gower

7 O–O Bf8–e7 8 Bc1–e3 O–O?!
The usual continuation is 8 ... c5xd4 9 c3xd4 Bc8–d7 10 Nb1–c3 Qd5–d6 with approximately equal chances. CRAY BLITZ was out of its openings book and believed that after 8 ... O–O 9 d4xc5 Rf8–d8 it would stand better.

9 d4xc5! Rf8–d8
Not 9 ... Be7xc5? 10 Bd3xh7+ winning a pawn.

10 Nf3–d4?!
Feeble. Better was 10 Bd3–e2 Qd5–f5 (not *10 ... Be7xc5 11 Qd1xd5 Rd8xd5 12 c3–c4* when Black loses material) 11 Nb1–d2 with a slight edge for White.

10 ... Be7xc5 11 c3–c4! Qd5–d6 12 Nd4xc6 b7xc6
If 12 ... Qd6xc6 13 Be3xc5 Qc6xc5 14 Bd3xh7+.

13 Be3xc5 Qd6xd3 14 Qd1–a4?!
Putting the queen offside. After 14 Nb1–a3 White would have retained a slight edge.

14 ... Nf6–e4! 15 Bc5–b6!
Not 15 Qa4xc6?? Bc8–d7 16 Qc6–c7 Rd8–c8 winning the bishop.

15 ... Rd8–d7 16 Bb6–a5?
Wasting more time. White had to play 16 Nb1–a3, in order to complete its development.

16 ... Bc8–b7 17 Nb1–c3 Ne4–c5 18 Qa4–b4 Qd3–d4 19 Ra1–d1?
A natural looking move, but 19 Nc3–e2 was better. Now Black begins to get the upper hand.

19 ... Nc5–d3 20 Qb4–a4 Qd4–g4 21 c4–c5 Qg4–f5

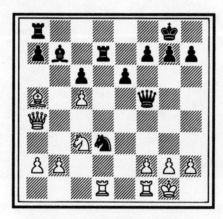

Figure 6.6 After 21 ... Qg4–f5

22 b2–b4?

White could have equalized with 21 Qa4–e4, and if 21 ... Qf5xc5 22 Rd1xd3 Rd7xd3 23 Qe4xd3 Qc5xa5 24 Qd3–d7. Instead BELLE decided to sacrifice its queen in return for a rook and bishop, and for getting a rook to the seventh rank.

22 ...   Nd3–b2   23 Rd1xd7 Nb2xa4   24 Nc3xa4 Qf5–c2   25 Rd7xb7 Qc2xa4 26 Rf1–a1 e6–e5!   27 f2–f3 Qa4–c2   28 Rb7–c7 Qc2–d3   29 Ra1–f1 Qd3–d5 30 a2–a3 g7–g5 31 Rc7–e7 f7–f6 32 Re7–c7 h7–h5 33 h2–h3 Kg8–h8 34 Kg1–h2 a7–a6   35 Rf1–e1 Ra8–e8   36 Re1–e4

36 a3–a4 would have a little more bite.

36 ...   f6–f5   37 Re4–e2 g5–g4 38 h3xg4 f5xg4 39 f3xg4 h5xg4 40 Re2–f2 e5–e4 41 Rf2–f7 Qd5–e5+!   42 g2–g3 e4–e3   43 Rf7–h7+ Kh8–g8   44 b4–b5 c6xb5 45 Ba5–e1 Qe5–b2+   46 Kh2–g1 Qb2–a1   47 Kg1–g2 Qa1–f6!   48 Kg2–h2 Re8–d8   49 Rh7–d7 Rd8–f8

CRAY BLITZ could also win quickly by trading rooks followed by ... Qf6–f1, but it prefers to play for mate.

50 Rd7–d6 Qf6–b2+   51 Kh2–g1 Qb2–b1   52 Kg1–h2 Qb1–c2+   53 Kh2–g1 Qc2–f5! White resigns.

Mate cannot be stopped.

Eyeball to Eyeball
with Grandmasters

CRAY BLITZ confirmed its superiority at the 1984 ACM tournament in San Francisco, but by the following year Hans Berliner's HITECH had made a big leap in playing strength and was a convincing winner in Denver. BEBE, meanwhile continued to slowly improve, but never quite made it to the top. In both 1984 and 1985 it lost key games to the tournament winners.

White: **CRAY BLITZ**
Black: **BEBE**
15th ACM NACCC, San Francisco 1984
Sicilian Defense

1 e2–e4 c7–c5 2 d2–d4 c5xd4 3 Ng1–f3 Nb8–c6 4 Nf3xd4 Ng8–f6 5 Nb1–c3 d7–d6 6 f2–f4 Qd8–b6 7 Nd4–b3 e7–e5 8 Qd1–e2 Bc8–g4 9 Qe2–b5 Qb6xb5 10 Bf1xb5 a7–a6?
This wastes time. Better was 10 ... Bg4–d7

11 Bb5xc6+ b7xc6 12 O–O
12 f4–f5 Nf6xe4 12 Nc3xe4 Bg4xf5 and 14 ... Bf5xc2 gives three pawns for the pi ece.

12 ... Ra8–b8?!
Black should do something about the precarious situation of its g4-bishop.

13 Nb3–a5
If 13 f4–f5 d6–d5 14 h2–h3 d5–d4 saving the bishop.

**13 ... Bg4–d7 14 Rf1–d1 Nf6–g4? 15 h2–h3 Ng4–f6 16 Na5–c4 Rb8–b4
17 b2–b3! d6–d5 18 e4xd5 Bf8–c5+ 19 Kg1–h2 Bc5–d4 20 d5xc6 Bd7xh3
21 Nc4–d6+**
White can also win with 21 Kh2xh3 Bd4xc3 22 c6–c7 Ke8–e7 23 Bc1–a3.

21 ... Ke8–e7 22 Kh2xh3 Ke7xd6
Or 22 ... Bd4xc3 23 Bc1–a3 winning material.

**23 Bc1–a3 a6–a5 24 Ba3xb4+ a5xb4 25 Nc3–b5+ Kd6xc6 26 Nb5xd4+ e5xd4
27 Rd1xd4 Nf6–d5 28 a2–a3 b4xa3 29 c2–c4 Nd5–b4 30 Ra1xa3 Rh8–e8**
If 30 ... Nb4–c2 31 Ra3–a6+ Kc6–b7 32 Rd4–d6.

**31 Ra3–a7 Re8–e3+ 32 Kh3–h4 Kc6–c5 33 Rd4–d8 Re3xb3 34 Rd8–c8+
Kc5–d4 35 Ra7xf7 Rb3–c3 36 g2–g3 Black resigns.**

Figure 7.1 Hans Berliner in Edmonton, 1989

White: **BEBE**
Black: **HITECH**
16th NACCC, Denver 1985
Ruy Lopez

1 e2–e4 e7–e5 2 Ng1–f3 Nb8–c6 3 Bf1–b5 a7–a6 4 Bb5–a4 Ng8–f6 5 O–O b7–b5 6 Ba4–b3 Bc8–b7 7 Rf1–e1 Bf8–c5 8 c2–c3 d7–d6 9 d2–d4 Bc5–b6 10 a2–a4 h7–h6 11 a4xb5 a6xb5 12 Ra1xa8 Qd8xa8 13 Nb1–a3 e5xd4 14 c3xd4?
Better is 14 Na3xb5 O–O 15 Nb5xd4 Nc6xd4 16 Nf3xd4 Bb7xe4 with equality (this variation is all "book").

14 ... Bb7–a6?
Correct is 14 ... O–O 15 Na3xb5 Nc6–a5 and Black will win back the pawn with the better game.

15 e4–e5! d6xe5 16 d4xe5 Nf6–g4
Here HITECH expected 17 Re1–e2 b5–b4 18 Na3–c4 Qa8–a7 19 Nc4xb6 Qa7xb6 but BEBE finds a more interesting continuation.

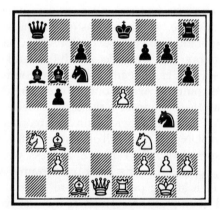

Figure 7.2 After 16 ... Nf6–g4

17 Bb3xf7+!?
So that if 17 ... Ke8xf7 18 Qd1–d7+ and 19 Qd7xg4.

17 ... Ke8–e7! 18 Kg1–f1?
A horrible move in a position which offered a number of good possibilities. For example 18 Re1–e2, 18 Qd1–d5 or 18 Bc1–e3.

18 ... b5–b4+! 19 Na3–c4 Rh8–d8 20 Qd1–c2 Ke7xf7?
HITECH should have played 20 ... Nc6–d4 21 Nf3xd4 Rd8xd4, and if now 22 Qc2–g6 Ng4xh2+ 23 Kf1–g1 Rd4–g4 winning for Black.

21 Qc2–f5+ Ng4–f6 22 Qf5–c2?
Why? BEBE could have maintained its winning position with 22 e5xf6
Ba6xc4+ 23 Kf1–g1 g7–g6 24 Qf5–f4 threatening both 25 Qf4xc4+ and
25 Qf4xh6.

22 ... b4–b3! 23 Qc2–e2
Or 23 Qc2xb3 Nc6–a5 winning.

**23 ... Nc6–d4! 24 Nf3xd4 Rd8xd4 25 Kf1–g1 Ba6xc4 26 Qe2–f3 Qa8xf3
27 g2xf3 White resigns.**

With the 1986 World Championship tournament due to take place in Cologne,
West Germany, it looked very much as though the world of computer chess
was going to have a new champion. When the tournament began HITECH
was firm favorite, especially after CRAY BLITZ unexpectedly lost to the low
ranked BOBBY program from West Germany in round 2. Before the last round
HITECH was a point clear of CRAY BLITZ, BEBE and Jonathan Schaeffer's
SUN PHOENIX (Canada), and was due Black against CRAY BLITZ. All that
HITECH needed was a draw and the title would have been Berliner's, a just
reward for all the effort he had expended on computer chess during the
previous 17 years or more. (Berliner was one of the very first to enter a
program in a computer tournament — at the 1st ACM Championship in New
York in 1970 his program JBIIT [Just Because It Is There] scored 50 percent.)
The CRAY BLITZ—HITECH game in Cologne was controversial, and in the
end it was the supercomputer which outanalyzed its more knowledgeable
opponent. To the suprise of almost everyone in Cologne, and as a result of a
tie-breaking system, CRAY BLITZ was again declared World Champion over
HITECH, BEBE and SUN PHOENIX all of which tied for first place. Perhaps
even more surprising than CRAY BLITZ' success was the performance
of a rank outsider, Ed Schroeder's REBEL program, written for a 6502
microprocessor, which at one point looked to have a realistic chance of
winning the World Championship. This was the first occasion on which a
microprocessor based program came close to winning a major title ahead of
the world's best big computers.

Having retained its World Championship title in Cologne, CRAY BLITZ
did not turn out for the 1986 ACM tournament in Dallas, which was won by
BELLE who entered the tournament at the last moment. One of the programs
that scored 50 percent in Dallas was CHIPTEST, created at Carnegie Mellon
University by Feng-hsiung Hsu. CHIPTEST was only a new born babe at the
time of the 1986 Dallas tournament and the event served more as a debugging
trial than a measure of the true potential of the program. Hsu had created on
a chip a faster version of BELLE. Once debugged this machine was so
powerful that at the following year's ACM event, also in Dallas, CHIPTEST
swept the board, pushing CRAY BLITZ into a tie for second place. Hsu later
predicted that with existing technology he could achieve well in excess of one

million evaluations per second, and that 14-ply searches were a realistic possibility within the forseeable future.

Although CRAY BLITZ was still World Champion in 1988 it was clear that CHIPTEST was the stronger program and most computer chess experts were of the opinion that HITECH was also stronger than CRAY BLITZ. Hsu and Berliner were becoming serious rivals at Carnegie Mellon University, even though CHIPTEST had been permitted to use some of the program code originally written for HITECH. In 1988 Hsu removed all traces of the Berliner code from his program and renamed it DEEP THOUGHT. It was under its new name that the program reasserted its position in the computer chess hierarchy by winning the 18th ACM Championship in Orlando, Florida.

White: **DEEP THOUGHT**
Black: **HITECH**
19th NACCC, Orlando 1988
Alekhine's Defense

1 e2–e4 Ng8–f6
HITECH's creator, Hans Berliner, used Alekhine's Defense extensively throughout his own chess career.

2 e4–e5 Nf6–d5 3 d2–d4 d7–d6 4 Ng1–f3 Nb8–c6 5 c2–c4 Nd5–b6 6 e5–e6!
White sacrifices a pawn to gum up Black's position.

6 ... f7xe6 7 Nf3–g5 g7–g6
7 ... e6–e5 is an interesting alternative.

8 Bf1–d3 Nc6xd4 9 Ng5xh7 Nd4–f5 10 Nh7xf8 Ke8xf8 11 O–O c7–c5
Once again 11 ... e6–e5 was called for.

12 b2–b3 d6–d5 13 Nb1–d2 Qd8–d6 14 Nd2–f3 Nb6–d7 15 Rf1–e1 d5–d4

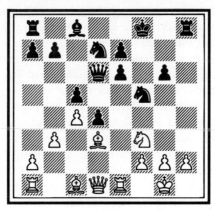

Figure 7.3 After 15 ... d5–d4

16 Nf3–e5! Nd7xe5 17 Bc1–f4 Rh8–h7
Black misses the last chance to stay in the game: 17 ... Ne5xd3 18 Bf4xd6
Nd3xe1 19 Bd6–e5 Rh8–h4 20 Qd1xe1 b7–b6 with balanced material and the
possibility of mobilizing the central mass of black pawns. Now, however,
White's attack becomes devastating.

18 Re1xe5
Threatening 19 Re5xf5+ and 20 Bf4xd6.

18 ... Qd6–b6 19 g2–g4 Nf5–h4 20 Bf4–g3 Bc8–d7 21 Re5–h5!!
Smashing open the black king.

**21 ... g6xh5 22 Bd3xh7 e6–e5 23 Bg3xh4 Bd7xg4 24 Qd1–d3 Ra8–c8 25 Ra1–e1
Qb6–e6 26 f2–f3! Bg4–h3 27 Qd3–g6 Qe6xg6+ 28 Bh7xg6 Rc8–c6 29 Bg6xh5
Rc6–e6**
If 29 ... Rc6–h6 30 Re1xe5.

**30 Bh4–g3 Re6–a6 31 a2–a4 d4–d3 32 Re1xe5 Ra6–d6 33 Re5–e1 Rd6–b6
34 Bg3–f4 a7–a5 35 Bf4–e3 Rb6xb3 36 Be3xc5 d3–d2 37 Bc5xe7+ Kf8–g7
38 Re1–d1 Rb3–e3 39 Be7–h4 Re3–a3 40 Bh5–e8 Ra3xf3 41 Bh4–g5**
If 41 Rd1xd2?? Rf3–f1 mate.

**41 ... Rf3–f8 42 Be8–b5 Kg7–g6 43 Bg5–e3 Rf8–f3 44 Be3xd2 Rf3–d3 45 c4–c5
Rd3–d5 46 c5–c6 b7xc6 47 Bb5xc6 Rd5–d6 48 Bc6–f3 Rd6–d4 49 Bd2xa5
Rd4xa4 50 Rd1–d6+ Kg6–f5 51 Ba5–c3 Ra4–a2 52 Rd6–h6 Bh3–g4 53 Bf3–d5
Ra2–c2 54 Rh6–c6 Rc2–e2 55 h2–h4 Kf5–f4 56 Rc6–c4+ Kf4–g3 57 Bc3–a5
Black resigns.**

Shortly after Orlando, DEEP THOUGHT stunned the chess world by finishing in a tie for first place in a tournament for grandmasters at Long Beach,
California. This result amazed even the greatest skeptics. Sharing first place
with the program was GM Tony Miles, for many years England's leading
player. Among those who finished behind the program were many times U.S.
Champion, GM Walter Browne (who beat the program in their individual
encounter); the former World Champion Mikhail Tal; and the Danish GM
Bent Larsen. Perhaps even more remarkable than winning the tournament
was the fact that DEEP THOUGH won its game against Larsen, the first
time that a program had ever defeated a world class grandmaster under
tournament conditions. It is true that a few months earlier HITECH had won
a match against Arnold Denker, but to be fair one must admit that Denker in
his seventies is not the player he used to be, and his GM title was awarded on
an emeritus basis — he had not achieved the necessary "norms."
    Here is DEEP THOUGHT's historic defeat of the great Dane. The Miles—
DEEP THOUGHT "play-off" exhibition game, played a year later, follows.

White: **Larsen**
Black: **DEEP THOUGHT**
American Open, Long Beach 1989
English Opening

1 c2–c4 e7–e5 2 g2–g3 Ng8–f6 3 Bf1–g2 c7–c6 4 Ng1–f3 e5–e4 5 Nf3–d4 d7–d5
6 c4xd5 Qd8xd5 7 Nd4–c2 Qd5–h5 8 h2–h4 Bc8–f5 9 Nc2–e3 Bf8–c5
10 Qd1–b3 b7–b6 11 Qb3–a4 O–O 12 Nb1–c3 b6–b5 13 Qa4–c2 Bc5xe3
14 d2xe3 Rf8–e8 15 a2–a4 b5–b4 16 Nc3–b1 Nb8–d7 17 Nb1–d2 Re8–e6
18 b2–b3 Ra8–d8 19 Bc1–b2 Bf5–g6 20 Nd2–c4 Nf6–d5 21 O–O–O Nd7–f6
22 Bg2–h3 Bg6–f5 23 Bh3xf5 Qh5xf5 24 f2–f3 h7–h5 25 Bb2–d4 Rd8–d7
26 Kc1–b2 Rd7–c7 27 g3–g4 h5xg4 28 Rh1–g1 c6–c5 29 f3xg4 Nf6xg4
30 Bd4xg7 Re6–g6 31 Qc2–d2 Rc7–d7 32 Rg1xg4 Rg6xg4 33 Nc4–e5 Nd5xe3
34 Qd2xd7 Ne3xd1+ 35 Qd7xd1 Rg4–g3 36 Qd1–d6 Kg8xg7 37 Ne5–d7
Rg3–e3 38 Qd6–h2 Kg7–h7 39 Nd7–f8+ Kh7–h8 40 h4–h5 Qf5–d5
41 Nf8–g6+ f7xg6 42 h5xg6+ Kh8–g7 43 Qh2–h7+ Kg7–f6 White resigns.

White: **Tony Miles (International Grandmaster)**
Black: **DEEP THOUGHT**
American Open, Long Beach 1989
Queen's Gambit Accepted

1 d2–d4 d7–d5 2 c2–c4 d5xc4 3 e2–e4 Ng8–f6
Varying from the move 3 ... Nb8–c6 which had brought it so much distress
in the games against Kasparov and HITECH.

**4 Nb1–c3 e7–e5 5 Ng1–f3 e5xd4 6 Qd1xd4 Bf8–d6! 7 Bf1xc4 O–O 8 Bc1–g5
Nb8–c6 9 Qd4–d2 h7–h6 10 Bg5–h4 Bc8–g4 11 O–O–O Bg4xf3 12 g2xf3**

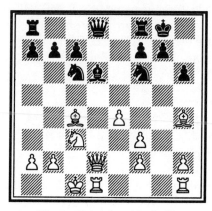

Figure 7.4 After 12 g2xf3

12 ... Nf6xe4! 13 Bg5xd8 Ne4xd2 14 Bd8xc7 Bd6xh2!!
Presumably Miles had overlooked this move when contemplating his 12th,
and had only considered the possibilities 14 ... Bd6xc7 15 Kc1xd2 and
14 ... Nd2xc4 15 Bc7xd6.

**15 Bc7xh2 Nd2xc4 16 Rd1–d7 b7–b6 17 f3–f4 Ra8–d8 18 Rh1–d1 Rf8–e8
19 b2–b3 Rd8xd7 20 Rd1xd7 Re8–e1+ 21 Nc3–d1 Nc4–a5 22 Kc1–d2 Re1–h1
23 Bh2–g3 h6–h5 24 f4–f5 h5–h4 25 Bg3–f4 Nc6–b4 26 a2–a3 Nb4–c6
27 Rd7–d3 Nc6–d4! 28 b3–b4**
Not 28 Rd3xd4 Nd2xb3+ 29 Kd2–c3 Nb3xd4 when the d1-knight is still
hanging.

**28 ... Na5–c6 29 f5–f6 g7xf6 30 Nd1–c3 Nd4–e6 31 Nc3–d5 Kg8–g7 32 Bf4–d6
Ne6–g5 33 Kd2–e2 h4–h3 34 Rd3–d1**
If 34 Rd3–c3 Nc6–e5 35 f2–f4 Rh1–e1+!! 36 Kd2xe1 h3–h2 and Black wins.

**34 ... Rh1xd1 35 Ke2xd1 Nc6–e5 36 Nd5–e3 h3–h2 37 Ne3–f5+ Kg7–g6
38 Nf5–g3 Ng5–e4! 39 Ng3–h1**
Or 39 Bg3xe5 Ne4xg3 and 40 ... h2–h1=Q.

39 ... Ne4xd6 White resigns.

Following its success in Long Beach DEEP THOUGHT won the 1989 World
Championship held in Edmonton in May with a 5–0 score. In its crucial last
round game against HITECH, Berliner's program built up a strategically
overwhelming position, but then played a few feeble moves and was crushed.
In Edmonton it was announced that Hsu and two of his colleagues had been
hired by IBM, who had earmarked a few million dollars with the goal of
creating a Kasparov beating machine within 5 years!
   In November of 1989 at the ACM's 20th Championship in Reno, DEEP
THOUGHT lost its only game to another computer — a dramatic encounter
with MEPHISTO. It had a perfect 4–0 score entering the last round and only
needed a draw to win the tournament, but MEPHISTO played a strong
positional game and avenged a loss from the previous year. DEEP THOUGHT
finished in a first place tie with HITECH. The HITECH—DEEP THOUGHT
game appears in Chapter 1 on pages 17–18.

White: **MEPHISTO**
Black: **DEEP THOUGHT**
20th ACM Championship, Reno, November 1989
Queen's Gambit Accepted

**1 d2–d4 d7–d5 2 c2–c4 d5xc4 3 Ng1–f3 Ng8–f6 4 e2–e3 Bc8–g4 5 Bf1xc4 e7–e6
6 h2–h3 Bg4–h5 7 Nb1–c3 Nb8–d7 8 g2–g4 Bh5–g6 9 Nf3–h4 Bg6–e4?!
10 Nc3xe4 Nf6xe4 11 Nh4–f3 Ne4–d6 12 Bc4–b3 Qd8–e7? 13 Bc1–d2 h7–h5**

14 Rh1–g1 h5xg4 15 h3xg4 O–O–O 16 Bd2–a5 b7–b6? 17 Ba5–b4 a7–a5
18 Bb4xd6 Qe7xd6 19 Qd1–c2 Bf8–e7 20 O–O–O Rh8–h3 21 Nf3–d2 c7–c6
22 Rg1–h1 Rd8–h8 23 Rh1xh3 Rh8xh3 24 Nd2–e4 Qd6–c7 25 Kc1–b1 g7–g5
26 Rd1–c1 Kc8–b7 27 Bb3–a4 Nd7–b8 28 Ne4–d2 Qc7–d7 29 Ba4–b3 Nb8–a6
30 Qc2–e4 Na6–b4 31 a2–a3 Nb4–d5 32 Qe4–g2 Rh3–h8 33 Nd2–e4 f7–f6
34 Qg2–g3 Rh8–g8 35 Rc1–h1 f6–f5 36 g4xf5 e6xf5 37 Qg3–h3 Rg8–f8
38 Ne4–d2 Be7–f6 39 Qh3–h7 Rf8–f7 40 Qh7–h6 Qd7–e6 41 Qh6–g6 Rf7–g7
42 Rh1–h7 Rg7xh7 43 Qg6xh7+ Bf6–e7 44 Kb1–c1 Kb7–c7 45 Nd2–f3 Kc7–d8
46 Nf3–e5 g5–g4 47 Qh7–h8+ Kd8–c7 48 Kc1–d2 Kc7–b7 49 Ne5xc6! Qe6xc6
50 Qh8–e5 Nd5–c7 51 Qe5xe7 Qc6–g2 52 Qe7–h4 f5–f4 53 e3xf4 Qg2–e4
54 Qh4xg4 Qe4xd4+ 55 Kd2–c1 Qd4xf2 56 Qg4–f5 Qf2–f3 57 Kc1–c2 Kb7–c6
58 Qf5–e5 Nc7–d5? 59 Qe5–e6+ Kc6–c5 60 Bb3xd5 Qf3xd5 61 Qe6xd5+
Kc5xd5 62 Kc2–d3 a5–a4 63 Kd3–c3 Kd5–c5 64 f4–f5 Black resigns.

At the end of 1989 DEEP THOUGHT put the crowning touch on an excellent year when it played a 4-game match in London against David Levy. This match was for the $5,000 "Omni" prize, and it was the first time that Levy had ever played a program rated higher than he was at his best. Although the program was clearly the better player, many pundits felt that Levy's understanding of how chess programs "think" would provide sufficient compensation to make the match interesting, and perhaps even give the human player a chance. Levy himself predicted before the match that the computer would wipe him out with a 4–0 score. The London bookmakers

Figure 7.5 Fidelity International Inc.'s special tournament machine, 1989

William Hill took the opposite position, and started the odds at 3 to 1 against
DEEP THOUGHT. At the end of the day Levy was correct — the layers of rust
caused by an 11 year layoff from serious chess made the human no match for
the machine, and Levy's prediction of 4–0 was vindicated.

Even before the end of the 1980s chess programs had risen above the level
of human achievement in more than one area of the game. It had been the case
since 1981 that the world's leading human chess problem solvers were no real
match for the best problem solving programs. The speed with which even
microprocessor based programs can solve chess problems of the type "White
to play and mate in 3 moves," renders a man versus machine problem-contest
somewhat pointless. But it is in the realm of endgame play that chess
programs have emphatically proved their worth. The first occasion on which
a program's ability to play certain endgames perfectly was useful to human
players was at a Soviet tournament in 1975. There, in Vilnius, Grandmaster
David Bronstein was able to use a database created by the KAISSA team to
help him analyze an adjourned game, which he subsequently won. This was
the ending of queen and knight's pawn (g-pawn or b-pawn) against queen,
the most difficult of all queen and pawn endings. An amusing side effect of
this type of database work is that the Rules Commission of the International
Chess Federation (FIDE) changed the "50-move rule" as a result of some of
Ken Thompson's results. Using his program BELLE, Thompson was able to
prove that there are some positions with rook and bishop against rook in
which the side with the bishop can force a win but not in 50 moves or less.
Since the 50-move rule would make it impossible for a human player to win
one of these positions against best play, FIDE changed the rule to allow the
player with the extra bishop 100 moves to try for a win. This rule change
caused great practical problems in a few international tournaments because
defending such an ending for 12 hours is sheer torture, and ruins the
tournament schedule by creating the need for extra adjournment sessions. So
the rule was later changed back to 50 moves, but when DEEP THOUGHT
reached this ending in Long Beach against Alex Fishbein, whose USCF rating
was 2572 at the time, the program needed just 23 moves to win.

As more and more programmers have easy access to computers, so the
amount of effort that goes into chess programming increases. New ideas are
generated by those working with microprocessors and the financial rewards
to be obtained by writing strong programs has provided a great incentive. The
best microprocessor based chess programs had absolutely no chance when
they first competed against the mainframe programs in the late 1970s, but by
1986 the gulf had narrowed considerably. In 1988 the two leading micro based
programs, MEPHISTO and CHESS CHALLENGER, both came within an
ace of winning the 19th ACM Championship in Orlando. In fact, CHESS
CHALLENGER shared first place on points with the mighty DEEP THOUGHT
but lost out on tie-break. One year later in Reno, we saw MEPHISTO defeated
DEEP THOUGHT in the last round. The trend is clear for those who are
watching closely. By the time that there is an electronic Kasparov, it will
probably be small enough to fit into a briefcase, if not a matchbox!

CHAPTER

8

Endgame Play and Endgame Databases

In 1966, when the Soviet program at the Institute for Theoretical Physics took on the Kotok/McCarthy Program, games were agreed drawn when they entered the endgame. In this way, both sides were able to avoid an embarrasing public demonstration of their programs' weak play at this stage of the game. Their programmers realized that the numerous concepts particular to the endgame and easily understood by humans were totally unknown to their programs. In part, this was because the concepts had simply not been programmed into their programs' scoring functions. But it was also because many endgame positions require searches to depths beyond the capabilities of the fastest computers of those years even if they had had the best of scoring functions. It seemed then that computers even thousands of times faster would still be unable to play endgames correctly.

Many endgame concepts turned out to be easier to encode in a program's scoring function than originally imagined. For example, code that gives credit for maintaining the defending king in the square of an advancing passed pawn is now part of the scoring function of all the best current programs. The scoring function calculates the distance of each passed pawn to its queening square and then compares this figure with the distance of the defending king.

The situation can become complicated when both sides have several passed pawns, but humans get confused in such situations also. Most scoring functions include code that gives credit for king support for advancing pawns. Programs also understand gaining control of promoting squares and squares in front of advanced passed pawns. They also understand that certain endgames such as KNK (white king and knight versus black king) and KBK (white king and bishop versus black king) are drawn. DEEP THOUGHT even has certain endgame databases available such as KRK and KQK which can be accessed during the search. Scoring functions also give credit for trading pawns when behind and trading pieces when ahead, avoiding the trade of the last pawn when it is crucial to maintaining an option of winning, say, a KNNPKNP endgame.

The concepts of opposition and zugzwang once were raised as problems for computers. Opposition is said to occur whenever the two kings are on the same row, column or diagonal and are separated by an odd number of squares. The king that gains the opposition is often able to force the opponent's king away from a square that the latter would like to remain on or move to. For example, in the position in Figure 8.1a with White to play, White wins by moving its king into opposition with 1 Kd5–d6. White only draws after 1 d2–d4 Kd8–d7 when Black has the opposition. A good player understands the principle of opposition and would immediately play 1 Kd5–d6 in this position, but a computer that did not have the concept in its scoring function might equally prefer to play 1 d2–d4. It might be saved however because scoring functions usually give credit for king centrality, and here 1 Kd5–d6 keeps the black king on the side of the board.

A player is in zugzwang when he is on the move and has only moves that are seriously damaging. White is in zugzwang in Figure 8.1b. He only has five moves all of which draw. If he could pass, the game would be an easy win. The situation is similar for Black. If he is on the move, he, too, is in zugzwang. His best move is to pass thereby placing White in zugzwang! But he has to move his king, giving up a pawn and the game. It is very difficult to program an understanding of zugzwang into a scoring function.

Exactly what defines an endgame is rather arbitrary. Some programs count material and when the total drops to some predetermined level, the game is declared to have reached the endgame. Others take into account the specific pieces on the board. Whatever the approach, this decision is often crucial. Scoring functions, which prior to the endgame give a penalty for king centrality, reverse this policy and give credit for this feature in the endgame. If a program prematurely decides the game has reached the endgame, the king can march toward the middle of the board at a most inopportune time.

In 1977, a king and pawns versus king and pawns endgame program called PEASANT was written by Newborn and tested on the set of 16 positions shown in Figure 8.2. These positions represent a small sampling of positions that are used to illustrate endgame principles in Fine's *Basic Chess Endings*. PEASANT showed that a brute force search using a simple scoring function and searching from 4 to 13 levels in 2 minutes could solve a fair

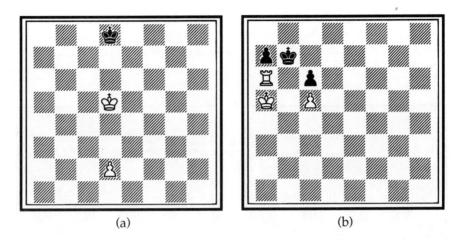

(a)   (b)

Figure 8.1 (a) An endgame illustrating the concept of opposition
(b) An endgame illustrating the concept of zugzwang

percentage of Fine's problems — 9 of them to be precise — but that several
were way beyond the program's capabilities. The program would have been
much more effective if it had had transposition tables. It was, in fact, the
introduction of transposition tables into chess programs that was the major
factor in their endgame improvement. These same 16 positions, when
attempted recently by HITECH and CRAY BLITZ, were all solved correctly in
less than a minute or so. The performances of PEASANT and CRAY BLITZ
are compared below each figure. When solving these problems, CRAY BLITZ
used a small 16,000-entry transposition table and searched approximately
200,000–250,000 positions per second on a 4-processor Cray Y-MP.

The position shown in Figure 8.2i vividly illustrates the effectiveness of a
transposition table. It is a win for White, but the win requires a search to a great
depth, requiring an eon to be found by a program without a transposition
table. However, programs with transposition tables can find the correct line
of play in less than a minute. CRAY BLITZ found the solution in 2 seconds.
Note that with no pawn moves available, the white king can reach a total of
only 13 different squares after 3 moves (i.e.: a1, a2, a3, b1, b2, b3, c1, c2, c3, c4,
d1, d2, d3) while the black king can reach at most 10. This gives 130 different
positions to consider after a search of 6 plies, a far cry from somewhere in the
neighboorhood of (assuming each king averages 5 moves per position) 5^6 =
15625 positions that a 6-level search by a program without a transposition
table would consider. Fine's analysis gives 1 Ka1–b1! Ka7–b7 2 Kb1–c1
Kb7–c7 3 Kc1–d1 Kc7–d7 (if 3 ... Kc7–c8, White wins with 4 Kd1–d2 Kc8–d7
5 Kd2–c3 Kd7–c7 6 Kc3–d3!) 4 Kd1–c2 Kd7–d8 5 Kc2–c3 Kd8–c7 6 Kc3–d3
whereupon Black is unable to maintain opposition. For White to see that it can
eventually capture either the a5-pawn or the f5-pawn requires a very deep
search by the computer. The earliest that the f5-pawn can be captured,
assuming Black does not attempt to defend it, is after an 18-ply search, and

then to see that this leads to a win requires several more moves. Thus, to correctly solve this problem, a computer must find a continuation of almost 30 half-moves. When a transposition table is used, this can be done, and was done by CRAY BLITZ!

(a) PEASANT sees the correct solution with a 5-ply search; CRAY BLITZ finds d4–d5 in less than a second.

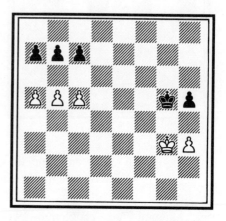

(b) PEASANT solves this problem with a search of 8 plies; CRAY BLITZ finds b5–b6 after a 14-ply search in negligible time.

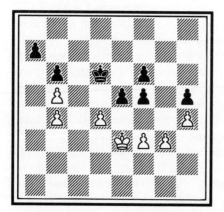

(c) PEASANT correctly selected g3–g4 but did not realize that was the winning move; CRAY BLITZ calculates for 1 minute looking to a depth of 13 plies and finds g3–g4 lead to a five pawn advantage.

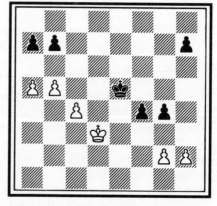

(d) PEASANT selects the correct move c4–c5 but again did not understand why. CRAY BLITZ calculates for 30 seconds and to a depth of 11 plies, plays c4–c5, but does not see the win.

(e) PEASANT fails to solve this problem. CRAY BLITZ sees that Kh6–h5 leads to mate in 19 in 10 seconds.

(f) PEASANT selects the wrong move. CRAY BLITZ sees Ke3–e4 wins 2 pawns when looking to a depth of 21 plies in 2 seconds.

(g) PEASANT vascillates between c4–c5 and the correct move d4–d5 from one iteration to the next, but not seeing any win. CRAY BLITZ sees d4–d5 leads to a score of +2.3 pawns for White after looking 19 plies in one minute.

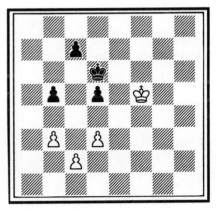

(h) Possibly the most difficult problem. PEASANT plays b3–b4 on early iterations, but chooses Kf5–f4 on an 8-ply search. CRAY BLITZ plays b3–b4, the correct move, but sees no better outcome than a draw after looking 18 plies in 1.5 minutes.

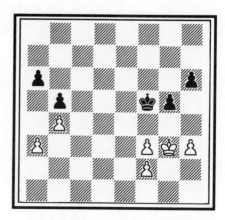

(i) PEASANT plays Ka1–b2 and has no understanding of the position. CRAY BLITZ sees Ka1–b1 wins when looking 18 plies deep, but it was able to look 30 plies in approximately 4 seconds.

(j) PEASANT selects h3–h4 and again has no understranding of the position. CRAY BLITZ see f3–f4 wins material after searching to a depth of 17 plies in 4 seconds.

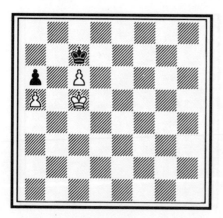

(k) An easy problem for both PEASANT and CRAY BLITZ. Kc5–d5 is necessary in order to avoid losing a pawn.

(l) PEASANT sees the correct move, Ke5–e4, though does not see the win. A shallow search will show that any other move is inferior. CRAY BLITZ sees Ke5–e4 wins after searching 23 plies in 1 second.

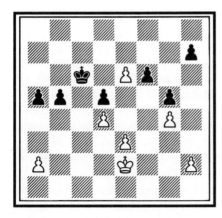

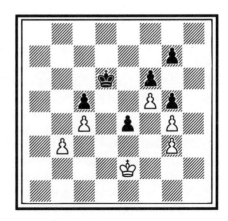

(m) PEASANT, on a 6-ply search, plays e3–e4, seeing that it holds the pawn on e6. CRAY BLITZ sees e3–e4 wins a pawn. In 35 seconds it searched to a depth of 13 plies.

(n) This problem involves triangulation and opposition. PEASANT sees Ke2–f2 is necessary in order to avoid disaster. CRAY BLITZ sees Ke2–f2 wins a pawn. It looked 18 plies in 48 seconds.

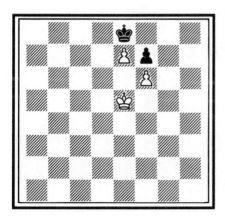

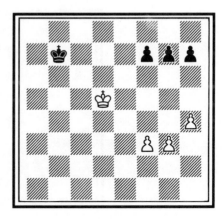

(o) PEASANT plays the correct move Ke5–f4 with an 11-ply search. CRAY BLITZ sees Ke5–f4 wins, searching 17 plies in negligible time.

(p) PEASANT stopped after searching to a depth of 8 plies, needing one more to see the correct continuation. CRAY BLITZ sees Kd5–d6 wins 3 pawns looking 15 plies deep in 1 minute and 9 seconds.

Figure 8.2 Endgame positions

Thus now, almost 25 years after the match between the Kotok/McCarthy Program and the ITEP Program, chess programs play endgames, perhaps not with the prowess of their middlegame tactical play but nevertheless, most respectably. CHESS 4.6 was first to show it could win an endgame from a strong player. Warren Stenberg (USCF 1969), a professor of mathematics at the University of Minnesota, had the distinction of being the first Class A player to lose to a computer, and he did so because his opponent, CHESS 4.6, didn't misplay an endgame. It was in February of 1977 when Stenberg and CHESS 4.6 battled for 24 moves to the position shown in Figure 8.3. Stenberg was playing White and CHESS 4.6 was Black. The game, beginning with White to play the 25th move, appears below. Data on each move made by CHESS 4.6 is included to give the reader some insight into the program's mind. The reader can see that CHESS 4.6 took between 1 minute and 6 minutes to make a move, and that it searched approximately 200,000 to 1,000,000 positions per move. Search depths ranged between 8 and 10 plies. These figures might be compared with those associated with CRAY BLITZ's performance on the 16 endgame positions. CRAY BLITZ is currently searching trees about 100 times as large as those searched by CHESS 4.6, while DEEP THOUGHT is searching trees approximately 300 times larger — and all this has happened in only 12 years.

Figure 8.3 After Black's 24th move

White: **Stenberg**
Black: **CHESS 4.6**
Minnesota Open Championship, 1977

After each move, the principal continuation calculated by CHESS 4.6 is given followed (surrounded by parentheses) by the time taken in seconds, the depth of search in plies, and the number of positions searched.

25 e3–e4 Rh8–c8
26 f2–f4 Rc8–c4 27 Nd1–f2 f6–f5 28 g2–g3 Rc4xe4 29 Nf2xe4 f5xe4 (58; 7; 183,842). CHESS 4.6 seems willing to exchange its rook for a knight and a pawn along with some positional gains, but this would give White the advantage.

26 Nd1–e3 f6–f5
27 Ne3xf5 Bg7xb2 28 Rf1–b1 Rc8–c2 29 Nf5–e3 Rc2–e2 30 Ne3–c4 (197; 8; 669,233).

27 b2–b3 f5xe4
28 Ne3–c4 Rc8–g8 29 Rf1–d1 Bg7–c3 30 d5–d6 h5–h4 31 d6xe7+ Kd7xe7 (97; 7; 342,981).

28 Ne3–c4 Rc8–g8
29 Rf1–d1 Bg7–c3 30 d5–d6 e7–e5 31 Kg1–h2 Kd7–e6 (83; 7; 267,663).

29 Rf1–d1 f7–f5
30 d5–d6 e7–e6 31 Rd1–d2 Kd7–c6 32 Rd2–a2 Kc6–b5 (117; 7; 375,313).

30 d5–d6 e7–e6
31 Rd1–d2 Kd7–c6 32 d6–d7 Kc6–c7 33 Rd2–d6 a6–a5 34 Kg1–f1 (167; 8; 567,651).

31 Nc4–b6+ Kd7–c6
32 Nb6–c4 Kc6–c5 33 Rd1–d2 Bg7–f6 34 Rd2–a2 Rg8–a8 35 Ra2–c2 (90; 8; 307,245).

32 Nb6–c4 Rg8–d8
33 Rd1–d2 Kc6–c5 34 Rd2–a2 Rd8–a8 35 Ra2–a5+ Kc5–d4 (130; 7; 415,153).

33 Nc4–a5+ Kc6–d7
34 Na5–c4 Bg7–c3 35 g2–g3 e6–e5 36 Kg1–g2 Kd7–e6 37 Rd1–c1 Rd8–g8 (297; 9; 989,004).

34 Na5–c4 Bg7–c3
35 g2–g3 e6–e5 36 Kg1–g2 Kd7–e6 37 Rd1–c1 Rd8–g8 (7; 7; 232,663).

35 Kg1–f1 Rd8–g8
36 g2–g3 Bc3–f6 37 Kf1–e2 h5–h4 38 Nc4–b6+ Kd7–c6 (69; 7; 222,322).

36 Nc4–d2 h5–h4
37 Nd2–c4 f5–f4 38 Nc4–d2 f4–f3 39 Nd2xe4 f3xg2+ 40 Kf1–g1 (83; 7; 260,734).

37 Nd2–c4 f5–f4
38 Nc4–d2 Bc3xd2 39 Rd1xd2 f4–f3 40 g2xf3 e4xf3 41 Kf1–e1 (211; 8; 746,997).

38 Nc4–d2 Bc3xd2
39 Rd1xd2 a6–a5 40 Rd2–d4 f4–f3 41 g2xf3 e4xf3 42 Kf1–e1 (96; 8; 363,181).

39 Rd1xd2 f4–f3
40 g2xf3 e4xf3 41 Rd2–d3 Rg8–f8 42 Rd3–d4 a6–a5 43 Kf1–e1 (100; 8; 350,800).

40 g2xf3 e4xf3
41 Rd2–d3 Rg8–f8 42 Rd3–d4 a6–a5 43 Rd4xh4 Kd7xd6 44 Rh4–h7 Kd6–d5 45 h3–h4 (112; 9; 448,606).

41 Rd2–d3 Rg8–f8
42 Kf1–e1 Rf8–f5 43 Ke1–d2 Rf5–d5 44 Rd3xd5 e6xd5 45 Kd2–e3 Kd7xd6 46 Ke3xf3 (260; 10; 1,002,080).

42 Kf1–e1 Rf8–f4
43 Ke1–d2 Rf4–f5 44 Kd2–e3 Rf5–d5 45 Rd3xd5 e6xd5 46 Ke3xf3 Kd7xd6 (96; 9; 372,796).

43 Ke1–d2 Rf4–f5
44 Kd2–e3 Rf5–f6 45 Ke3–e4 Rf6–f7 46 Rd3xf3 Rf7xf3 47 Ke4xf3 Kd7xd6 48 Kf3–e4 (213; 10; 753,462).

44 Kd2–c2 Rf5–c5+
45 Kc2–b2 Rc5–e5 46 Rd3xf3 Re5–e2+ 47 Kb2–c1 Kd7xd6 48 Rf3–f7 e6–e5 (264; 8; 923,960).

45 Kc2–b2 Rc5–g5
46 Rd3xf3 Rg5–g2 47 Kb2–c2 Kd7xd6 (133; 9; 464,549). This continuation lead to a position in the transposition table, and the remainder of the continuation was thus not available.

46 Kb2–c2 Rg5–f5
47 Kc2–d2 a6–a5 48 Kd2–e3 Rf5–d5 49 Rd3xd5 e6xd5 50 Ke3xf3 Kd7xd6 (175; 9; 613,761).

47 Rd3–d4 Rf5–c5+
48 Kc2–d1 Rf5–d5 49 Rd4xd5 e6xd5 50 Kd1–d2 Kd7xd6 51 Kd2–e3 Kd6–e5 52 Ke3xf3 (135; 9; 520,486).

48 Kc2–b2 a6–a5
49 Rd4–d3 Rc5–f5 50 Kb2–c2 Rf5–f7 51 Kc2–d2 Kd7–c6 52 Kd2–e3 e6–e5 (175; 9; 650,408).

49 Rd4–d3 Rc5–e5
50 Rd3xf3 Re5–e2+ 51 Kb2–c1 Kd7xd6 52 Rf3–d3+ Kd6–e5 53 Rd3–d2 Re2–e4 (185; 9; 656,255).

50 Rd3xf3 Re5–e2+
51 Kb2–c1 Kd7xd6 52 Rf3–f8 Kd6–e5 53 Rf8–f7 Re2–a2 (83; 9; 302,371). Again, the continuation ends at a position in the transposition table.

51 Kb2–c1 Kd7xd6
52 Rf3–d3+ Kd6–e5 53 Rd3–e3+ Re2xe3 54 f2xe3 Ke5–e4 55 Kc1–d2 e6–e5 (51; 8; 184,078).

52 Kc1–d1 Re2–a2
53 Rf3–d3+ Kd6–e5 54 Rd3–d2 Ra2xd2+ 55 Kd1xd2 Ke5–d4 56 f2–f3 e6–e5 57 Kd2–e2 (170; 10; 647,082).

53 Rf3–d3+ Kd6–c5
The data for this move is not available.

54 Kd1–e1 e6–e5
55 Rd3–d2 Ra2–a3 56 Rd2–b2 Kc5–d4 57 Ke1–d2 a5–a4 58 Kd2–c2 Ra3–a1 (95; 9; 340,505).

55 f2–f4 e5xf4
56 Ke1–d1 Ra2–f2 57 Kd1–e1 Rf2–h2 58 Ke1–d1 Kc5–c6 59 Rd3–f3 Kc6–d5 60 Rf3xf4 Rh2xh3 (99; 9; 395,263).

56 Rd3–f3 Kc5–d4
57 Rf3–f2 Ra2xf2 58 Ke1xf2 Kd4–e4 59 Kf2–e2 f4–f3+ 60 Ke2–f2 (11; 8; 48,988).

57 Rf3xf4+ Kd4–e3
58 Ke1–d1 Ke3xf4 59 Kd1–c1 Ra2–e2 60 Kc1–b1 Re2–e3 61 Kb1–a2 Re3xh3 62 Ka2–b2 (44; 10; 197,344).

White resigns.
Black is threatening to capture the rook and to mate, and White cannot defend against both threats. Even without stepping into this mess, White has been unable to outplay Black.

The current strength of endgame play can be appreciated by following through Edward Formanek's game against HITECH. HITECH entered the endgame with a pawn advantage, but no clear way to win. This victory gave HITECH the 1988 Pennsylvania State Championship. The game is presented beginning at move 29 in the position shown in Figure 8.4.

White: **Edward Formanek (2461)**
Black: **HITECH (2400)**
Pennsylvania State Championship, 1988

Figure 8.4 After Black's 28th move

29 Nb5–d4 Rc8–c3 30 Rf1–e1 Be8–d7 31 Qf2–f3 Bd7–c8 32 Kg1–f2 f7–f6
This eliminates back-rank mate threats which often give computers difficulties.

**33 Re1–a1 Bc8–b7 34 Ra1–b1 Rc3–c7 35 Rb1–b6 Kg8–f7 36 Rb6–e6 Qe5–g5
37 Qf3–g3 Rc7–c2+ 38 Nd4xc2**
White must exchange pieces now at a time when it is not to its advantage to do so.

**38 . . . Qg5xg3+ 39 Kf2xg3 Kf7xe6 40 Nc2–d4+ Ke6–e5 41 Kg3–f3 h7–h5
42 h3–h4 g7–g5 43 g2–g3 Bb7–c8 44 Nd4–c6+ Ke5–d6 45 Nc6–d4 Bc8–g4+
46 Kf3–f2 Kd6–e5 47 Nd4–b5 Bg4–d7 48 Nb5–d4 Ke5–e4 49 Nd4–c2 Bd7–b5
50 Nc2–d4 Bb5–a6 51 Nd4–e6 Ba6–c8 52 Ne6–d4 Bc8–d7 53 Nd4–c2 g5xh4
54 g3xh4 Bd7–g4 55 Nc2–d4 f6–f5 56 Nd4–e6 f5–f4**
HITECH is playing its best chess!

**57 Ne6–c5+ Ke4–f5 58 Nc5–d3 d5–d4 59 e3xd4 Kf5–e4 60 Nd3–e5 Ke4xd4
61 Ne5–f7 Bg4–e6 62 Nf7–g5 Be6–d5 63 Ng4–h3 Kd4–e4 64 Nh3–g1 Ke4–f5
65 Ng1–e2 Kf5–g4 66 Kf2–g1 f4–f3 67 Ne2–c3 Bd5–c6 68 Kg1–f2 Kg4xh4
69 Nc3–d1 Kh4–g4 70 Nd1–e3+ Kg4–f4 71 Ne3–f1 h5–h4 72 Nf1–h2 h4–h3
73 Nh2–f1 Bc6–b5 74 Nf1–g3 h3–h2 75 Ng3–h5+ Kf4–g4 76 Nh5–g3 Bb5–f1**
White resigns.

While those concerned with developing strong chess programs have concentrated their efforts on building good scoring functions and efficient search techniques, there are two other interesting areas where work on endgames has been carried out. At one extreme, with computers getting larger and faster, certain endgames have been completely analyzed by computers. Large databases that permit perfect play have been developed for these endgames, even though the databases provide no understanding of the principles required to force a win or draw as appropriate. At the other extreme, researchers are trying to use endgames as domains for learning how to build expert systems. Let us first review what has been accomplished on endgame databases.

Consider the simple endgame of king and queen versus lone king (KQK endgame). In the December 1985 issue of the *ICCA Journal*, H. J. J. Nefkens, of Delft University of Technology, describes how a microcomputer with 64k bytes of memory can construct a database for this case. The number of positions in the database is determined as follows. First, the black king can be placed on the board on any of 64 squares, although from the standpoint of symmetry, there are only 10 squares that need be considered as shown in Figure 8.5. Once the black king has been placed, there are at most 64 x 64 different ways to place the 2 white pieces. The KQK database must thus contain information on 10 x 64 x 64 = 40,960 positions: for each position, the database must know whether White wins and in how many moves.

Figure 8.5 Squares of black king that must be considered in KRK database

The database is created by a process called retrograde analysis. To begin, each of the 40,960 entries is initially set to zero (See Figure 8.6a). Let the first entry correspond to the position BK on a1, WK on a1, and WQ on a1, denoted <a1–a1–a1>, and the second entry correspond to the position BK on a1, WK on a1, and WQ on b1, denoted <a1–a1–b1>. The 129th entry would then correspond to the position <a1–c1–a1>, the 130th entry to the position <a1–c1–b1>, and the last entry to the position <d4–h8–h8>. Retrograde analysis then performs the following three steps until the table is complete.

1. First, determine all positions with the black king in check and all positions which are illegitimate. Illegitimate positions are those in which the two kings occupy the same square or are adjacent to one another. Positions with the black king and white queen occupying the same square are not illegitimate because they turn out to be necessary to determine those positions in which the black king must capture the white queen. The first 128 positions in the table are found to be illegitimate because the two kings either occupy the same square or are within a distance of one from each other. The 129th position finds the black king in check. At the end of this step, the database appears as in Figure 8.6b.
2. Next, all mate-in-one positions are determined as follows. For each of the positions with the black king in check, see whether Black has a safe move. If there is none, mark all positions in which White can move to the checking position as a mate-in-one for White, excluding positions which are checking positions or illegitimate, and record these in the table. Position 129 is the first position in the table with the black king in check. Black has three possible moves, Ka1–b1 (illegitimate position), Ka1–b2 (illegitimate position), or Ka1–a2 (still in check), and thus Black has no safe move. Now White's positions that are not checking or illegitimate and that have moves that lead to this position are determined and indicated in the table as such. There are the 12 positions <a1–c1–b3>, <a1–c1–b4>, . . . , <a1–c1–b8> and <a1–c1–c2>, <a1–c1–d3>, . . . , <a1–c1–h7>, and they are all mate-in-one.
3. Starting with n equal to 1, recursively determine all positions that are mate-in-(n+1) from positions that are mate-in-n. The first mate-in-two on the list is <a1–d1–b4>. In this position, White plays Kd1–c1 and then mate on the next move. When there is no mate-in-n for some n, stop.

In the worst case KQK endgame, shown in Figure 8.7, White mates in 10 moves. There is only one such position, apart from symmetry, that attains this maximum. This means that the KQK endgame requires only four bits per position for a total of 20480 bytes for the entire database. If White had a rook instead of a queen, mate would have been assured in 16 moves, and while it seems that five bits per position would have been required, Nefkens showed that it was possible to get by with only four.

Building a database for an endgame with pawns on the board turns out to have some added subtleties. In particular, games do not all end in mates or draws but transform themselves into other endgames. A KPK endgame transforms itself into a KQK game, for example, when the pawn queens. Thus to build a database for a KPK endgame, the KQK database must be used.

British computer scientist Michael R. B. Clarke first used retrograde analysis on KPK endgames reporting his work in *Advances in Computer Chess*, Volume 1 in 1977. Clarke's results differed slighty from those of individuals who tried to repeat his procedure. The conflicting results seem to have been straightened out only in 1989 by Hans Zellner of Mallersdorf, West Germany in an article in the *ICCA Journal*. Of the 64 x 64 x 24 = 98304 ways to place the two kings on a board while restricting the pawn to one side, 62480 are wins for

Position	Information On Position
<a1-a1-a1>	0
<a1-a1-b1>	0
...	.
...	.
<a1-a1-h8>	0
<a1-b1-a1>	0
<a1-b1-b1>	0
...	.
...	.
<a1-c1-a1>	0
<a1-c1-b1>	0
...	.
...	.
<a1-c1-h8>	0
...	.
...	.
<d4-h8-h8>	0

(a)

Position	Information On Position
<a1-a1-a1>	illegitimate
<a1-a1-b1>	illegitimate
...	.
...	.
<a1-a1-h8>	illegitimate
<a1-b1-a1>	illegitimate
<a1-b1-b1>	illegitimate
...	.
...	.
<a1-c1-a1>	illegitimate
<a1-c1-b1>	in check
...	.
...	.
<a1-c1-h8>	in check
...	.
...	.
<d4-h8-h8>	in check

(b)

Figure 8.6 Building a KQK database (a) initial contents of database, and (b) contents after performing the first step

Figure 8.7 Worst-case position of KQK database: White mates in 10 moves

White. Of these, 12749 are wins in one — that is, the game can be transformed in one move to a won KQK or KRK endgame — for White. Earlier work had failed to realize that in the position shown in Figure 8.8, a white king move is necessary; promoting to a queen leads to a draw while promoting to a rook does no better. In any case, no victory requires more than 19 moves to queen the pawn and since the worst-case position for the KQK endgame (Figure 8.7) could not possibly arise as the result of a promotion, no won game requires more than 19 + 9 = 28 moves to mate.

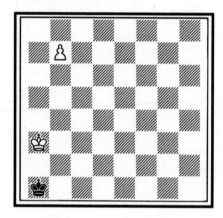

Figure 8.8 A KPK endgame with White to play and win

Ken Thompson has been the leader in developing databases that allow perfect play in certain endgames. His foremost work has been on five piece endgames, including in particular, the KBBKN, the KQPKQ, and the KRPKR endgames. In 1977, Thompson came to the World Computer Chess Championship in Toronto with a database that played a perfect KQKR endgame and it took on several masters. The players were surprised at how badly they played, being unable to win with the queen when they were sure they could. Thompson was disappointed and perplexed when several Grandmasters in attendance refused to test their talents, but several months after the championship, Walter Browne agreed to test his expertise. Browne played two games against BELLE. He had 2.5 hours to play 50 moves, while BELLE made its moves almost instantaneously. Browne was forced to accept a draw in the first game. The second game, played the following week, was won by Browne on the 50th move. Browne had prepared intensively during the interim.

There are two KQKR positions that are wins for White, either mates or rook captures, in 30 moves. All other wins take fewer moves. The two games with Browne begin in these positions.

Game 1
White: **Browne**
Black: **BELLE**

Figure 8.9 Position from BELLE's database:
White to play and win in 30 moves

**1 Ka8–b7 Re8–e7+ 2 Kb7–c6 Re7–e6+ 3 Kc6–d7 Re6–e7+ 4 Kd7–d8 Re7–e4
5 Qa5–c5 Re4–e5 6 Qc5–d4**
–1 move (that is, Browne's move set him back one move), 25 moves to victory:
correct is 6 Qc5–c3, 6 Qc5–c4, 6 Qc5–f8+, or 6 Qc5–g1.

**6 ... Kf6–f5 7 Kd8–d7 Re5–e4 8 Qd4–d3 Kf5–f4 9 Kd7–d6 Re4–e3 10 Qd3–d4+
Re3–e4 11 Qd4–f2+ Kf4–g4 12 Kd6–d5 Re4–e8 13 Qf2–f6 Re8–e3 14 Kd5–d4
Re3–f3 15 Qf6–g6+ Kg4–f4 16 Qg6–g2 Rf3–a3 17 Qg2–c6**
–3 moves, 17 moves to victory: correct is 17 Qg2–d2+ or 17 Qg2–e4+.

17 ... Ra3–a1 18 Qc6–c7+
–2 moves, 18 moves to victory: correct is 18 Qc6–c2.

18 ... Kf4–f5 19 Qc7–c2+
–1 move, 18 moves to victory: correct is 19 Qc7–c8.

19 ... Kf5–e6 20 Qc2–d2
–1 move, 18 moves to victory: correct is 20 Qc2–c4+.

20 ... Ra1–a7 21 Qd2–b4
–2 moves, 19 moves to victory: correct is 21 Qd2–e2+, 21 Qd2–h6+,
21 Qd2–e3+, or 21 Qd2–e1+.

21 ... Ra7–e7 22 Kd4–e4
–1 move, 19 moves to victory: correct is 22 Qb4–b3+, 22 Qb4–a5, 22 Qb4–c5,
22 Qb4–e1+, or 22 Qb4–c3.

**22 ... Ke6–f6+ 23 Ke4–f4 Kf6–e6 24 Qb4–d4 Re7–f7+ 25 Kf4–e4 Rf7–f6
26 Qd4–d5+**
–2 moves, 17 moves to victory: BELLE's database gives 26 Qd4–d8 Rf6–f7
27 Qd8–d5+ Ke6–f6 28 Ke4–f4.

**26 ... Ke6–e7 27 Ke4–e5 Rf6–h6 28 Qd5–b7+ Ke7–d8 29 Qb7–f7 Rh6–c6
30 Ke5–d5 Rc6–b6 31 Kd5–c5**
–1 move, 13 moves to victory: correct is 31 Qf7–f4.

31 ... Rb6–a6 32 Qf7–c4
–4 moves, 16 moves to victory: BELLE indicates 32 Qf7–d5+ Kd8–c7
33 Qd5–e4 Ra6–a5+ 34 Kc5–b4 Ra5–a6 35 Qe4–e7+ Kc7–c6 36 Qe7–e6+
Kc6–b7 37 Qe6–d7+.

32 ... Ra6–f6 33 Qc4–h4
–2 moves, 17 moves to victory: Browne can no longer win.

**33 ... Kd8–e7 34 Kc5–d5 Ke7–f7 35 Kd5–e5 Rf6–e6+ 36 Ke5–f5 Re6–d6
37 Qh4–c4+ Kf7–e7 38 Kf5–e5 Rd6–h6 39 Qc4–c7+ Ke7–f8 40 Ke5–f5**
–3 moves, 13 moves to victory.

**40 ... Kf8–e8 41 Qc7–c1 Rh6–d6 42 Qc1–c8+ Ke8–e7 43 Qc8–c7+ Rd6–d7
44 Qc7–c5+ Ke7–d8 45 Kf5–e6 Rd7–b7 Draw.**

Game 2
White: **Browne**
Black: **BELLE**

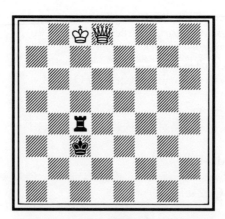

Figure 8.10 A second position from BELLE's database: White to play and
win in 30 moves

**1 Kc8–b7 Rc4–b4+ 2 Kb7–c6 Rb4–c4+ 3 Kc6–b5 Rc4–b4+ 4 Kb5–a5 Rb4–e4
5 Qd8–d6 Re4–d4 6 Qd6–e5**
–1 move, 25 moves to victory: correct is 6 Qd6–a3+

**6 ... Kc3–d3 7 Ka5–b5 Rd4–e4 8 Qe5–f6 Kd3–e3 9 Kb5–c5 Re4–f4 10 Qf6–g6
Rf4–a4 11 Qg6–g3+ Ke3–e2 12 Qg3–c3 Ra4–f4 13 Kc5–d5 Rf4–h4 14 Qc3–c2+
Ke2–e3 15 Qc2–d1 Ke3–f2 16 Qd1–d2+**
–1 move, 16 moves to victory: correct is 16 Qd1–d3

16 ... Kf2–f3 17 Qd2–e1
–3 moves, 18 moves to victory: correct is 17 Qd2–d3+.

17 ... Rh4–g4 18 Qe1–d1+ Kf3–f4 19 Qd1–e2
–3 moves, 20 moves to victory: correct is 19 Qd1–c1+.

**19 ... Rg4–g5+ 20 Kd5–d4 Rg5–f5 21 Qe2–e3+ Kf4–g4 22 Kd4–e4 Rf5–f7
23 Qe3–g1+ Kg4–h5 24 Qg1–g3 Rf7–f8 25 Ke4–e5 Rf8–f7 26 Ke5–e6**
–1 move, 14 moves to victory: correct is 26 Qg3–d3.

26 ... Rf7–f8 27 Qg3–a3
–2 moves, 15 moves to victory: correct is 27 Qg3–e5+.

27 ... Rf8–f4 28 Qa3–h3+
–2 moves, 16 moves to victory: correct is 28 Qa3–g3.

28 ... Kh5–g5 29 Qh3–g3+ Rf4–g4 30 Qg3–e5+
–1 move, 15 moves to victory: correct is 30 Qg3–e3+.

30 ... Kg5–h4 31 Qe5–h2+ Kh4–g5 32 Ke6–e5
–1 move, 14 moves to victory: correct is 32 Qh2–d2+.

32 ... Kg5–g6 33 Qh2–h8
–1 move, 14 moves to victory: correct is 33 Qh2–h3.

33 ... Rg4–g5+ 34 Ke5–e6 Rg5–g4 35 Qh8–g8+
–2 moves, 14 moves to victory: correct is 35 Qh8–e5.

35 ... Kg6–h5 36 Qg8–h7+ Kh5–g5 37 Ke6–e5 Rg4–g3 38 Qh7–g7+
Note the pattern!

38 ... Kg5–h4 39 Qg7–h6+ Kh4–g4 40 Ke5–e4 Rg3–g2 41 Qh6–g6+
And again!

41 ... Kg4–h3 42 Qg6–h5+ Kh3–g3 43 Ke4–e3 Rg2–g1 44 Qh5–g5+
–1 move, 6 moves to victory, no room for an error! Correct is 44 Qh5–e5+.

**44 ... Kg3–h2 45 Qg5–h4+ Kh2–g2 46 Ke3–e2 Rg1–a1 47 Qh4–e4+ Kg2–h3
48 Qe4–h7+ Kh3–g3 49 Qh7–g7+ Kg3–h3 50 Qg7xa1 Black resigns.**

Others have worked on developing endgame databases, most notably the KRPKR database by the Soviet scientists Vladimir Arlazarov and Aron Futer in the late 1970s, and the KQPKQ database by Edik Komissarchik, Futer, and Arlazarov several years later. Most recently, Boston University graduate student Larry Stiller carried out a massively parallel retrograde analysis of eighty five piece endgames without pawns — essentially all five piece games of any interest — and eight classic endgames with pawns. He used a 32K-processor Connection Machine CM-2 — a computer with approximately 32,000 processors! — and created the eighty non-pawn endgame databases using 227 minutes of computing time, an incredible accomplishment! Each of the 32,000 processors of the Connection Machine is very small, and in some sense, can process only one bit of information at a time. His results confirmed Thompson's with several small exceptions: Thompson's program did not consider underpromotions in some cases while Stiller's did.

Thompson's work in the early 1980s shook up the chess world when he found that certain endgames could be won, but that they required more than 50 moves without advancing a pawn or capturing material. Until this discovery, the rules of chess considered a game drawn if 50 moves passed and no pawn advanced or piece was captured.* It had been believed that a game was drawn if neither side was able to make any progress towards a win after 50 such moves. In particular, the following endgames have positions that require the number of moves enclosed in parentheses to mate or to convert the game by captures into a simpler won endgame: KNBKN(77), KBBKN(66), KRBKR(59), KQRKQ(60), KQKNN(63), and KQKBB(71). Figure 8.11 shows a KBNKN position requiring 77 moves for White to win. Figure 8.12 shows a KNNKP(d4) endgame in which White can force a win, but it requires 83 non-capturing, non-pawn moves to do so.

With essentially all five piece endgames solved, attention by researchers has now turned to six piece endgames. Each additional piece increases the number of positions in the database by a factor of about 64. Further, a program that solves six piece endgames must also have available the outcomes of relevant five piece endgames. There are 256 six piece endgames with four white pieces and two black pieces, another 256 with three pieces per side, and still another 256 with two white pieces and four black pieces. Many of this total of 768 endgames are not of interest because of the large material imbalance. There are several hundred that are, however, such as KRBKNN, KQNKRR, KQBKRN, etc.

---

* There is one exception: KNNKP where the pawn is safely blockaded in certain situations. In this case, FIDE allowed 100 moves.

Endgames with several pawns and pieces will also receive attention in the coming years. The KRP(a2)KBP(a3) has already been the subject of several papers in the *ICCA Journal*, the most recent of which is by H. J. van den Herik, I. S. Herschberg and N. Nakad. This database has 8,388,608 positions since with the two pawns fixed, the remaining four pieces can be on any of 64 x 64 x 64 x 32 squares. There are 523 positions where it takes more than 50 moves to win, the maximum being 54 moves, of which there are 12 such positions.

Figure 8.11 A KBNKN endgame with White to play and win in 77 moves

White: **king, bishop and knight**
Black: **king and bishop**
White to win beginning in position shown in Figure 8.11. Note that in the following, moves in parentheses are equally good alternatives.

1 Bh2–g3 Nb2–c4 2 Kc1–d1 Nc4–e3+ 3 Kd1–e2 Ne3–f5 4 Bg3–f2 Nf5–e7 5 Ke2–f3 Ne7–c6 6 Kf3–g3 Nc6–d4 7 Kg3–g4 Nd4–c6 *(7 ... Nd4–b3)* **8 Kg4–h3 Nc6–b4** *(8 ... Nc6–e5)* **9 Bf2–b6 Nb4–d3 10 Ne1–c2 Nd3–f2+ 11 Kh3–g3 Nf2–e4+ 12 Kg3–f4 Ne4–d2 13 Nc2–e3 Kh1–h2 14 Kf4–g4 Nd2–b3 15 Bb6–a7 Nb3–c1 16 Ba7–d4 Nc1–d3 17 Kg4–h4 Nd3–f2 18 Bd4–e5+** *(18 Bd4–c5 or 18 Bd4–b6)* **Kh2–g1 19 Be5–c3** *(19 Be5–g3)* **Nf2–e4** *(19 ... Nf2–h1)* **20 Bc3–e1 Ne4–f6** *(20 ... Ne4–d6 or 20 ... Ne4–c5 or 20 ... Ne4–f2 or 20 ... Kg1–h1 or 20 ... Kg1–h2)* **21 Kh4–g5** *(21 Kh4–g3 or 21 Kh4–h3)* **Nf6–d7** *(21 ... Nf6–e4+)* **22 Kg5–f4** *(22 Kg5–g4)* **Nd7–c5 23 Kf4–f3 Nc5–e6** *(23 ... Kg1–h2)* **24 Be1–c3 Kg1–h2 25 Kf3–g4 Ne6–d8** *(25 ... Ne6–c5)* **26 Bc3–e5+** *(26 Bc3–a5)* **Kh2–g1 27 Kg4–g3 Nd8–e6 28 Be5–f6** *(28 Be5–h8 or 28 Be5–c3 or 28 Be5–b2 or 28 Be5–a1)* **Ne6–c5 29 Bf6–d4 Nc5–b3 30 Bd4–a7 Nb3–d2 31 Ne3–c4+ Kg1–h1 32 Nc4–e5** *(32 Nc4–b2)* **Nd2–c4 33 Ne5–d3** *(33 Ne5–g4)* **Nc4–d6** *(33 ... Nc4–d2)* **34 Kg3–h3 Nd6–f7 35 Ba7–e3 Nf7–e5 36 Nd3–f4** *(36 Nd3–f2+)* **Ne5–c4 37 Be3–d4** *(37 Be3–c5 or 37 Be3–a7 or 37 Be3–f2)* **Nc4–d6** *(37 ... Nc4–d2)* **38 Nf4–h5** *(38 ... Nf4–d3)* **Nd6–e4 39 Bd4–e3 Ne4–f2+ 40 Kh3–g3 Nf2–e4+** *(40 ... Nf2–d3)*

41 Kg3–f3 Ne4–d6 42 Be3–f4 Nd6–c4 43 Kf3–f2 Nc4–a5 44 Nh5–f6 Na5–b7
45 Kf2–f3 Nb7–d8 *(45 ... Nb7–a5)* **46 Bf4–d6** *(46 Nf6–e4)* **Kh1–g1 47 Nf6–e4**
Nd8–c6 *(47 ... Nd8–e6)* **48 Ne4–d2 Nc6–d4+ 49 Kf3–e4 Nd4–e2 50 Ke4–e3**
Ne2–c3 51 Bd6–e5 Nc3–a2 52 Ke3–f3 Na2–b4 53 Kf3–g3 Kg1–h1 54 Be5–d4
Nb4–c6 55 Bd4–c5 Nc6–d8 56 Nd2–e4 Nd8–b7 57 Bc5–b4 Nb7–d8 58 Bb4–a5
Nd8–e6 59 Ba5–b6 Ne6–g5 60 Ne4–f2+ Kh1–g1 61 Kg3–f4 Ng5–f7
62 Nf2–g4+ Kg1–g2 63 Ng4–e3+ Kg2–h3 64 Ne3–f5 Kh3–g2 *(64 ... Kh3–h2)*
65 Bb6–c5 Nf7–h8 *(65 ... Nf7–d8 or 65 ... Kg2–h2)* **66 Nf5–d4 Kg2–h3 67 Kf4–f5**
Kh3–h4 68 Nd4–e6 Kh4–h5 69 Bc5–e3 Nh8–f7 70 Ne6–g7+ Kh5–h4
71 Be3–f4 Nf7–h8 *(71 ... Kh4–h3)* **72 Ng7–e6** *(72 Kf5–f6)* **Nh8–f7 73 Kf5–g6**
(73 Kf5–f6) **Nf7–h8+ 74 Kg6–g7 Kh4–g4 75 Bf4–h6** *(75 Bf4–d6 or 75 Bf4–c7 or*
75 Bf4–b8 or 75 Bf4–d2 or 75 Bf4–c1 or 75 Bf4–h2) **Kg4–h5** *(75 ... Kg4–f5)*
76 Ne6–f4+ Kh5–h4 *(76 ... Kh5–f4)* **77 Kg7xh8 with conversion to KBNK.**

Figure 8.12 KNNKP(d4) endgame with White to play and win in 84 moves

White: **king and two knights**
Black: **king and pawn**
White to win in 84 moves beginning in position shown in Figure 8.12

1 Na2–b4+ Ka6–b6 2 Nb4–d3 Kb6–c7 3 Na7–b5+ Kc7–c6 4 Nb5–a3 Kc6–b6
5 Ka8–b8 *(5 Na3–c4+ or 5 Na3–c2)* **Kb6–c6 6 Na3–c4** *(6 Na3–c2)* **Kc6–b5**
7 Nc4–e5 Kb5–b6 8 Kb8–c8 Kb6–a6 *(8 ... Kb6–a5 or 8 ... Kb6–b5)* **9 Kc8–c7**
(9 Kc8–d7) **Ka6–b5 10 Kc7–d6 Kb5–a4 11 Kd6–c5 Ka4–b3 12 Kc5–b5 Kb3–c3**
13 Kb5–a4 Kc3–c2 14 Ka4–b4 Kc2–d1 15 Kb4–b3 Kd1–d2 16 Kb3–b2 Kd2–d1
17 Ne5–c4 Kd1–e2 18 Kb2–c2 Ke2–f3 19 Kc2–d2 *(19 Kc2–d1)* **Kf3–g3**
(19 ... Kf3–e4) **20 Kd2–e2** *(20 Nc4–e5)* **Kg3–g2 21 Nc4–e5 Kg2–g3 22 Ke2–f1**
Kg3–h4 23 Kf1–g2 *(23 Kf1–f2)* **Kh4–g5 24 Kg2–f3 Kg5–f5 25 Ne5–c4 Kf5–f6**
26 Kf3–f4 Kf6–e6 27 Kf4–e4 Ke6–f6 28 Ke4–d5 Kf6–e7 29 Kd5–e5 Ke7–f7
30 Ke5–d6 Kf7–f6 31 Nc4–d2 Kf6–f5 32 Kd6–e7 Kf5–g6 33 Ke7–e6 Kg6–g7
(33 ... Kg6–g5) **34 Nd2–e4 Kg7–g6 35 Ke6–e5 Kg6–g7 36 Ke5–d6 Kg7–h7**
(36 ... Kg7–h6) **37 Ne4–d2** *(37 Ne4–f2)* **Kh7–g7 38 Kd6–e6 Kg7–f8 39 Nd2–e4**

(39 Nd2–c4) **Kf8–e8 40 Ne4–f6+** *(40 Ne4–d6+)* **Ke8–f8** *(40 ... Ke8–d8)* **41 Nf6–h5 Kf8–e8 42 Nh5–g7+ Ke8–d8 43 Ke6–d6 Kd8–c8 44 Ng7–e6 Kc8–b8** *(44 ... Kc8–b7)* **45 Kd6–c5 Kb8–a7 46 Kc5–c6 Ka7–a6 47 Ne6–c5+** *(47 Ne6–g5)* **Ka6–a5 48 Nc5–b3+** *(48 Nc5–e4)* **Ka5–a4 49 Nb3–d2 Ka4–a5 50 Kc6–c5 Ka5–a6 51 Nd2–c4 Ka6–b7 52 Kc5–d6 Kb7–c8 53 Nc4–a5 Kc8–d8 54 Na5–b7+ Kd8–e8 55 Kd6–e6 Ke8–f8 56 Nb7–d6 Kf8–g7 57 Ke6–f5 Kg7–h6 58 Kf5–f6 Kh6–h5 59 Nd6–f7** *(59 Nd6–e4)* **Kh5–g4 60 Nf7–g5 Kg4–h4 61 Kf6–f5 Kh4–g3 62 Kf5–e4 Kg3–g4 63 Ng5–f7 Kg4–h5** *(63 ... Kg4–g3)* **64 Ke4–f5 Kh5–h4 65 Nf7–e5 Kh4–h5 66 Ne5–g4 Kh5–h4 67 Ng4–f6 Kh4–h3 68 Kf5–e5 Kh3–g3 69 Ke5–e4 Kg3–h3 70 Ke4–f3 Kh3–h4 71 Kf3–f4 Kh4–h3 72 Nf6–e8** *(72 Nf6–e4 or 72 Nf6–h5)* **Kh3–h4 73 Ne8–g7 Kh4–h3 74 Ng7–f5 Kh3–g2** *(74 ... Kh3–h2)* **75 Kf4–g4 Kg2–h2** *(75 ... Kg2–f1 or 75 ... Kg2–g1 or 75 ... Kg2–h1)* **76 Nf5–d6** *(76 Nf5–g3)* **Kh2–g2** *(76 ... Kh2–g1 or 76 ... Kh2–h1)* **77 Nd6–c4** *(77 Nd6–e4)* **Kg2–h2** *(77 ... Kg2–g1)* **78 Nc4–d2 Kh2–g2 79 Kg4–h4 Kg2–h2** *(79 ... Kg2–g1)* **80 Nd3–f4** *(80 Nd3–e1)* **Kh2–g1 81 Kh4–g3 Kg1–h1 82 Nd2–f3** *(82 Nf4–e2 or 82 Nf4–h3)* **d4–d3 followed by 83 Nf4–h3 d3–d2 84 Nh3–f2 mate.**

Running in parallel with efforts to built large databases by retrograde analy-sis has been the study of endgames in an attempt to understand how expert knowledge can be synthesized and then used, a problem central to the field of

Figure 8.13 Donald Michie in Edmonton, 1989

artificial intelligence. For many years, Donald Michie has compared chess' role in this discipline to that of the fruit fly in genetics, and the case seems even stronger for endgames. With all the apparent complications of the middle game gone, endgames present a clear challenge — how does one concisely specify a simple set of rules for optimal play. Michie has led this effort to study endgame play in the context of expert systems. He has been interested in the process of developing rules which allow perfect play if possible, while settling for strong play if perfect play cannot be achieved. Torres y Quevedo's mechanical wonder of the early 20th century used rules to guide its play in KRK endgames, but Michie has been interested in more complex endings.

Alen Shapiro, while working with Michie on his doctoral dissertation in the early 1980s, studied the Kp(a7)KR endgame. A list of rules was established that permitted strong play by White. The top-level rule used to determine whether a position with White to move is won for White or not is:

KP(a7)KR is won for White if and only if:
        The BR can be captured safely
        OR none of the following is true:
                A Black piece controls the Queening square
                OR there is a simple delay to White's Queening the pawn
                OR one or more Black pieces control the Queening square
                OR the White King is in stalemate
                OR there is a good delayed skewer threat.

Additional rules made this top-level rule more explicit. For example:

There is a simple delay to White's Queening the pawn if and only if:
        There is a good delay because there is a mate threat
        OR there is a good delay because the WK is on square a8
        OR there is a good delay because the White King is in check
        OR there is a good delay because of a double attack threat
        OR there is a good delay because there is a hidden check.

Michie's work continues to evolve with better ways to write the rules and with more elaborate rules. However, in complex endgames, there seems to be a fair percentage of positions which defy finding rules for guiding play.

Michie has been concerned with the implications of machines solving complex problems other than chess. In an article that appeared in the *ICCA Journal* of September 1989, Michie wrote that

Combinatorial domains of importance in empirical science are today facing something of the same impasse as computer chess. That is to say, solutions to particular instances of a scientific problem (analogous to particular legal positions in a complex domain of chess) can be laboriously obtained, perhaps by prohibitively costly analysis, yet the solutions are opaque. What is required is the extraction from such solved cases of a manageable set of general rules by which solutions to newly encountered instances can expeditiously be obtained — the extraction, preferably on a computer-aided basis, of operational theories.

9

Search Techniques Used by Chess Programs

The progress of chess programs, from rank beginners to grandmasters over a period of about 30 years, is due to the development and refinement of search techniques particularly suited to the capabilities of computers, and to the rapid improvement of computer hardware. In the remainder of this chapter, the search techniques will be described. Chapter 10 surveys advances in computer hardware. The description of search techniques appropriately begins with the minimax algorithm. This algorithm serves as the foundation of all chess programs and was originally proposed for that purpose in papers by Claude Shannon and Alan Turing in the late 1940s. A description of the alpha-beta algorithm, a powerful addition to the minimax algorithm, follows. After that, material is presented on how moves are generated, how the main line of play called the principal continuation is found, and how the computationally cheap but effective killer heuristic is used by chess programs. Pruning techniques, which eliminate obviously bad moves from the search, and variable depth quiescence searches, which follow crucial lines of play deeper into the tree than other lines, are discussed next. Then hash tables and hashing techniques are described, followed by iteratively deepening search and the use of search windows. The subject of the efficient use of time concludes the chapter.

The Chess Tree and the Minimax Algorithm

When the game of chess begins, White has a choice of 20 moves. Following White's 1st move, whatever the move, Black has 20 replies (See Figure 9.1). Thus 400 different positions arise after only 1 move by each side. After 2 moves the number grows to over 20,000, becoming astronomical after several more moves. The entire *chess tree* has more positions than there are atoms in the Milky Way although, because of the rules of the game, the number is finite. According to the rules, a game is normally drawn if 50 moves pass without the capture of a piece or the advancement of a pawn, implying that a game can last at most 3150 moves, and consequently the chess tree can have only so many different positions. If it were possible to examine this entire tree, to search out all lines of play to their conclusion, it would be possible to determine precisely the best initial move. However, in practice, the tree is far too large to consider this approach. Even at positions in the middle of the game, determining the best move by searching the chess tree rooted at these intermediate positions is impossible. At best, it is possible to search only a small part of the tree, hoping to gather sufficient information to decide correctly what move is best. Humans use this approach as do computers. Exactly how humans do it is not clear. The following describes the general approach taken by computers.

In the early 1970s, programs searched chess trees at rates of approximately 200 positions per second. Today, DEEP THOUGHT is searching 2,000,000 positions per second, or about 400,000,000 positions per tournament-speed move, an increase of a factor of 10,000 over the last twenty years. The better programs examine all sequences of moves for approximately 8 to 10 levels (or plies) in the tree — 4 or 5 moves for each side. Crucial lines of play such as checking lines and capturing sequences are searched even deeper. In the jargon of chess programs, a *6-ply brute force search* thus means a search of all moves by both sides to a depth of 6 levels (3 moves by each side) and deeper along highly tactical lines.

For a given chess tree, the minimax algorithm provides the rule for deciding which move the first player, assumed to be the computer, should make. The minimax algorithm begins by calculating a numerical value or score for the position at the end of each continuation. Such positions are called *terminal positions* and their scores are calculated by an *evaluation function* or *scoring function*. The evaluation function attempts to measure how good the position is. A positive score signifies that the computer is winning; a negative one means that the opponent is ahead. The larger the score, the better the position, and conversely, the more negative the score the worse the position. Exactly how scores are determined is discussed shortly.

The minimax algorithm understands that the goal of the first player is to steer the game toward the terminal position with the highest score, while the goal of the opponent is to do exactly the opposite. This is equivalent to saying that at even levels in the tree where it is the computer's turn (the root is at level 0, although the moves at the root are said to be at level 1), the minimax algorithm should assign each *nonterminal position* a score equal to the

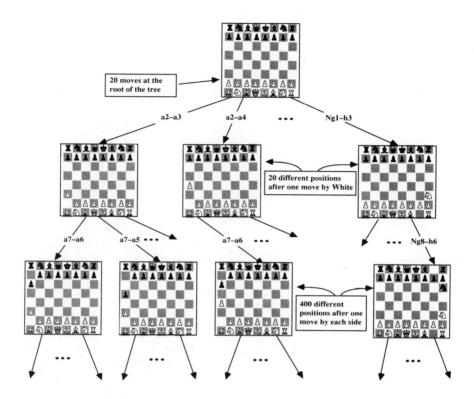

20 moves at the root of the tree

a2–a3   a2–a4   • • •   Ng1–h3

20 different positions after one move by White

a7–a6   a7–a5 • • •   a7–a6 • • •   • • •   Ng8–h6

400 different positions after one move by each side

Figure 9.1 The first two levels of the chess tree

maximum score of any of its successor positions. That is, the computer is assumed to pick the move leading to the position at the next level with the maximum score. At odd levels in the tree where it is the opponent's turn, the minimax algorithm should assign each nonterminal position a score equal to the minimum score of any of its successors. Since the scores of a nonterminal position's successors must be known in order to assign that position a score, the scores of the terminal positions must be determined first and then the remaining nonterminal positions can be assigned scores by *backing up* scores assigned to the terminal positions towards the root.

A small 2-level tree is shown in Figure 9.2. The computer is assumed to be playing White and is on the move. Not all moves in each position are shown; for the purpose of illustrating the minimax algorithm, only two moves in each position are shown. The minimax algorithm first calculates the scores of the four terminal positions. Their scores are based only on the difference in material, where white pieces are assigned the following values: pawn=1, knight=3, bishop=3, rook=5, and queen=9. In terminal position **D**, the material is even and thus the score is **0** as indicated alongside. In the second terminal position **E**, a score of **+2** is assigned since White is ahead an exchange, i. e., a rook for a bishop. The bottom 2 terminal positions are assigned scores of **-4** and **-2** respectively. Next, the scores of positions **B** and **C** at the 1st level are determined by assuming the opponent plays the move in each of these 2 positions leading to the position at level 2 with the minimum score. In position

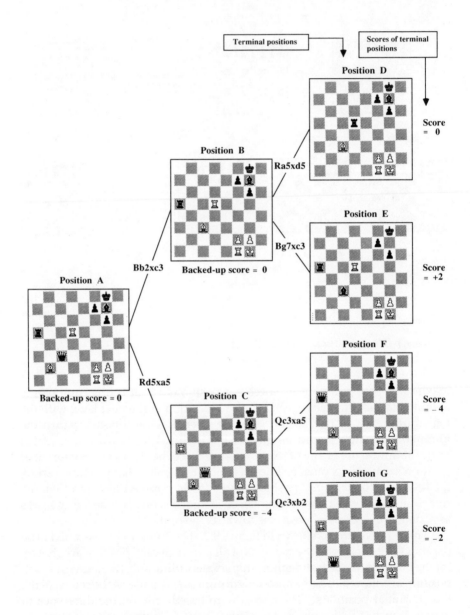

Figure 9.2 Tree showing how the minimax algorithm backs up scores

B, this is move **1 ... Ra5xd5** and in position **C**, this is move **1 ... Qc3xa5**. Thus position **B** is assigned a backed-up score of **0**, while position **C** is assigned a backed-up score of **-4**. Lastly, the score of the root is determined by assuming the computer plays the move leading to the position at the level 1 with the maximum score. Move **1 Bb2xc3** can be seen to be best, leading to a score of **0**, and thus the root is assigned a score of **0**. The sequence of moves **1 Bb2xc3 Ra5xd5** is called the *principal continuation*, the line of play that the minimax algorithm calculates both sides should follow.

A larger 4-level tree is shown in abstracted form in Figure 9.3. This tree is used throughout the remainder of this chapter to illustrate the minimax algorithm and modifications that can be made to it to improve its effectiveness. The tree has 12 terminal positions; scores are assumed to be assigned to these positions by some scoring function. Their scores are shown in the column at the right side of the figure. Moves are labeled with letters from **a** to **p**. Some moves appear at several positions in the tree. Move **d** appears four times, for example. This is typical of chess trees where the same move can be made in many different positions. Positions to which the minimax algorithm assigns a score equal to the maximum (minimum) of its successors is denoted by a square (circle).

Figure 9.3 shows how backed-up scores are assigned to nonterminal positions by the minimax algorithm. The algorithm first determines a score for each nonterminal position at the 3rd level by backing up to each of these positions the minimum score of any of its terminal position successors. From top to bottom these backed-up scores can be seen to be **4, 30, 56, 10, 4**, and **–8**. Next, each position at the second level is assigned a score equal to the maximum of any of its successors. Again, from top to bottom, these scores are **30, 56**, and **4**. Then, each position at the 1st level is assigned a score equal to the minimum score of any of its successors giving a score of **30** to the top position and **4** to the bottom position. Finally the root is assigned the maximum score of any of its successors, i. e., a score of **30**. In this case, the minimax algorithm instructs the computer to play move **a** leading to the terminal position with a score of **30**. Move **b**, the other choice, leads to a lower score of **4**. The sequence of four moves **a-c-e-d** leading to the position with the score of **30** is the principal continuation. If either side chooses to deviate from this line of play, it can only be to its disadvantage. For example, if in reply to move **a** by the first player, the second player chooses to play move **d** instead of move **c**, the first player can reply with move **f** leading to a score of **56**.

Depth-First Minimax Search

Programs carry out the minimax algorithm by searching the chess tree in a *depth-first* fashion, as contrasted with breadth-first or some other sort of best-first search. When using depth-first search, a maximum depth of search is initially selected. Then the search proceeds in such a way that whenever there is a choice of which position to search next, it is always the deepest unsearched

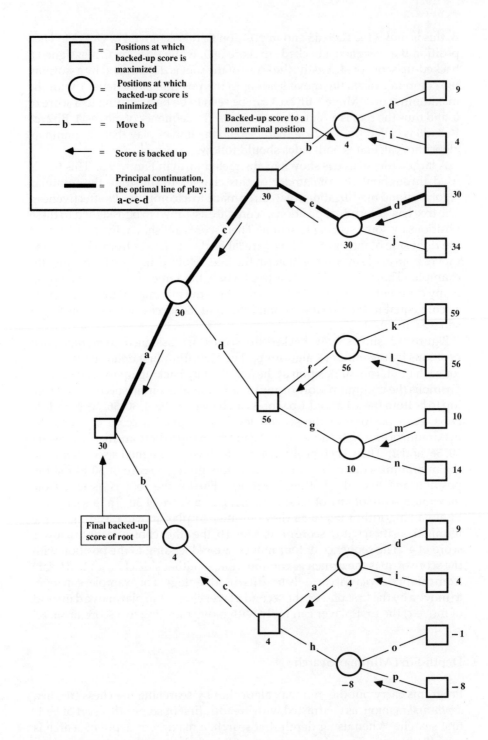

Figure 9.3 Continuing example: backing up scores by the minimax algorithm

position in the tree. This differs from breadth-first search in which the choice is always the shallowest unsearched position. With best-first search, the most promising position, as determined by a heuristic function, is the choice.

There are several reasons why depth-first search has become so standard. Most importantly, depth-first search requires very little memory space. Memory space requirements grow linearly with the depth of search as opposed to exponentially when breadth-first search or best-first search is employed. This was particularly important in the 1960s and the 1970s when memory space was at a premium. Today, with memories measured in megabytes, this advantage is no longer significant for programs developed in a research environment, but it remains important for commercial chess machines. Second, the control strategy used by depth-first search is simpler than that used by other search strategies: deciding where next in the tree to search is well defined; there is no jumping around in the tree as there is with other types of search. Third, depth-first search can be parallelized more easily than other types of search. As a small fourth advantage, printouts of trees produced by depth-first search are easier to understand than those produced by other types of search.

Chess programs carry out the minimax algorithm by storing and processing information kept in various data structures. These structures typically are:

1. A representation of the 64 squares of the chess board, usually an 8x8 array of 64 integers, BOARD(8,8). A 0 indicates a blank square, +1 a white pawn, +2 a white knight, +3 a white bishop, +4 a white rook, +5 a white queen, and +6 a white king. Black pieces are represented by corresponding negative numbers. The initial position is as shown in Figure 9.4.

2. An array in which the moves at each level in the search tree are stored as they are generated, MOVE(100,40) — allowing for at most 100 moves in any position and a search to a depth of 40 levels. Chess notation for the

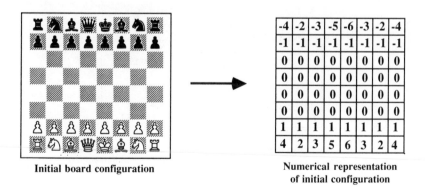

Initial board configuration

Numerical representation
of initial configuration

Figure 9.4 Initial position and equivalent computer representation

individual squares of the board and the corresponding computer encoding of the squares is shown in Figure 9.5a. A move can be specified by giving the "from" and "to" square of the moving piece, and this information can be stored in 2 computer bytes (1 byte is 8 bits), 1 byte for the "from" square and 1 byte for the "to" square. Actually only 6 of the 8 bits of a byte are required to represent the 64 squares, leaving 2 free for other purposes. A partial listing of the 20 moves for White at the start of a game in both chess notation and their equivalent computer encodings are shown in Figure 9.5b. This format is satisfactory for all but promoting moves, where the move must use 2 of the extra 4 bits to indicate the new piece, queen, rook, bishop, or knight.

3. An array of move pointers, MP(40). MP(i) points to the move at level i which is currently under search. In Figure 9.3, for example, when the

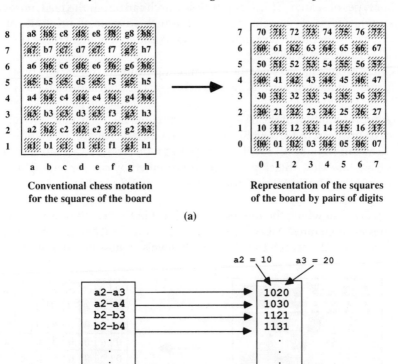

Figure 9.5 (a) Notation for the squares of a chess board, (b) moves in chess notation and computer notation

terminal position with a score of 10 (the seventh from the top) is reached, the values of the move pointers are: MP(1) = 1, MP(2) = 2, MP(3) = 2, and MP(4) = 1.

4. An array to keep track of the backed-up scores to positions in the tree. This array, SCORE(40) has elements SCORE(0), ... , SCORE(39). SCORE(i) keeps track of the best score found so far by the search at level i in the tree. The nature of depth-first search requires that only one score per level be kept. When searching, say, the 4th move at the root, SCORE(0) will contain the maximum score backed up to the root after searching the first 3 moves at the root.

5. A triangular array, PC(40,40) which keep track of the principal continuation as it is being formed. When search finishes, the principal continuation is stored in the top row of this array.

6. A stack called CLIST(1000) which saves the changes to the board and other data structures when the search moves from a position to one of its successors. When backing up from a position to its predecessor, CLIST is examined to see what changes must be undone.

7. In addition, the program needs two variables: DMAX denotes the maximum depth of search, while PLY indicates the current depth of the search.

The data structures MOVES(40,100), SCORE(40), PC(40,40), CLIST(1000), DMAX, and PLY are shown in Figure 9.6. In addition to these data structures, some programs have a killer moves array and a large hash table. These data structures are discussed later in this chapter.

Greatly oversimplified, the minimax algorithm can be described in terms of how five major subroutines work: GENERATE_MOVES, EVALUATE_POSITION, UPDATE_POSITION, RESTORE_POSITION, and PC_UPDATE.

GENERATE_MOVES accepts the current board position and the value of PLY as inputs. It creates a list of legal moves in the position, placing them in the MOVE array in MOVE(0,PLY), MOVE(1,PLY) , ... , MOVE(q–1,PLY).

EVALUATE_POSITION, the scoring function, determines a score for a terminal position. It has for input a position and it returns a score. No two programs have the same scoring function, but most take into account material balance, factors concerned with pawn structure, mobility, king safety, center control (related to mobility), as well as such factors as trading pieces when ahead, avoiding draws when playing a weaker player, and mating in the fewest number of moves when two or more mating sequences are available. Programs generally assign the pawn some value and the remaining pieces

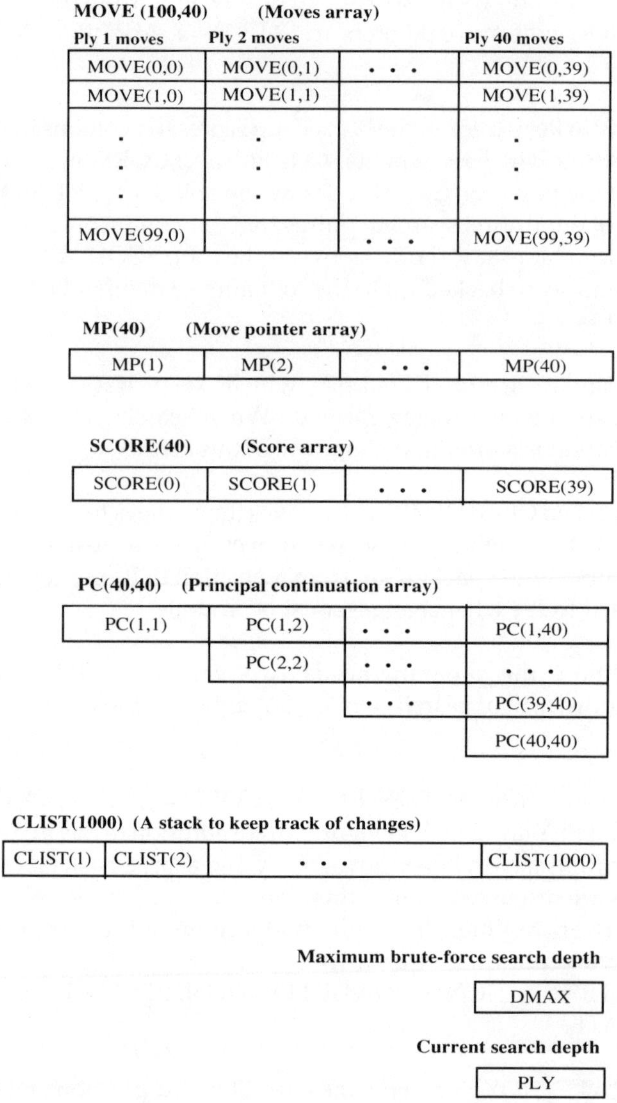

MOVE (100,40)   (Moves array)

Ply 1 moves	Ply 2 moves		Ply 40 moves
MOVE(0,0)	MOVE(0,1)	• • •	MOVE(0,39)
MOVE(1,0)	MOVE(1,1)		MOVE(1,39)
.	.		.
.	.		.
.	.		.
MOVE(99,0)		• • •	MOVE(99,39)

MP(40)   (Move pointer array)

MP(1)	MP(2)	• • •	MP(40)

SCORE(40)   (Score array)

SCORE(0)	SCORE(1)	• • •	SCORE(39)

PC(40,40)   (Principal continuation array)

PC(1,1)	PC(1,2)	• • •	PC(1,40)
	PC(2,2)	• • •	• • •
		• • •	PC(39,40)
			PC(40,40)

CLIST(1000) (A stack to keep track of changes)

CLIST(1)	CLIST(2)	• • •	CLIST(1000)

Maximum brute-force search depth

DMAX

Current search depth

PLY

Figure 9.6 Data structures used by chess programs

values relative to the pawn. For example, the pawn is typically given a value of 100 and the remaining pieces values as follows: knight=300, bishop=320, rook=500, and queen=900. These values may vary during the course of a game, being conditional on situations that might arise. Two bishops versus two knights, for example, generally results in a small bonus. Programs vary on the precision of their evaluation function, but typically quantize features of a position to approximately 1/100 of a pawn.

Many factors taken into account by the scoring function can be updated incrementally when going from one position to another in the search tree. Material, for example, must only be updated when a move is a capture or a promotion. Other factors such as pawn structure, once computed for one configuration of pawns, can be saved in a hash table and retrieved for use on other positions having the same pawn configuration.

UPDATE_POSITION has for its input the current position and the current move under consideration. It updates the board based on the move and saves the changes on CLIST. It also assigns a score to the new position equal to $-\infty$ at even levels in the tree and $+\infty$ at odd levels in the tree.

RESTORE_POSITION has for input the current board and the changes on CLIST that were made to its predecessor to yield the current board. It restores the board to its predecessor. It also backs up the score of the position to its predecessor if it is better than the current score of the predecessor. This backed-up score is called a *provisional score* until all successors have been scored; it is then called a *final score*. Initially assigning a position at even (odd) levels a score of $-\infty$ ($+\infty$) assures that the first successor searched in each position will have its score backed up.

PC_UPDATE updates the principal continuation array PC whenever a good move is found. That is, when the search of move **m** in position **P** at depth PLY results in backing up an improved score to position **P**, PC_UPDATE is called. PC_UPDATE then (1) places move **m** in PC(PLY,PLY), and then (2) places the remainder of the principal continuation following move **m**, which is in PC(PLY+1,PLY+1), PC(PLY+1,PLY+2), ... , PC(PLY+1,DMAX), into PC(PLY,PLY+1), PC(PLY,PLY+2), ... , PC(PLY,DMAX) (i.e., it moves the continuation up one row in the array). In order to obtain the principal continuation, it is necessary to save the best continuation found as the search progresses at every position on the continuation under search. Thus for a depth DMAX search, DMAX continuations must be kept of lengths DMAX, DMAX − 1, DMAX − 2, ... , 1, and this is done in rows 1, 2, 3, ... , DMAX − 1, DMAX respectively of the triangular PC array. When search ends, the continuation of length DMAX in the top row of the array is the principal continuation.

Consider now Figure 9.7 and Figure 9.8 which show in detail the operation of depth-first minimax search. The minimax algorithm searches the tree by following the path shown by the arrows. The path begins at the root of the tree and ends there. When the search arrives at each non-terminal position, it calls GENERATE_MOVES. When it arrives at each terminal position, it calls EVALUATE_POSITION. The search moves from one position to another along the path shown by calling UPDATE_POSITION when moving deeper into the tree, and by calling RESTORE_POSITION when backing up in the tree. Each right-directed (left-directed) arrow in the figure corresponds to

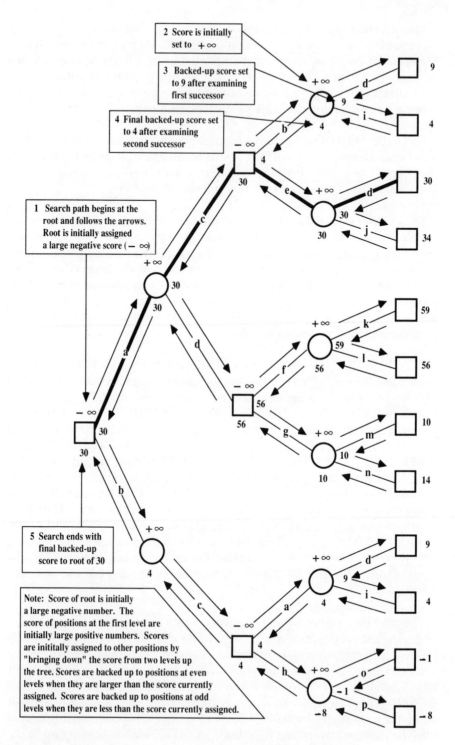

Figure 9.7 Continuing example: depth-first minimax search

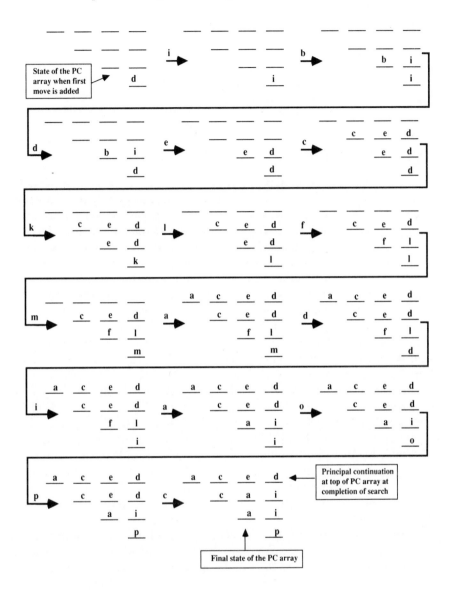

Figure 9.8 Continuing example: placing moves in the PC array

calling UPDATE_POSITION (RESTORE_POSITION). Following the search path to the first terminal position, it can be seen that calls were made to the subroutines in the following order: G,U,G,U,G,U,G,U,E where each letter corresponds to the first letter in the name of the five subroutines. When the first terminal position is evaluated, its score is backed up to its parent and move **d** is placed in the PC array in location PC(4,4). The search trace continues: P,R,U,E,P,R,P,R,U,G,U,E upon which a score of 30 is found. Note that during the course of the search, GENERATE_MOVES was called 12 times, EVALUATE_POSITION was called 12 times, UPDATE_POSITION and RESTORE_POSITION were each called 23 times, and PC_UPDATE was called 15 times. The state of the PC array after each of the 15 calls to it is shown in Figure 9.8. Above each arrow is indicated the move placed in the PC array that transforms the array from one state to the next.

The Alpha-Beta Algorithm

A careful study of the minimax algorithm leads to the observation that there are many paths within the search tree that need not be examined because they have no effect on the outcome of the search. This may have been realized first in the late 1950s by John McCarthy who was then a professor at MIT. Hart and Edwards, also of MIT, published a memorandum describing the algorithm in 1961, while A. L. Brudno described the algorithm in the Soviet literature in 1963. The elimination of these unnecessary paths is the function performed by the alpha-beta algorithm. Essentially, the alpha-beta algorithm is the minimax algorithm supplemented by a few lines of code that decide which paths have no bearing on the outcome of the search and thus need not be searched.

The alpha-beta algorithm is illustrated by reconsidering the depth-first minimax search of the tree shown in Figure 9.2. When re-searched by the alpha-beta algorithm (See Figure 9.9), only 3 of the 4 terminal positions need be scored as the following explains. The alpha-beta search path shows that the 1st terminal position scored is **D**. After assigning a score to position **D** of 0, a provisional backed-up score can be assigned to position **B** of 0. Because a score is backed up to position **B** only if it is lower than the current score of **B**, the score of 0 establishes an upper bound on the eventual score of **B**. Next position **E** is scored. Its score of +2 implies that 1 ... Ra5xd5 is the better move in position **B**, and that the final backed-up score of position **B** is 0. The root can now be assigned a provisional score of 0; no matter what score the 1st level move 1 Rd5xa5 leads to, the root score is at least 0. Next, position **F** is found to have a score of –4. Given that the score backed up to position **C** is the minimum of the scores of its successors, no matter what score any other move in position **C** leads to, the score of **C** can be at most –4. Given this knowledge, it would be an error for the first player to play 1 Rd5xa5 when 1 Bb2xc3 has already been found to lead to a score of 0. And since the score of the position that any other move in position **C** leads to is irrelevant, there is no reason to search futher at position **C**. We say that the move 1 ... **Qc3xa5** is a *refutation* of move 1 **Rd5xa5**, or equivalently that 1 **Rd5xa5** was *refuted* by 1 ... **Qc3xa5**; search at position **C** was *cut off* after examining only one move, 1 ... **Qc3xa5**. The net result of this alpha-beta search is that only 3 of the 4 terminal positions must be examined, yet the same principal continuation was found. On larger trees, more dramatic savings in effort are achieved as is discussed shortly.

More generally, the alpha-beta algorithm says that a move **y** in position **Y** refutes its immediate predecessor move **x** in position **X** at even levels (at odd levels) if the current provisional score of *any* position at even levels (at odd

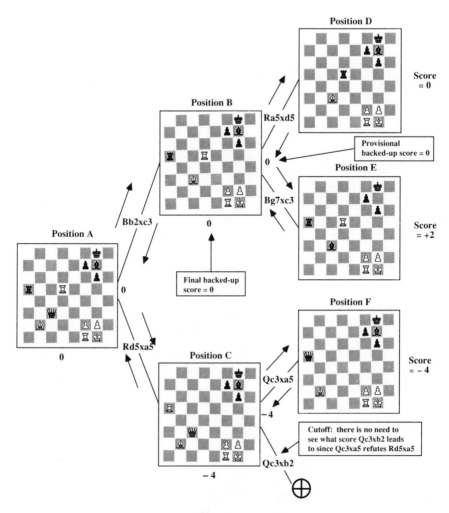

Figure 9.9 Illustration of the alpha-beta algorithm

levels) on the continuation from the root to position **X** has a score greater than or equal to (less than or equal to) the backed-up score assigned to position **Y** by move **y**. The cutoff described in the last paragraph satisfies this condition. But *deep cutoffs* can also occur as illustrated by the partially drawn 4-level chess tree shown in Figure 9.10. Here, it is shown that **1 Bb2xc3** is searched first and returns a material score of **0**. Then the search proceeds out to position **F** which is assigned a score of **–3** by the scoring function. A backed-up score of **–3** is then assigned to position **E**. This score of **–3** is less than the provisional score of the root, implying that move **2 ... Bg7xd4** is a refutation of **2 Bb2xd4**, and that no other move in position **E** requires search. Move **2 ... Bg7xd4** leading to position **F** is said to have caused a deep cutoff.

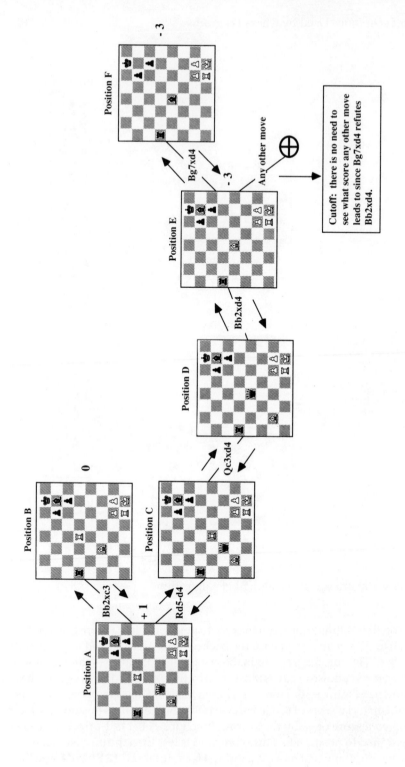

Figure 9.10 Part of a 4-level tree showing how deep cutoffs occur in an alpha-beta search

The programming modifications that must be made to the minimax algorithm to incorporate the alpha-beta algorithm are very minor. For a few lines of code, very large time savings can be achieved. Most simply, rather than having UPDATE_POSITION assign an initial score of $-\infty$ or $+\infty$ to a position, a position is assigned a score equal to that of the position 2 levels higher up the tree. That is, a score is *brought down* from the position 2 levels higher. This has the effect of assigning to a position the maximum score of any position on the path from the root to that position and having the same parity level in the tree. This, in turn, simplifies the test for a refutation: a move **y** in position **Y** refutes its predecessor move **x** in position **X** at even levels (at odd levels) if the current provisional score of position **X** is greater than or equal to (less than or equal to) the backed-up score assigned to position **Y** by move **y**. The root position and positions at the 1st level are exceptions; they are still initially assigned values of $-\infty$ and $+\infty$ respectively since scores cannot be brought down to them from higher levels.

Figure 9.11 Alex Brudno in Moscow, 1988

Consider the continuing example redrawn in Figure 9.12 to show the result of an alpha-beta search. There are 3 cutoffs denoted by small circled crosses; 4 moves are refutations, although only 3, moves **f**, **d** and **o**, resulted in cutting off the search. Move **c** refuted move **b** at the root, but there were no additional moves at the root that remained to be searched when the refutation occurred. Moves **d** and **o** caused deep cutoffs. Note that during the course of the search, GENERATE_MOVES was called 11 times, EVALUATE_POSITION was called 8 times, UPDATE_POSITION and RESTORE_POSITION were each called 18 times, and PC_UPDATE was called 10 times.

In 1969, James Slagle, one of the United States' top blind chess players and a distinguished computer scientist, and J. Dixon showed that for a uniform tree — a tree with the same number of moves (or branches) B in each position and in which all terminal positions are at the same depth DMAX — the number of terminal positions scored by the alpha-beta algorithm must be at least $2B^{DMAX/2} - 1$ for DMAX even, and $B^{(DMAX+1)/2} + B^{(DMAX-1)/2} - 1$ for DMAX odd. In chess, there are about 36 moves in the typical position. Modeling this by a uniform tree with branching factor 36, we find that for a depth 2 search, i.e., DMAX = 2, at least $2 \times 36 - 1 = 71$ terminal positions must be scored. For a uniform tree of depth three, at least $36^2 + 36 - 1 = 1{,}331$ positions must be scored, and at least $2 \times 36^5 - 1 = 3{,}359{,}431$ must be scored for a tree of depth 10 and branching factor 36. Essentially, the minimum tree that must be searched increases in size, on average, by a factor of 6 (i.e., the square root of 36) for every extra level searched. This implies that to search one level deeper, a computer either must run 6 times faster or take 6 times as long.

Because moves are not ordered optimally at each position, chess programs search more than the minimal tree. In an attempt to find out how much more, several studies have been carried out on models of abstract game trees in which the terminal positions are assigned random scores. In 1975, Donald Knuth and R. E. Moore showed that for a uniform tree of depth 2 in which terminal positions are assigned random numbers for scores, of the B^2 terminal positions, on average $B^2 / (\log_2 B - .923)$ are scored. Two years later Newborn showed that for the same uniform trees of depth 2 and branching factor B, if the score of each terminal position is the sum of random scores assigned to the branches on the path from the root to that position, then far fewer terminal positions are scored on average. This branch-dependent model for assigning scores of terminal positions seems to model chess trees better than the first model. In chess, the score of a terminal position is dominated by material, and material at a terminal position is very dependent on the captures that take place on the path from the root to it. Newborn showed that for this branch-dependent model, on average approximately $2B\log_2 B$ positions are scored. For deeper trees the question is still somewhat open for the branch-dependent case, but it could quite well be that on average of the order of $B^{(DMAX/2)}\log_2 B$ positions are scored. This implies that the alpha-beta algorithm performs quite effectively when the scores of terminal positions are sums of random branch scores as is the case in chess. In effect, a program that uses the alpha-beta algorithm can search to almost twice the depth as one that does not.

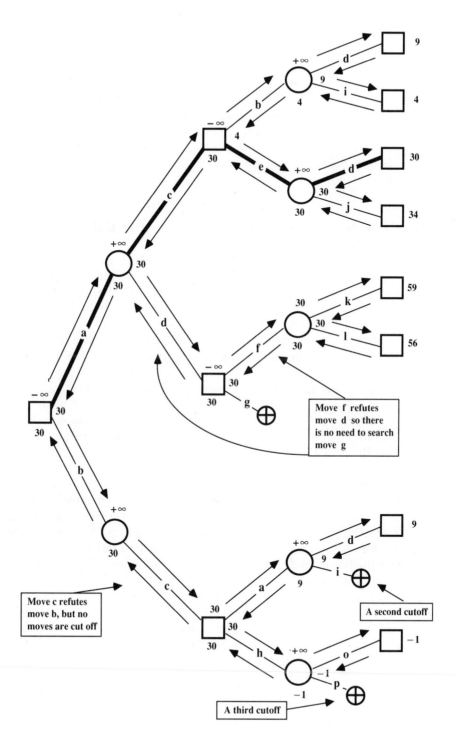

Figure 9.12 Continuing example: alpha-beta search

In searches carried out on real chess trees, the number of terminal positions is typically far less than the number predicted by the random models. Information gathered during the search can be used to order moves at each position from best to worst quite effectively. This reduces the actual number of positions examined by chess programs to very near the theoretical minimum. In the limit when moves are ordered from best to worst at each position, the alpha-beta algorithm examines the minimum number of positions and trees grow in size by a factor of approximately 6 for each additional level searched. Several techniques used to order moves are discussed in the following section.

Move Generation, the Principal Continuation and the Killer Heuristic

GENERATE_MOVES is a very sophisticated algorithm in chess programs. More time is consumed by this subroutine than by any other. It is primarily the generation of moves that special purpose chess hardware has been designed to perform at high speeds. The exact order in which moves are generated and listed is crucial to the speed of the alpha-beta algorithm. It is very important that good moves are placed at the top of the list. With good move ordering, the number of refutations is maximized, and correspondingly the number of cutoffs.

Move generation can be viewed as a two step process: (1) generate a list of moves, and (2) order the list so that good moves are placed at the top. Programs integrate these two steps in various ways. For example, a move generator can generate king moves last in the opening and middlegame, while generating them first in the endgame. The move generator needs simple, quick, reliable algorithms for identifying good moves.

The easiest good moves to identify are captures, and most programs can determine whether moves are captures very quickly and then place them at or near the top of the list of moves. In 1986, P. Bettadapur carried out experiments that showed captures should be ordered from the capture of the biggest piece to the capture of the smallest piece for best results. Further, the capture of the last-moved piece of the opponent is often a particularly good capture and deserves special placement.

The killer heuristic is used by most chess programs to identify good moves quickly. Jim Gillogly used it in his chess program TECH in 1972. Essentially, when a move is found to be a refutation at level k in the search tree, it is placed on killer_list$_k$. (There is one killer list for every level of the search tree; killer_list$_k$ is the killer list for moves at level k.) Then when moves are generated at each position in the search tree, the relevant killer_list is scanned and if a move is found to match a legal move in the position, it is ordered to the top or near the top of the list of legal moves.

Figure 9.13 illustrates the killer heuristic. It is White's turn to move. A program playing White would probably try the move **1 Ng4xh6** first of all, because it captures a rook for nothing. After examining Black's replies, it would eventually find that **1 Ng4xh6** can be answered with **1 ... Ra3-a1** mate. Now, each time the program examines another move for White, the first Black move it tries in reply will be **1 ... Ra3-a1**, because if that move is legal, there is a good chance it might again be mate. The killer heuristic thus tells the program that the move **1 ... Ra3-a1** is worthy of serious consideration as a reply to each White move, and each time **1 ... Ra3-a1** does refute White's initial move, the search cuts off, with possibly considerable savings in search effort and time.

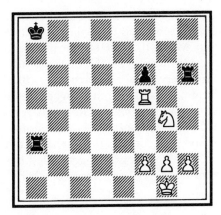

Figure 9.13 Position illustrating the killer heuristic

Various strategies exist for saving killer moves and using them. Most simply, the killer lists are kept short—one or two moves. Only the most recent refutations are kept in the array. Alternatively, each refutation in the array can have a count of the number of times it has caused a cutoff. When a new move is added, it replaces the least successful move in the array. By using killer moves, the number of cutoffs is higher than otherwise, and the overall efficiency of the alpha-beta algorithm improves. In place of killer lists, Jonathan Schaeffer's PHOENIX uses two 64 by 64 arrays to keep track of all moves by each side and how often each causes a refutation. Schaeffer claims this "history heuristic" is an improvement on the simpler killer heuristic. The principal continuation array also provides a good source of killer moves as was pointed out by Selim Akl and Newborn in 1977.

Pruning Techniques and Variable-Depth Quiescence Search

The early chess programs used forward pruning to reduce the effective branching factor at each position in the search tree as exemplified by Newell, Shaw, and Simon's program developed in the late 1950s. Based on short-term considerations, programs typically tried to intelligently choose to search the relevant moves while attempting to filter out those that were not at each position. Some chess heuristics, rules of thumb, were used to include certain classes of moves while other heuristics were used to eliminate moves. Heuristics such as "Include at least one move for each piece" or "Try all capturing moves" were used to include moves while "Do not bring out your queen too early" or "Do not put your knights on the edge of the board," were used to reduce the number of "sensible" moves that need to be examined. However, forward pruning heuristics were undependable and programs too often weeded out the wrong moves, throwing out, in Botvinnik's words, "the baby with the bathwater." Gradually throughout the 1970s, heuristics that filtered out moves were removed from most successful chess programs.

Although forward pruning has been unsuccessful, the best programs carry out variable depth searches beyond the arbitrary value of DMAX set at the beginning of the search. Moves that put the king in check are usually searched deeper as are certain capturing moves. HITECH extends the search one level deeper than DMAX for every equalizing recapture. BEBE does the same for pawn advances to the 6th, 7th, and 8th ranks. When describing their program in *Chess Skill in Man and Machine*, David Slate and Larry Atkin report that the typical search tree of CHESS 4.9 contains about half of its positions at depths greater than DMAX, and they contend this is an effective balance.

In 1987, DEEP THOUGHT's programmers added the singular extension heuristic to their program as described in the December 1988 issue of the *ICCA Journal*. It

uses a modified brute-force search to provide on-line measures of the forcedness of a move. A move is declared *singular* if it returns a value "much better" than all alternative moves, and whenever a move is found *singular* **and** *likely to affect the outcome of the search if its value changes*, the position arising from the move is researched one more ply than the normal positions. For chess, depending on the criteria used in selecting the types of singular moves extended, the overhead can be as low as 5 percent to as high as 20 percent for quiet positions. For tactical chess positions, the overhead can grow to more than doubling the nodes searched at a given depth. But since the extensions allow the program to see the outcome of a tactical skirmish somewhat earlier and occasionally a lot earlier, the overhead usually pays for itself handsomely.

When a program decides that a position is terminal, a *swap-off* routine is called to refine the score of the position. Programs attempt to carry out an exchange of all pieces that can be exchanged without actually searching beyond the position. Different strategies are used. Some programs swap-off pieces on the square of the last-moved piece. Others keep a list of captures available by both sides and play them off. Captures not on the board, but created due to moves of the capturing pieces, are overlooked and can lead to erroneous evaluations. Swap-off routines provide a cheap and usually improved score for terminal positions.

Hash Tables (Transposition Tables)

Consider a partial tree of the moves that can be made starting at the intial position as shown in Figure 9.14. Note that moves **1 d2–d4 d7–d5 2 e2–e4** lead to the same position, denoted **T**, as do moves **1 e2–e4 d7–d5 2 d2–d4**. Identical positions result when White's 1st and 2nd moves are *transposed*. The moves **1 d2–d3 d7–d6 2 d3–d4 d6–d5 3 e2–e4** also lead to **T** but this sequence of moves is more complex and cannot be described by a simple transformation. Furthermore, while moves **1 d2–d4 d7–d6 2 e2–e4 d6–d5** also lead to a position with pieces on identical squares, in this case it is White's turn and thus the positions cannot be considered identical. Two positions can be considered identical only when, in addition to having pieces on identical squares, castling rights, en passant options, and whose turn it is are identical.

Suppose position **T** in Figure 9.14 had been reached via **1 d2–d4 d7–d5 2 e2–e4** and had been assigned a score by the scoring function or by backing up a score to it. Then, when position **T** is arrived at through **1 e2–e4 d7–d5 2 d2–d4**, it is not necessary to search beyond **T** or even score **T** if the results of the first examination of **T** was saved and provided sufficient information. Chess programs use large *hash tables* (sometimes called *transposition tables*) to save this information. When the search arrives at each position, the hash table is examined to see whether information about that position was saved previously. If it was, and if the information is sufficient (what constitutes sufficient information is discussed shortly) then that position need not be searched again. It can be considered a terminal position and assigned the score found in the hash table. When search backs up to a position, the hash table is searched for a match. It no match is found, a new entry is placed in the table. If the position has already been entered, the information regarding it is updated if appropriate.

As a chess game progresses, a higher and higher percentage of identical positions crop up, especially as a result of king moves. In deep endgames, programs with hash tables can often find principal continuations 20 plies long and sometimes longer. In Chapter 8, a set of 16 positions from Fine's *Basic Chess Endings* vividly show how effective hash tables can be. The position in Figure 8.2j cannot be solved by a program unless it has a hash table; a program with a hash table can solve it in less than a minute. More typically in middlegame play, hash tables provide speedups ranging from 20 percent to 50 percent.

In rigorous terms, when the search backs up to some position **P**, the computer knows the following information about **P** :

1. The score of **P**, denoted SCORE(**P**). This is either the exact value or an upper or lower bound
2. An indication whether the score is exact or an upper or lower bound, denoted by BOUND_SCORE(**P**)
3. The depth of the brute-force search beyond position **P**, denoted by DEPTH(**P**)

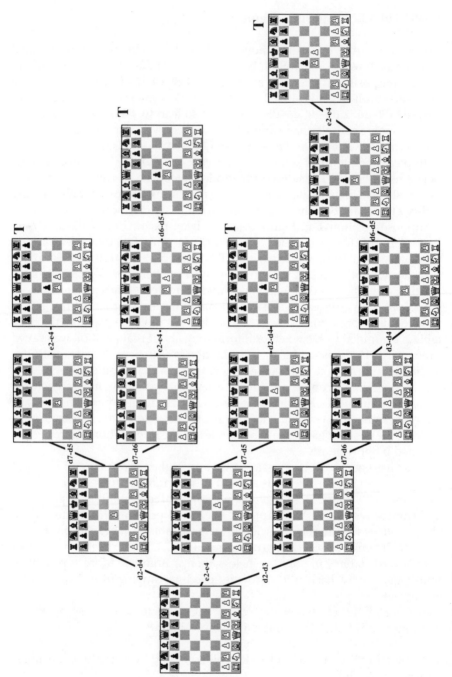

Figure 9.14 Partially drawn tree rooted at the initial chess position

4. The best move to make in position **P**, denoted BEST_MOVE(**P**)
5. Position **P**, itself, whose turn to move, en passant information, and castling rights

   The computer now examines the hash table to see whether there is a position that is the same as **P**. If so, and if the new information found about **P** is better than that currently stored, the entry in the hash table is updated appropriately. The improved information may be a more precise score rather than only a bound, it may be a better bound, or it may be a larger value for DEPTH(**P**).

   When the search arrives at any position **Q** at depth PLY in the tree, the hash table is initially searched for a match. If successful and if the following two conditions are satisfied by the entry, then **Q** is considered a terminal position and given the score found in the hash table:

1. The value of DEPTH(**Q**) in the table is equal to or greater than DMAX − PLY,
2. The score found in the table entry is exact, or if not exact, the bound on the score is sufficient to cause the move leading to **Q** to refute its predecessor.

   If **Q** does not satisfy these two conditions, then if **Q** is a terminal position it is assigned a score by the scoring function. Otherwise a search of the successors of **Q** is required. The move found best the last time **Q** was searched, BEST_MOVE(**Q**), is in the hash table and it should be searched first on this try.

   Figure 9.15 illustrates various situations that can occur when hash tables are used. Position **T** arises in four different places. When completing the search of the first occurence of **T**, its score can be assigned an upper bound of **18** and saved in the hash table. When the search arrives at **T** the second time, **T** will be found in the hash table and the score saved with it can be used to cut off search. When the search arrives at **T** the third time, the bound of **18** is insufficient to cut off search, and thus its successors must be searched. When they have been searched, an exact value of **16** is assigned to this third **T** and the transposition table entry updated accordingly. In addition, move **y** is saved as the best move to make in position **T**. When the search arives at **T** the 4th time, it is at the 1st ply in contrast with the 3rd ply for each of the other 3 times. This time the position is too shallow in the tree to permit the score obtained previously for **T** (at the 3rd ply) to be used to terminate the search. If it were used, then not all positions in the tree would have been searched to a depth of 4 plies, contrary to the goal of the search. Move **y**, however, was previously stored in the table entry as the best reply in position **T**, and as the search tree shows, this move is searched first this time. After the tree rooted at the fourth occurrence of **T** has been searched, an exact value of **17** is determined for **T**.

   In Figure 9.16, the effect of using a hash table on the continuing example is illustrated. It is assumed that moves that transpose lead to the same positions. That is, move sequence **a-c-b** leads to the same position as does the sequence **b-c-a**. In Figure 9.16, one position, the shaded circle, at the end of the move sequence **b-c-a** was found in the hash table with a useful score of **4**. Note that

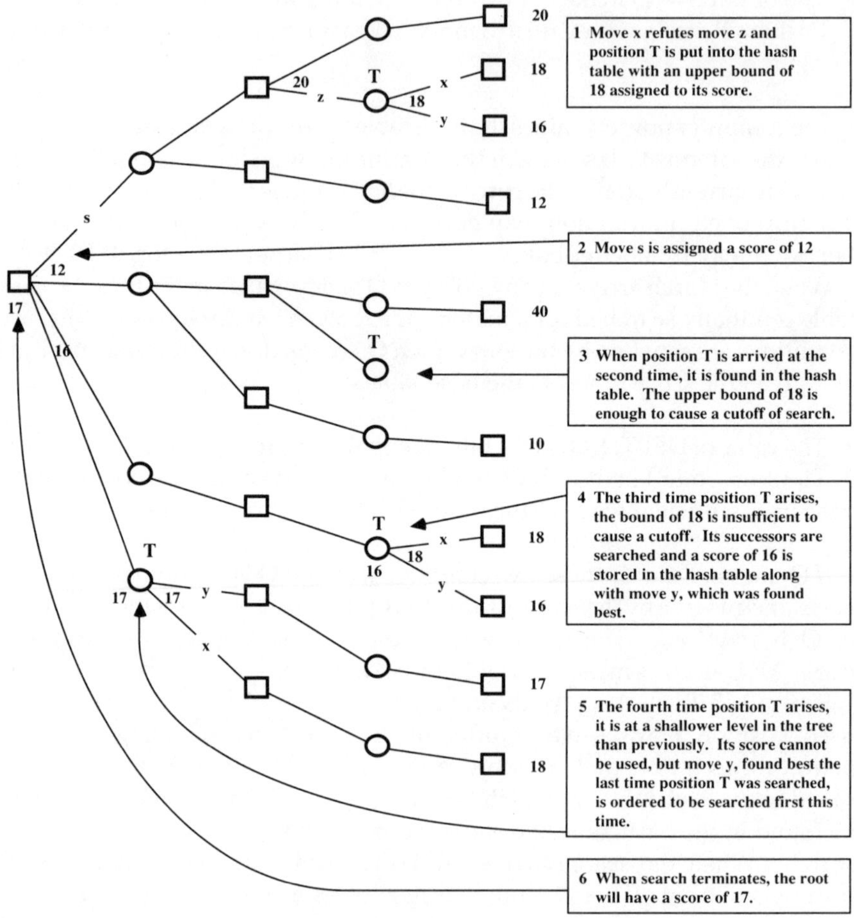

20
18
16
12
40
10
18
16
17
18
T
x
y
z
s
20
18
12
17
16
T
T
18
16
T
17
17
y
x
1 Move x refutes move z and position T is put into the hash table with an upper bound of 18 assigned to its score.
2 Move s is assigned a score of 12
3 When position T is arrived at the second time, it is found in the hash table. The upper bound of 18 is enough to cause a cutoff of search.
4 The third time position T arises, the bound of 18 is insufficient to cause a cutoff. Its successors are searched and a score of 16 is stored in the hash table along with move y, which was found best.
5 The fourth time position T arises, it is at a shallower level in the tree than previously. Its score cannot be used, but move y, found best the last time position T was searched, is ordered to be searched first this time.
6 When search terminates, the root will have a score of 17.

Figure 9.15 An example showing how a hash table works

during the course of the search, GENERATE_MOVES was called 10 times, EVALUATE_POSITION was called 7 times, UPDATE_POSITION and RESTORE_POSITION were each called 17 times, PC_UPDATE was called 9 times, and the hash table allowed 1 position at a depth less than DMAX to be considered a terminal position.

Hash tables were the focus of experiments in machine learning conducted by Slate in 1987 and extended by Tony Scherzer the following year. Their experiments are the most significant work carried out in this challenging area. In Slate's experiment, a special hash table was used to store information on root positions found troublesome during the course of a game. The information was retrieved and used when the same position appeared in a future game, although the second time the position might come up deep in the tree. Troublesome positions are positions for which a deep search finds a

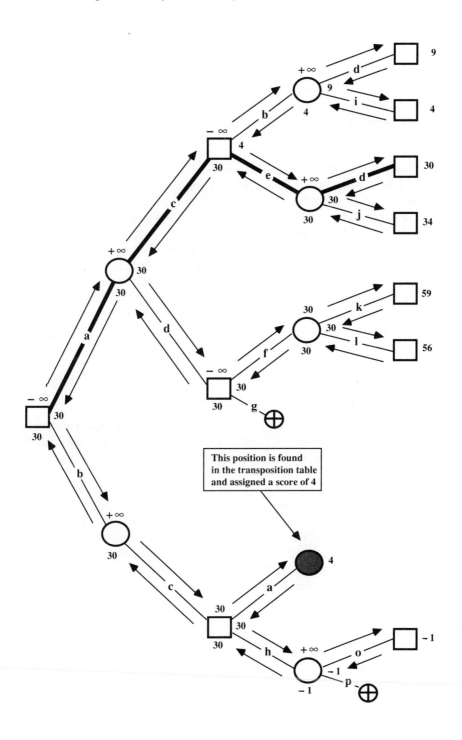

Figure 9.16 Continuing example: alpha-beta search with a hash table

score significantly different than a shallow one. Of the total number of chess positions, only a very small percentage are troublesome. Suppose, now, a program searches all moves to a depth of 8 plies, and suppose on the 8th move of some game, a troublesome position **T** is found and saved in the special hash table, and that the trouble only appeared on the 7th iteration. Suppose later, another game is played that follows the same line of play for the first 5 moves. Then, on the 6th move, **T** will be a position somewhere at the 4th level in the search tree. Without the hash table, it would have been searched an additional 4 plies and assigned an unreliable score. However, using the special transposition table, **T** will be given a more reliable score, one based on the previous 8-ply search. The program, then, will less likely make a move leading to the same trouble twice. It will also save some time.

Scherzer extended Slate's idea by storing information on all root positions, not just troublesome ones, in a "Long Term Memory" and using the information when appropriate at a later time. He described his work at the 6th World Computer Chess Championship in Edmonton in May of 1989. He reported that his program learned quite effectively to avoid making the same mistakes. He said this strategy allowed him to come to a tournament and not worry about modifying or correcting his opening book between rounds; the hash table took care of this.

Hashing Positions

Hash tables are designed to be as large as memory space allows. The number of entries is usually a power of 2, although this is not necessary. Typical sizes range from as small as 4,000 positions to as large as 4,000,000. Each entry stores information about 1 position, say **P**. The board, itself, is not usually stored. That would require storing the contents of the 64 squares. Instead, a program stores a compressed encoding of the board called a *hash code* as calculated by a *hash function*. The hash code for **P**, denoted HASH_CODE(**P**), is typically 36 to 64 bits. This, of course, means that since more than 64 bits are necessary to uniquely describe a chess position, two different positions can be assigned the same hash code. Hash functions are designed to minimize this likelihood. The more bits in the hash code, the less likely two different positions will be assigned the same hash code.

A position is assigned a location in a hash table of size 2^k by using the least significant k bits of the position's hash code as an address. For example, in a hash table having $2^{12}=4096$ entries (i.e., k = 12), if a position **P** is assigned a 32-bit hash code, HASH_CODE(**P**) = 01011100110011110000100010000110, then the information about **P** would be stored in hash table location 100010000110_2 or 2179_{10}. Typically the information stored in that entry would be SCORE(**P**), BOUND_SCORE(**P**),   DEPTH(**P**), BEST_MOVE(**P**), and HASH_CODE(**P**). This is illustrated in Figure 9.17. In Figure 9.17a, the format of a hash table entry is presented. In Figure 9.17b, the information stored in the hash table entry for position **T** from Figure 9.15 is shown. The first time

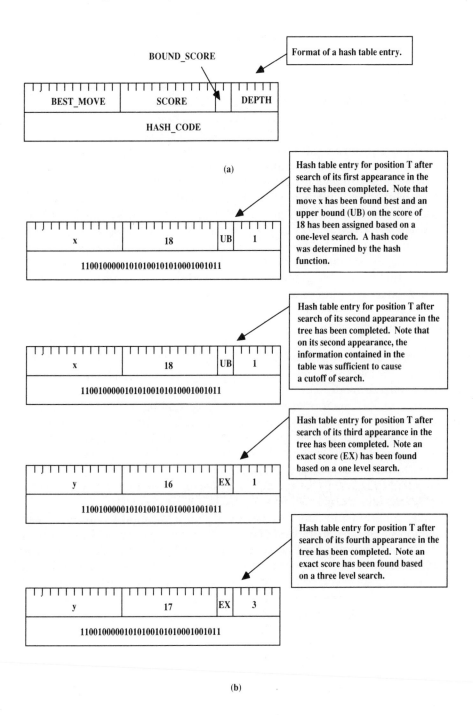

BOUND_SCORE

Format of a hash table entry.

BEST_MOVE	SCORE		DEPTH

HASH_CODE

(a)

Hash table entry for position T after search of its first appearance in the tree has been completed. Note that move x has been found best and an upper bound (UB) on the score of 18 has been assigned based on a one-level search. A hash code was determined by the hash function.

x	18	UB	1

1100100000101010010101010001001011

Hash table entry for position T after search of its second appearance in the tree has been completed. Note that on its second appearance, the information contained in the table was sufficient to cause a cutoff of search.

x	18	UB	1

1100100000101010010101010001001011

Hash table entry for position T after search of its third appearance in the tree has been completed. Note an exact score (EX) has been found based on a one level search.

y	16	EX	1

1100100000101010010101010001001011

Hash table entry for position T after search of its fourth appearance in the tree has been completed. Note an exact score has been found based on a three level search.

y	17	EX	3

1100100000101010010101010001001011

(b)

Figure 9.17 (a) Format of a hash table entry, and (b) contents of the hash table entry corresponding to position **T** in Figure 9.15 as the search progresses

position **T** is encountered, only an upper bound of **18** is available for its score based on a 1-ply search. The second time it is encountered, the bound on the score of **18** is enough to cause the search to cutoff. On the third encounter, it is found that the successors of position **T** must be searched. Upon searching them, a new score of **16** and a new best move **y** are found and stored in the hash table. On the fourth encounter, the score cannot be used to cause a cutoff, but the 1st move searched this time is move **y**. It turns out that move **y** is best, based this time on a 3-ply search, and the score of **T** changed to **17**.

When searching a tree, a program may assign two different positions identical values for the k least significant bits of their hash code. A *clash* results when an attempt is made to store the second of these positions in the hash table; this second position is assigned the same memory location as the first. A *hashing error* can also occur when two different positions are assigned the same hash code. It should be obvious that the greater the number of bits in the hash code, the smaller the probability of a hashing error.

Programs have various strategies for deciding what to do when a clash occurs. Some programs attempt to store the position at the next location. If that location is found to be occupied also, the program can give up or it can replace the older of the two entries just examined. Most programs try more than once to find an unoccupied location; CRAY BLITZ tries eight times. Some programs have frequency-of-hit counts saved with each table entry, and entries with low frequency counts are thrown out of the table first when a choice must be made.

CRAY BLITZ, the former World Champion among computer programs, uses a six million word hash table with 64 bits per word. Each table entry requires two words of memory, with the hash code consuming 40 bits. BEBE uses a home-brewed hash table with 96-bit words. It can hash up to 256K positions with each position requiring one word: 32 bits for a hash code, 16 bits for DEPTH, 16 bits for the move, 16 bits for a lower bound on the score, and 16 bits for an upper bound.

Most programs determine a hash code for a position by using a hash function similar to the one described in 1970 by Al Zobrist in a University of Wisconsin technical report. Hash functions make use of a *piece-square table* of 12 (pieces) by 64 (squares) random numbers each of k + m bits. A position is assigned a hash code by exclusive-or'ing the random numbers assigned to appropriate piece-squares. The "exclusive-or" operation (symbolized by $\oplus$) is defined as follows:

$$0 \oplus 0 = 0,$$
$$0 \oplus 1 = 1,$$
$$0 \oplus 1 = 1,$$
$$1 \oplus 1 = 0.$$

The exclusive-or of two n-bit binary numbers, say A and B, is an n-bit binary number formed by performing the exclusive-or operation on each of the corresponding bits of A and B. For example, suppose A and B are 101110 and

001101. Then A ⊕ B is 100011. Now, suppose random numbers are assigned to the piece-square entries in the table as shown in Figure 9.18a. Then the position shown in Figure 9.18b is assigned a hash code by exclusive-or'ing the five random numbers in the piece-square table corresponding to WK on c3, WN on f3, WP on a2, BK on f5, and BP on h7. To take into account that positions are different if castling opportunities are different, if en passant opportunities are different, or even if whose turn it is to move is different, extra entries can be included in the piece-square table.

The beauty of this hash function is the ease of computing the hash code of a position that results by making a move in a given position. For a move that is the transfer of a piece to a vacant square, it is necessary only to remove the piece from its original square square by exclusive-or'ing the random number of the corresponding original piece-square and the hash code of the original position. The piece is then placed on its destination square by exclusive-or'ing

Piece-Square Table

Piece-square	16-bit random number
WK on a1	1001010011110101
WK on b1	1001010001010001
.	.
.	.
WK on c3	0100101000101010
WK on d3	1101000101010111
.	.
.	.
WK on h8	1010010100010111
.	.
.	.
WN on f3	0000100101110101
.	.
.	.
WP on a2	1001001010100101
.	.
.	.
BK on f5	0100111101010001
.	.
.	.
BP on h7	0011010001110101

(a)

Position P

Hash code for this position P as given by piece-square table is:

       0100101000101010 (WK on c3)
⊕   0000100101110101 (WN on f3)
⊕   1001001010100101 (WP on a2)
⊕   0100111101010001 (BK on f5)
⊕   0011010001110101 (BP on h7)
=   1010101011011110

(b)

Figure 9.18 (a) Piece-square table, and (b) determining the hash code of a chess position

the modified hash code and the random number corresponding to the new piece-square. That is, two exclusive-or operations are required to obtain the hash code of a position's successor given the hash code of the original position. Minor extensions of this idea are necessary for capturing moves, pawn promotions, en passant moves, and castling moves. Figure 9.19 shows how to obtain the new hash code for the position that results when **Kc3–d3** is played in the position in Figure 9.18b. This is done by exclusive-or'ing the hash code of **P** and the piece-square random number for a WK on c3 and the piece-square random number for a WK on d3.

Hash tables are also used in chess programs for hashing scores given to pawn structure and king safety. These hash tables can be much smaller than those for transposition tables. Harry Nelson reported that hit rates by CRAY BLITZ were quite high, resulting in significant savings in time when compared with the alternative of recalculating the value of these factors at each position.

Iterative Deepening

One of the problems early chess programmers encountered was correctly setting the search depth, DMAX, before beginning the search. It turned out

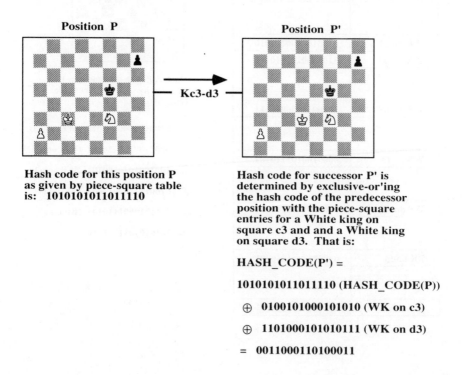

Figure 9.19 Obtaining the hash code of a successor position

to be a very difficult problem. If DMAX was set too shallow, the program made moves unnecessarily fast, failing to take advantage of the allotted time. If DMAX was set too large, the program might take an excessive amount of time — an hour, for example, when the target was three minutes. In the early programs, if DMAX was set too large, time might expire before the best move at the root was searched.

Iteratively deepening searches became popular in the middle 1970s and they solved this problem. Slate and Atkin introduced iterative deepening into their program in 1975 at the suggestion of Peter Frey, Northwestern University psychology professor. Over the next two years, the technique became a part of every chess program. More recently the technique is finding applicability in other problems in artificial intelligence, in particular automated theorem proving. When proving a theorem, all possible proofs in 1 step can be attempted first, then 2 steps, and so on. One of the leading theorem-proving programs, developed in the middle 1980s at Stanford Research Institute by M. Stickel and W. Tyson, uses essentially this approach.

With iterative deepening, rather than carry out one depth-first search to some arbitrarily predetermined depth, a sequence of increasingly deeper depth-first searches are carried out, beginning with a depth of one, then two, and continuing until time expires. Each iteration finds a principal continuation which is searched first on the next iteration. Each iteration also saves many positions in the hash table for use on subsequent iterations. The net result is an improvement in the efficiency of the alpha-beta algorithm, more than compensating for the time required to carry out the extra shallower searches. More importantly, iterative deepening allows the search to stop at any time with no serious negative consequences. At worst, when stopping in the middle of the n-th iteration, the computer has available the best continuation from the (n-1)st iteration. When using iterative deepening, the search is balanced, i.e., every move receives almost equal treatment. Stopping in the middle of an iteration will miss the best move on that iteration only if the best move is ordered below the stopping move on that final iteration. This happens when this best move was also not found best or good enough on the penultimate iteration to warrant being ordered above the stopping move on the final iteration.

Windows

In the late 1970s, *windows* began to be used in chess programs in conjunction with iterative deepening. Their use increases the overall search efficiency by increasing the number of cutoffs. Windows are based on the idea that it is worth gambling that the score found on the current iteration probably will be almost the same as the score found on the previous iteration. When using windows, an expected root score (RS) is guessed at the beginning of each iteration, usually the score backed up to the root by the previous iteration, and a narrow search window is placed about that score. Then during the course of the search, cutoffs occur at positions where backed-up scores are not inside the window. The *width* of the window is typically 2 pawns, i. e., 2P. At the beginning of each iteration, SCORE(0) is initialized to RS–P and whenever the search arrives at a new position at level one, SCORE(1) is assigned a value of RS+P, where P is the value of a pawn. These values correspond to values of $-\infty$ and $+\infty$ when windows are not used. The window is said to be initialized to < RS–P, RS+P >. The search then procedes as usual. If a move is found with a score within the window when the iteration terminates, the next iteration begins with a window again 2 pawns wide but centered about the newly obtained root score. If no move is found with a score within the window, the search is said to fail — *high* if the root score is equal to or greater than RS + P, *low* if the root score is equal to or less than RS – P. If the search fails, the iteration must be repeated to find the true root score and correct principal continuation. In the case of a high failure, the window must be set to <RS+P, $+\infty$> to ensure that the *second pass* will not also fail. Similarly, in the case of a low failure, the window must be set to <$-\infty$, RS–P>. The narrower the window, the faster the first pass proceeds, but the greater the chance of failure. When windows are used, each iteration should be viewed as consisting of two passes, the second pass being unnecessary if the first is successful.

When using a window of < 15, 35 > to search the continuing example, one additional position is cut off as shown in Figure 9.20. The search terminates with success, finding a score of 30 for the root, within the limits of the window. Note that during the course of the search, GENERATE_MOVES was called 10 times, EVALUATE_POSITION was called 6 times, UPDATE_POSITION and RESTORE_POSITION were each called 16 times, and PC_UPDATE was called 8 times.

The windowing strategy described above can be improved as follows. First, if some move at the root causes the search to fail high on the first pass, the search can be stopped immediately and a second pass started with a revised window < RS+P,$+\infty$> . More effectively, the window can be raised and narrowed to < RS+P, RS+P+1 > and the first pass continued. If a second move at the root causes the search to fail high again, a second pass becomes necessary. When a second pass is necessary due to two high failures, a re-search is required only of those 2 moves that caused the search to fail high and of those moves ordered below the 2nd of these 2 moves. If another high failure does not occur, the best move, the one that caused the failure, is known at the end of the 1st pass although only a lower bound on its score is available. Generally, it is unnecessary to know the precise score and thus gambling that the search will not fail high twice is more effective than initiating a 2nd pass after one failure. This technique has been used by BELLE for a number of years.

The process is illustrated in Figure 9.21. Suppose moves **a**, **b**, **c**, **d**, and **e** have minimax scores of **7, 19, 12, 22,** and **10**, respectively, and suppose the first pass begins with a window of **< 2, 16 >** . A subtree is rooted as shown at each position at the 1st level. Shaded regions denote subtrees searched. On the first pass, search fails high for the first time when searching move **b**. The window

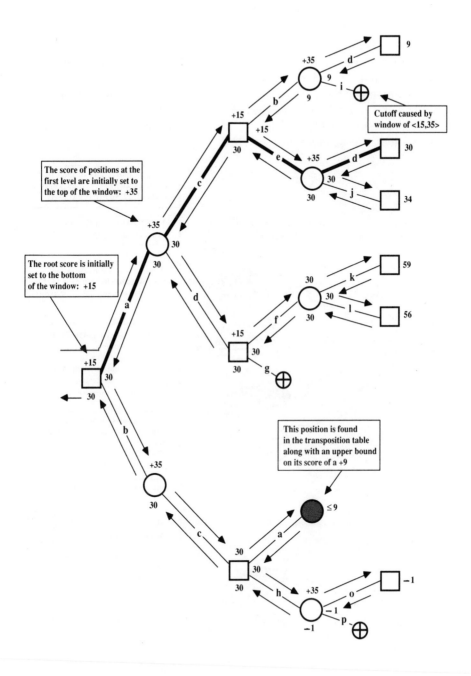

Figure 9.20 Continuing example: alpha-beta search with a hash table and a window of <15,35>

is raised to **< 16,17 >** for the remaining moves. Move **c**'s subtree, with a score below **16**, fails low. When searching move **d**, the search fails high for a 2nd time, causing the 1st pass to terminate. On the 2nd pass, it is not necessary to re-search moves **a** and **c**. Futhermore, move **d** should be searched first followed by move **b** since move **d** failed with the higher score and, knowing only this, it is more likely to be the better move. As shown, move **d** leads to a score of **22**, sufficient to allow moves **b** and **e** to be refuted before the entire trees rooted at these mores are searched.

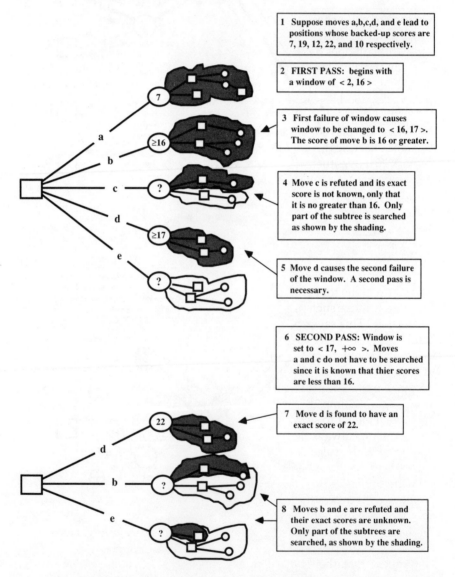

1 Suppose moves a,b,c,d, and e lead to positions whose backed-up scores are 7, 19, 12, 22, and 10 respectively.

2 FIRST PASS: begins with a window of < 2, 16 >

3 First failure of window causes window to be changed to < 16, 17 >. The score of move b is 16 or greater.

4 Move c is refuted and its exact score is not known, only that it is no greater than 16. Only part of the subtree is searched as shown by the shading.

5 Move d causes the second failure of the window. A second pass is necessary.

6 SECOND PASS: Window is set to < 17, +∞ >. Moves a and c do not have to be searched since it is known that thier scores are less than 16.

7 Move d is found to have an exact score of 22.

8 Moves b and e are refuted and their exact scores are unknown. Only part of the subtrees are searched, as shown by the shading.

Figure 9.21 Search tree that results from a two-pass alpha-beta search using a narrow window

The windowing schemes described above carry out re-searches only at the root of the tree. More sophisticated windowing strategies that allow setting windows and carrying out re-searches of subtrees at all positions in the tree are used by a number of programs. These recursive procedures are described in papers by J. Pearl in 1980 and A. Reinefeld et al. in 1985.

The Efficient Use of Time

On each move, a chess program must make a very important decision: how much time does this position deserve? Easy positions deserve less time, while more difficult ones deserve more time. Of course, deciding what is an easy position and what is a difficult one is tricky, just as is deciding what is less time and what is more time! But over the years, programmers have developed reasonably good algorithms for making this decision. Hyatt describes how CRAY BLITZ handles time in a 1984 paper.

Games are played under two types of time control rules. The more conventional rules give each side 2 hours to play the first 40 moves and 1 hour for each 20 moves thereafter. This is an average of 3 minutes per move. At the beginning of each move, a typical program determines the number of moves to time control, say N, and the time remaining to time control, say T. The ratio of T/N gives the base time, say B, allotted to that move. A maximum time is also set for the move — typically 4B — although this must be adjusted downward when near time control. The program then begins its iteratively deepening search. After searching for B/2 seconds, the program makes a decision on how much longer to search by taking into consideration the scores backed up to the root on successive iterations. If they indicate the computer has an easy move such as a queen recapture or a pawn promotion, the search terminates. This saves B/2 seconds for later moves. Otherwise the search continues until B seconds have passed, where again the computer makes a decision on how much longer to search. This time, the computer stops if the score of the root has not dropped off as the search progressed. If it has dropped off, indicating trouble on the horizon, the computer continues searching until time 2B. At time 2B, the program again makes a decision on how much longer to search. This time it quits unless it sees losing a piece or worse. Search always terminates after at most 4B seconds.

More recently, rules that give each side a fixed amount of time to play all moves have been used in a number of tournaments. The DEEP THOUGHT —Kasparov games in Chapter 1 were played with each player having 90 minutes. This makes the above algorithm more complex since it is not clear how long a game will last. Some programs assume a game will always continue for another 30 moves, and so N=30 in the paragraph above.

Computers are programmed to think while their opponent is on the move. They guess that their opponent will make the anticipated move on the principal continuation (found in PC(1,2)), and they procede to calculate a reply. If their guess turns out to be correct, they can either save time by replying immediately, or they can continue searching. If they are wrong, they simply restart their search. The best programs guess their opponents' moves 50 percent of the time, effectively giving them 50 percent more time. This is equivalent to running the program on a computer 50 percent faster.

CHAPTER

10

The Evolution of Computing Systems for Chess Programs

Over the last several decades, incredible progress has been made in computer hardware and software, and this progress has had an enormous impact on the development of chess programs. These advances include faster processors, larger memories, larger word sizes, smaller and more reliable circuitry, better software, special-purpose circuitry, and multiprocessors. This chapter surveys these advances.

Faster Processors

The speed of processing units has increased dramatically due to the rapid evolution of semiconductor technology. Computers have progressed from executing approximately 10,000 instructions per second when the first chess programs were written, to approximately 1,000,000,000 today. They are approximately 100,000 times faster now than they were then. Imagine if transportation speeds had increased as much during the same period. Airplanes flying at 1000 miles per hour in 1955 would now be traveling at speeds of 100,000,000 miles per hour; a trip to the sun would take about an hour, and a round trip visit to the nearest star Alpha Centauri, which is 4.5 light years away, would take only about 70 years.

Continued increases in processing speeds can be expected in the coming years, and a speedup by another factor of 100 in the next 10 years is not at all unreasonable to expect. By the year 2000, computers will be 10,000,000 times faster than they were when chess programming began. A round trip to Alpha Centauri would now take less than 1 year! Each 6-fold increase in speed gives a computer time to search approximately 1 level deeper. A speedup of 100 yields approximately 2.5 additional levels. With DEEP THOUGHT now searching to a depth of 9 to 10 levels on most moves, it is quite likely that search depths of 12 levels will be typical by the year 2000.

The effect of an increase in hardware speed on the performance of chess programs has been studied for many years. History has shown that ratings have improved by about 200 points for each additonal level searched. This is shown in Table 10.1 where search depths, years and ratings have been rounded slightly to dramatize the 200-point effect. What the table doesn't show is that many other improvements have been made to the programs on their journey to deeper search, and that simply running a program on a computer six times faster does not in itself yield a 200 point rating improvement.

In the late 1970s, Thompson had various versions of BELLE play one another in an attempt to measure performance as a function only of speed — to factor out the effects of other improvements. He actually measured performance as a function of search depth, but speed and search depth are very closely related as discussed two paragraphs ago. In his experiments, search depths ranged from 3 levels to 9 levels. Thompson's results showed that for rating ranging from 1400 to 2000 there were approximately 200 points in improvement for each additional level searched. However, as rating increased beyond 2000 and search depths exceeded 7, there was a decrease in this 200 point figure. A follow-up study by Newborn, which considered search depths from 3 to 13, found the same slowdown, but also found that ratings would nevertheless continue to increase as search depths increased. Faster computers, by themselves, would continue to yield significantly stronger programs for many years to come.

Table 10.1 Correlation between search depth and chess ratings

Depth of search	Year	Program	Rating
5	1972	CHESS 3.5	1600
6	1975	CHESS 4.0	1800
7	1978	CHESS 4.7	2000
8	1980	BELLE	2200
9	1986	HITECH	2400
10	1989	DEEP THOUGHT	2600

Larger Memories

Larger memories are also the result of the rapid evolution of semiconductor technology. The first chess programs ran on computers using magnetic core memories. In the early 1970s, semiconductor memories were introduced on the IBM 370 series computers. Just as computer speeds have increased by a factor of approximately 100,000, so too have memory sizes grown. This is particularly important for chess programs that use transposition tables. As computer speeds increase, proportionally larger memories are necessary to store the increased number of positions that are searched.

Just as it is reasonable to expect significant speedups in processor speeds in the coming years, memory sizes will continue to grow even more dramatically. Extremely large memories will be used by large hash tables, and the information stored in these hash tables will not be erased between games.

Larger Word Sizes

Word sizes have generally been growing, with some of the more impressive gains coming in the small computers. Intel's 80386 and their new 80486 are based on a 32-bit word size. At the other extreme, the Cray uses a 64-bit word size, particularly suited for chess programs, since the chess board, by good fortune, happens to have exactly 64 squares. Larger word sizes mean that an increased amount of information can be moved around in the computer during each clock cycle. It is unlikely that future computers will use larger word sizes although they can be expected to have greater flexibility in handling a wider variety of word sizes ranging from 1 bit to 64 bits.

Smaller Computers

Computers that once occupied a room now occupy a desktop, and the desktop computers of today are considerably more powerful. The processing units of the first computers used for chess occupied several cabinets of vacuum tubes totalling, for round numbers, 100 cubic feet or 172,800 cubic inches in volume. Today's microprocessors occupy less than 1 cubic inch and are much more powerful.

More Reliable Computers

Vacuum-tube computers used to break down every several hours. Nowadays, computers can be expected to run for a year without any problems. Further, fault tolerant computers are currently being marketed by several manufacturers. These computers will be able to function even when a number of their parts are no longer operating correctly.

Better Software

Better, more efficient software is available for editing, compiling, assembling, linking, and debugging programs. It is hard to quantify how much better software is today than before, although by any reasonable measure it has not improved by a factor anywhere near that which has taken place in the area of hardware. Nevertheless, gigantic strides have been made. Somewhat surprising in this regard has been the lack of development of special-purpose languages for chess.

Special-Purpose Hardware

Special-purpose hardware for chess appeared in the middle 1970s and will continue to get more sophisticated. The first such systems were designed using components that could be classified as medium scale integrated circuits; each chip consisted of from 10 to 100 logical components. The most recent circuits are designed using VLSI circuitry. The success of special-purpose hardware for chess is likely to encourage its use on other AI problems that depend on search.

Multiprocessors

In the long run, multiprocessing offers the greatest potential for further advances. Computers with thousands of processors have been built in recent years and computers with millions of processors are on the horizon. In addition to using multiprocessors to play more effective chess, they have been used by Ken Thompson and Larry Stiller to develop endgame databases. In the future, they may also be used to generate opening lines automatically.

A Chronology of Progress in Computing Systems for Chess

The first full-fledged game of chess was played on a computer in 1957. Alex Bernstein, Michael de V. Roberts, Timothy Arbuckle, and Martin A. Belsky did their programming on an IBM 704, one of the last in the series of IBM mainframe vacuum tube computers and one of the first of its scientific — as opposed to business — computers. The 704, which was introduced in 1955, was a much improved version of the 701, which appeared in 1953. IBM produced about 140 704s, renting them for approximately $20,000 per month. The principal designer was no less than Gene Amdahl, who had only recently graduated from the University of Wisconsin. Amdahl left IBM in 1970 to form his own company.

   The 704 was one of the first computers to use magnetic core memory technology, replacing the slower and less reliable cathode ray tube memories that were used on the 701. It was also one of the first to use special circuitry for performing floating-point arithmetic operations, a feature that distinguished early scientific computers from their data processing counterparts. In addition, it was the first computer to use index registers for increasing the flexibility of addressing information in memory. The 704 used a 4k 36-bit word magnetic core memory with a memory cycle time, i.e. the time between 2 successive memory accesses, of 12 microseconds. A fixed-point addition required 2 memory cycles or 24 microseconds, while a floating-point addition required 84 microseconds. Multiplication, though, was much slower, requiring 240 microseconds to calculate a fixed-point product. Chess programs, it might be pointed out, can be written without the need to perform very many multiplications, and programmers often make every effort to avoid them. In describing their program in the June 1958 issue of the *Scientific American*, Bernstein and Roberts indicated that the 704 executed 1,000,000,000 instructions in a day. With 86,400 seconds in a day, in round numbers, this amounts to the 10,000 instructions per second mentioned earlier in this chapter. A magnetic drum that was able to store 16,000 numbers was used for the long-term storage of information.

While the 704 is noteworthy for being the first computer to run FORTRAN, the chess program was written in MIDAS, an assembly language for the 704. The Bernstein Program searched to a depth of 4 plies examining exactly 7 moves at each node thus creating a tree with 2401 terminal positions. The program played only a few games, none of which could be characterized as good chess.

When the Kotok/McCarthy Program took on the ITEP Program in 1966, it used an IBM 7090 located at Stanford University. Announced by IBM in 1957, the 7090 was essentially a transistorized version of the IBM 709 which, in turn, was a slightly improved version of the 704. The 7090, which appeared in 1959, was much faster than the 709 having a memory cycle time of 2.18 microseconds and an add time of 4.36 microseconds. The one used by the Kotok/McCarthy Program had a magnetic core memory of 32K 36-bit words. The 7090 dominated the world of scientific computing throughout the early 1960s.

In the middle 1960s, Digital Equipment Corporation's computers began to appear on university campuses. A PDP-6, DEC's first large computer, was used by MACHACK VI at MIT. The PDP-6 was delivered to MIT with a 16K memory and no time-sharing, but by 1967, timesharing had been added along with a much larger 256K Fabritek memory. The memory cycle time of the PDP-6 was 1.75 microseconds, the add time was 4.4 microseconds, and the word size was 36 bits. Time-sharing made it possible for the average graduate student in a university to develop a chess program. Until time-sharing, access to computers was too costly and restricted to permit this. It was on a time-shared Control Data Corporation 6400 that a group of Northwestern University graduate students developed the chess program that won the 1st ACM NACCC in 1970. Five of the six participants in that event used large time-shared computers. These systems were a real bonanza to the development of chess programs, although anyone who ever used one in a tournament feared the other unknown users who always seemed to load down the main processor at a crucial stage of the game.

The CDC Cyber series computers initiated the modern era of supercomputers in 1975. That year, the CHESS 4.0 team found support at CDC from David Cahlander who arranged access to the Cyber series computers at CDC Headquarters. Cahlander assisted them for several years in adapting their program to the new environment. CHESS 4.4 used the Cyber 175 to win the 6th ACM NACCC in Minneapolis, finishing with a perfect 4-0 score. The following year, CHESS 4.5 used the superfast Cyber 176 when it won the 7th ACM NACCC in Houston. In 1977, the Cyber 176 was used by CHESS 4.6 when it won the 2nd World Championship in Toronto. The Cyber's add time was 55 nanoseconds (one nanosecond is a billionth of a second). An Amdahl computer appeared for the first time at an ACM tournament in 1975 when CHAOS used the powerful 470 model. CHAOS ran at the University of Michigan on Amdahl's very first 470 V/6 installation. Its add time was 64 nanoseconds and it had a 2 megabyte main memory. Amdahl 470 computers were compatible with IBM's 360/370 series computers although, dollar for dollar, a bit more powerful, and so some participants in the ACM tournaments would run on Amdahl computers one year and on IBM ones the next year.

Supercomputers were actually first used in 1970 when Hans Berliner entered J. BIIT in the 1st ACM North American Computer Chess Championship. Berliner ran J. BIIT on an IBM 360/91 at Columbia University. The 360/91 was the top of the line of IBM's 360 series computers at that time. Only a few were ever produced. It was one of the first computers to use pipelining of

Figure 10.1 The IBM 360/91, the first supercomputer used by chess programs

instructions to increase overall speed. It was also water cooled. If you held your hand on the console, you could feel the "heartbeat" of the machine pumping water through its pipes.

Currently, Cray Corporation's supercomputers are the favorite of the chess community. In 1980, CRAY BLITZ participated in the 11th NACCC with a Cray–I computer. Two years later, it ran on the 4-processor Cray X-MP when it participated in the 4th World Championship. The 8-processor Y-MP, introduced in 1988, is now the top of Cray's line and will probably be used soon by CRAY BLITZ in a major tournament. The X-MP has an 8.5 nanosecond clock cycle time and executes approximately 100,000,000 instructions per second on each of its 4 processors. The clock cycle time on the Y-MP is 6 nanoseconds. Memory sizes range to 16 million words on the X-MP. On the Y-MP, the main memory contains 32 million words, but a secondary solid-state memory with fast accessibility capabilities contains another 128 million words. Supercomputers, however, are very expensive to use and developing chess programs on them generally receives low priority.

In the late 1970s, several simultaneous revolutions in the computer world took place. With the falling cost of circuitry, the increasing ease of fabricating special-purpose devices, the growing awareness of the importance of speed as a factor in the strength of a chess machine, and the high cost of using supercomputers, part of the computer chess community broke from the traditional mainframe and minicomputer world to explore (1) microcomputers, (2) special-purpose circuitry, and (3) multiprocessing. Chapter 11 covers the fast-moving world of microcomputers in chess. The remainder of this chapter considers special-purpose circuitry and multiprocessing.

Special-Purpose Chess Hardware

The first special-purpose chess hardware was developed in 1976. Given that the most time-consuming part of most chess programs is the generation of moves, it was inevitable that this process would be built into hardware. The idea was to give a hardware move generator a position and have it return a list of moves — in the same way that a hardware multiplier receives two arguments and returns the product. Next to the generation of moves, the work done by a chess program's evaluation function is typically the most time-consuming, and a number of special-purpose hardware evaluators also have been built. Table 10.2 lists the programs, their year of introduction and the number of positions searched per second.

In 1976, Joe Condon and Ken Thompson developed a hardware prototype of a move generator for BELLE. Thompson had started work on BELLE in 1972 at Bell Laboratories in Murray Hill, New Jersey. By that time he already had developped the UNIX operating system and the C programming language, earning him a position in the US National Academy of Engineering, the youngest person ever so honored. BELLE participated in the 1973 ACM tournament, finishing in the middle of the field. The following year it

Table 10.2 Special-purpose hardware for chess

Program	Year of Introduction	Positions/Second
BELLE		
1st prototype	1976	200
2nd prototype	1978	5,000
3rd prototype	1980	120,000
CHEOPS	1977	150,000
BEBE	1980	40,000
HITECH	1985	200,000
DEEP THOUGHT	1986	700,000

improved somewhat, finishing with a 3-1 score. Then, in 1976, Joe Condon joined with Thompson and they designed their first 25-chip prototype move generator. BELLE participated in 1977 World Championship in Toronto, finishing in a tie for fourth place with CHAOS.

In 1977, CHEOPS was constructed at MIT by J. Moussouris, J. Holloway, and R. Greenblatt, although Ed Fredkin was instrumental in the original concept and design. It was essentially a brute-force searcher that could be linked to another chess program. It was capable of carrying out an exhaustive search of 6 to 8 plies in about 2 minutes.

CHEOPS was coupled with Alan Baisley's brute-force TECH II. Jim Gillogly, who created TECH at Carnegie Mellon University in the early 1970s gave his code to Baisley who subsequently made a number of modifications. TECH II played only slightly better than TECH, and after competing in the ACM tournaments in 1974 and 1975, it was retired from competition. TECH II was used by CHEOPS to develop an ordering of the moves at the root of the tree using various factors including pawn structure, control of center, and king safety. The resulting 1st level positions were given to CHOEPS, which then carried out an alpha-beta minimax search with material balance as an evaluator, returning a principal continuation.

CHEOPS was also coupled with MACHACK, and performed two different functions. First, running in parallel with MACHACK, it carried out a brute-force search of the position. The result of CHEOPS' search was compared with that of MACHACK, and if there was a difference, a final choice was made by a heuristic program. In addition, at MACHACK's request it carried out short tactical searches from positions within the game tree in order to improve the tactical play of MACHACK. CHEOPS and MACHACK played David Levy a two game match in late 1977 and lost both games (see pages 90-92).

An improved version of BELLE that searched approximately 5000 nodes per second appeared in 1978. It participated in the 9th ACM NACCC and finished 1st, winning all its games. This second prototype was much larger, consisting of 325 chips, and included special-purpose hardware for generating moves, evaluating positions and for handling a large transposition table.

According to Thompson and Condon, the host "PDP-11 now requested move generation, move making, and move unmaking from the move generator, position evaluation from the the the evaluator, and position match and store from the transposition device. The PDP-11 was still responsible for the alpha-beta algorithm and the proper coordination of the three devices." In contrast with their first prototype, moves were stacked in the move generator rather than being transmitted one at a time to the PDP-11, thus reducing communication between the move generator and the PDP-11. While the new BELLE was able to search 5000 nodes per second, the PDP-11 "was still a limitation to even faster performance." Nevertheless, BELLE won the 1978 ACM NACCC with a perfect 4-0 score. During the following year BELLE earned an official 1884 USCF rating based on 29 tournament games. According to Thompson and Condon, "the major flaw with the second machine was its inability to order legal moves. It could only generate moves in *from* square order. This was so intolerably slow for the alpha-beta algorithm that the software generated all of the legal moves five times in each position and selected the moves in five sorted subsets: a) principle variation move, b) favorable captures, c) killer moves, d) unfavorable captures, e) all other moves."

In 1980, BEBE, developed by Tony Scherzer, used a pipeline approach to generating moves and was able to search about 40,000 positions per second. BEBE participated in 3th World Championship in Linz and finished with a 2–2 score, drawing all four of its games. BEBE has continued to improve with its

Figure 10.2 The Cray Y-MP, currently the world's most powerful computer

best performance coming at the 6thWorld Championship in Edmonton in May 1989 where it finished in second place, although that was in part due to fortunate pairings.

BELLE's third prototype was completed in 1980 and also participated (via telephone) in Linz. It contained 1700 chips and searched approximately 120,000 positions per second. This machine included an alpha-beta microprocessor which supervised the operation of its three other circuits: a move generator, a position evaluator, and a transposition table manager. The entire system weighed 60 kilograms and occupied .2 cubic meters.

The move generator was much improved over the second prototype. It consisted of 64 transmitter circuits and 64 receiver circuits, corresponding to the 64 board squares. It was able to generate the move leading to the capture of the highest-valued enemy piece in one cycle.

The evaluation function was also designed around a similar set of 64 circuits. It used 8 cycles to evaluate "pins, discoveries, attacks, defenses, and other things in the general realm of square control. A second part of the evaluator machine uses the 8 cycles to scan the pawn structure, 3 files at a time, left to right over the chess board. This section detects passed pawns, blocked pawns, backward pawns, isolated pawns, open files, and half-open files. There is also a static part to the evaluation machine. This machine tracks the board changes and incrementally modifies an evaluation based on these changes. The major evaluation here is material, but other factors such as king safety are also included. This value, since it is immediately available, is used as a fast approximate evaluation for possible quick cutoffs."

The third prototype also included a 128K position transposition table. Each entry used 8 bytes; the hash code was 48 bits. The first 16 bits plus the "side-to-move" were used to address an 8-byte position in memory, while the other 32 bits were stored in the first 4 of the 8 bytes to reduce the probability of erroneous match. They calculated that false matches were still possible but only one a day. Two bytes were used to store the score of a position, 1 to store the depth in the tree, and 1 for flags. The last byte was used to represent whether the score was exact or only an upper or lower bound. This version of BELLE was the class of the field when it came out in 1980. It won the 3rd World Championship in Linz and in 1983 it became the first program to be awarded the title of Master by the USCF.

In 1985, a group of graduate students at Carnegie Mellon University under the supervision of Hans Berliner developed a hardware move generator and special-purpose circuitry to score positions at high speeds. Carl Ebeling, along with Andy Palay did most of the circuit design. Their program, HITECH, currently searches approximately 200,000 nodes per second. It has won the Pennsylvania State Championship 3 years running, playing against a strong group of human opponents and earning a performace rating of approximately 2400. HITECH won the 1985 ACM NACCC with 4-0 score. One of the strengths of its hardware is that extra terms can be added to the scoring function, and these terms can be computed in parallel with the other terms, thus not slowing down the evaluation of positions. In other words, adding intelligence to the scoring function could be done with virtually no computational overhead.

In 1986, a second group at Carnegie Mellon University, following the ideas in BELLE and to a lesser extent in HITECH, launched the strongest program to date. It still had bugs in it when it participated in the ACM's NACCC that year, finishing with a score of 2.5/5. Initially named CHIPTEST-M, renamed DEEP THOUGHT 0.02 in 1988, and simply DEEP THOUGHT the following year, it initially ran on a SUN 3 workstation with a VLSI move generator attached, the first move generator using VLSI technology. The system, developed by Feng-hsiung Hsu along with fellow graduate students Thomas Anantharaman, Murray Campbell, Mike Browne, and Andreas Nowatzyk was debugged and improved after its bug-ridden performance in 1986 to capture first place at the 18th and the 19th ACM NACCCs. In its current form the processor can search 700,000 positions per second.

Multiprocessing Systems

Beginning in 1981, multiprocessing systems found their way into computer chess competition. Programmers had a goal of obtaining an N-fold speedup using N processors. While this is an easily-stated objective, in fact, it has been impossible to achieve thus far for any large value of N. The programs used *tree decomposition* algorithms to divide up the search tree among the processors. But it turns out to be a very difficult programming exercise to divide up the tree in such a way that all processors are kept busy all the time, carrying out non-redundant search.

One major problem with multiprocessing systems are the difficulties faced when debugging programs. Debugging programs on multiprocessing systems is much more difficult than debugging programs running on single processors. It is particularly difficult to get a multiprocessing system to exactly repeat a computation. The processors run asynchronously and sometimes an event will occur on one processor before another event on a second processor, and at other times the events will occur in just the opposite order.

OSTRICH was the first program to compete in a major tournament using a multiprocessing system — five Data General 16-bit Nova series computers connected together by a high-speed communication package. The system was housed in the Parallel Processing Laboratory at McGill University. The program used what has become called the principal variation splitting algorithm as its strategy for dividing up the search of the tree among processors. In subsequent years, eight DG computers were used, and on the eight computers, a speedup of approximately 5 was achieved. A special eight-screen terminal was built so that all the calculations being carried out on the eight processors could be monitored simultaneously. Following OSTRICH, five other chess programs emerged running on parallel systems: CRAY BLITZ (1983), SUN PHOENIX(1986), CHESS CHALLENGER(1987), WAYCOOL(1987), and most recently DEEP THOUGHT(1989). Parallel systems have also been used for endgame studies. Table 10.3 summarizes the use of multiprocessing systems in computer chess.

The principal variation splitting algorithm and variations of it have served as the foundation for all parallel alpha-beta implementations. This algorithm is based on iterative deepening. Its success depends on the fact that when moves are ordered optimally for search at each node, almost fifty percent of the total search time is consumed in examining the 1st move in each position on the principal continuation. It is thus the search of replies to the 1st move in each position that should be divided up, and this is exactly what the PVSA does (See Figure 10.3). On the n-th iteration, all processors search along the principal variation found on the (n - 1)-st iteration to position $P(n-1)$ at the $(n-1)$-st level. Then the subtrees of depth one rooted there are dynamically divided up among the processors and searched. Upon completion, a final score can be assigned to position $P(n-1)$. The search then backs up one level to position $P(n-2)$, where again moves are dynamically divided up and this time 2-level subtrees rooted at $P(n-2)$ are searched, and again, upon completion a final score can be assigned to $P(n-2)$. Eventually, moves at position $P(0)$ are dynamically divided up and the n-level subtrees rooted at $P(0)$ are searched. Although interprocessor communication is not particularly a problem on a small to moderate number of processors, there is considerable waiting time by processors that have no work to do. It is very difficult to divide the tree up uniformly among the processors; subtrees vary widely in size by as much as a factor of 100-1. The granularity problem becomes more pronounced as the ratio of the number of processors to the number of root moves increases. Attempts by Schaeffer (SUN PHOENIX), Hyatt (CRAY BLITZ), and Ed Felton and Steve Otto (WAYCOOL) to remedy the inefficiency of the PVSA involve using more flexible decomposition rules.

Table 10.3 Data on multiprocessing systems used in computer chess

Program	Year	Processor	# of Proc's
OSTRICH	1981	Data General System	5
OSTRICH	1982	Data General System	8
CRAY BLITZ	1983	CRAY X-MP	2
CRAY BLITZ	1984	CRAY X-MP	4
SUN PHOENIX	1986	VAXs and Suns	20
CHESS CHALLENGER	1986	8086 microporcessors	20
WAYCOOL	1986	N/CUBE	128
WAYCOOL	1988	N/CUBE	256
DEEP THOUGHT	1989	SUNs & VLSI hardware	3
Stiller's Retroanalysis	1988	Connection Machine	32,000
Thompson's Retroanalysis	1986	Sequent Symmetry	30

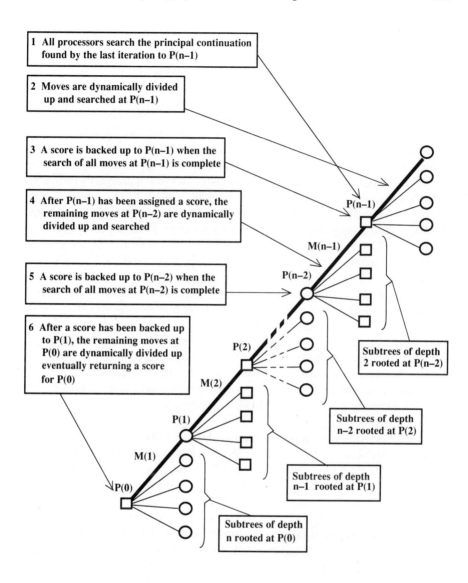

1 All processors search the principal continuation found by the last iteration to P(n–1)

2 Moves are dynamically divided up and searched at P(n–1)

3 A score is backed up to P(n–1) when the search of all moves at P(n–1) is complete

4 After P(n–1) has been assigned a score, the remaining moves at P(n–2) are dynamically divided up and searched

5 A score is backed up to P(n–2) when the search of all moves at P(n–2) is complete

6 After a score has been backed up to P(1), the remaining moves at P(0) are dynamically divided up eventually returning a score for P(0)

P(n–1)

M(n–1)

P(n–2)

Subtrees of depth 2 rooted at P(n–2)

P(2)

M(2)

Subtrees of depth n–2 rooted at P(2)

P(1)

M(1)

Subtrees of depth n–1 rooted at P(1)

P(0)

Subtrees of depth n rooted at P(0)

Figure 10.3 The principal variation splitting algorithm

Perhaps the most important architectural difference between parallel systems is whether or not the individual processors share memory with one another. With shared memory one common transposition table can serve all processors. This is the case on the Cray multiprocessors. On the other hand, the N/CUBE has no shared memory. WAYCOOL is programmed so that each processor contributes part of its memory to a shared transposition table.

The hash function maps each position to a particular computer and to a particular memory location. The programmers indicate that the overhead associated with using the table is only a small percent of the overall time and well worth using.

CRAY BLITZ had done well in the ACM tournaments leading up to the World Championship in 1983 but not quite well enough to win. In 1982, it finished with the same number of points as BELLE, but BELLE was given the title on tie-breaking points. Then in 1983, CRAY BLITZ was moved to a Cray X-MP and surprised everyone by defeating BELLE and then going on to win the 4th World Computer Chess Championship in 1983. It used only two of the X-MP's four processors. The following year, CRAY BLITZ used all four processors and finishing first at the 1984 ACM NACCC. CRAY BLITZ used the PVSA and a large hash table in shared memory to store positions.

In 1986, SUN PHOENIX used a network of 20 VAXs and SUNs when it participated in the 17th NACCC championship. Shaeffer decided to set aside 6 processors or so to search specifically for material gains, arguing that he was unable to obtain significant speedup by using all of the processors in a search carried out using the PVSA. By eliminating from these processors all the other overheads of a chess program, he was able to have them search typically two plies deeper than the rest of the parallel program. When they found that their material evaluation differed from the main parallel search program, a re-search was carried out. In general, one of the questions that remains unanswered is whether a parallel search in which processors are assigned to search for specific goals is a good idea. For example, should one processor be set aside to look for mates?

In 1986, Ron Nelson's parallel version of CHESS CHALLENGER participated at the 17th ACM NACCC. It used 20 8086 processors. WAYCOOL, developed at Cal Tech by Ed Felton, Steve Otto and Rod Morison, also appeared for the first time with a 64-processor N/CUBE. The following year, WAYCOOL participated in the 18th ACM NACCC using a 256-processor N/CUBE. Its programmers claim a speedup of 101. One year later, they came to the 19th ACM NACCC prepared to use a 512-processor N/CUBE, claiming that they were able to achieve a speedup of approximately 170. However, they were unable to use all 512 processors during the tournament, using 256 instead. Each processor ran at 7 MHz and contained 512k bytes of memory.

The Ultimate: Special-Purpose Hardware and Multiprocessing Systems

In 1989, DEEP THOUGHT was triplicated to run on three processors using the PVSA to divide up the search. In so doing, it searched approximately 2,000,000 positions per second while establishing new levels of performance. DEEP THOUGHT thus became the first system to combine parallel search at the level of tree decomposition and special-purpose chess circuitry. In the coming years, additional processors will be added, and DEEP THOUGHT will search yet larger trees.

11

Commercially Available Chess Computers and Software

The advent of the microprocessor at affordable prices brought a new dimension to computer chess in the late 1970s. Whereas this somewhat esoteric activity had previously been the province of only a few privileged computer scientists, who had access to free computer time on their mainframe at work or at university, computer chess was now available to all. One merely had to own a home computer – there were chess programs available on cassette (and later disk) for only a few dollars. Two of the early ventures in this field led to outstandingly successful careers for their programmers: SARGON, written by Kathe and Dan Spracklen (husband and wife team), was so successful as an item of commercially available software that the authors were encouraged to write a book on the program so that home computer owners could type SARGON into their computers and understand how it worked. The book became a best seller. Another notable success on cassette was Peter Jennings' MICROCHESS, which became the industry's first "golden casette," selling more than one million copies. Jennings became a millionaire and moved from Toronto to California where his business flourished. More recently David

Kittinger's CHESS MASTER 2000 and the Spracklen's CHESS MASTER 2100 have been the most prominent.

In 1977 the first dedicated chess computers came on the scene. One of these, called COMPUCHESS, had a short lived future under its own name but a much more successful existence in pirated form. The chess playing program in COMPUCHESS was copied by a Hong Kong manufacturer who marketed a product containing the program under the name "CHESS CHAMPION MK 1." The copy was exact — no attempt had been made to hide the fact by changing some of the program code. The CHESS CHAMPION MK 1 was an enormous marketing success and the manufacturer was able to buy a 57-foot yacht on the proceeds. Litigation followed, but in those days there was little or no copyright protection available to those who owned computer programs and the suit eventually fizzled out, after lawyers on both sides had no doubt benefited substantially.

Perhaps the most interesting success story of those days was that of Fidelity Electronics of Chicago. Fidelity was in the business of manufacturing hearing aids. A local engineer had built a neat little electronic gadget that could play chess. This news came to the attention of company President Sidney Samole, who seized the opportunity and marketed the program under the name CHESS CHALLENGER. The program played horrible chess by today's standards, but the novelty of the product made it an instant success. The fact that one could win a game by playing illegal moves did not detract from this success — after the moves 1 Nb1–e5 (by the user) 1 ... d7–d5 2 h2xf7, the computer would announce "I LOSE." It simply did not check to see if its

Figure 11.1 The original CHESS CALLENGER

opponent's moves were legal, and recognized that with a white knight on e5 and a white pawn on f7 Black has been checkmated! But bugs of this nature were not important. What mattered most was that Fidelity helped to create a worldwide market for chess computers, and for many years theirs was by far the most prominent brand name. The programmer of the original CHESS CHALLENGER, Ron Nelson, is still with the company 13 years later, and Fidelity International Inc. is still one of the world's major forces in the chess computer market.

During the period from 1977 to 1980 the market for dedicated chess computers grew rapidly. In the United States Fidelity's main rival was a product called Boris (no one was foolish enough to try to name a chess computer Bobby!). Boris had a scrolling display which would output various jokey messages at random, such as "I expected that" or "Don't tell David Levy about that move." While the United States had been the birthplace of chess computers, Hong Kong was quick to react. Two Hong Kong companies, Novag and Scisys-W, each had their own range of chess computers before the end of 1980, and a third Hong Kong company, Cassia, soon entered the market.

The leading European chess computer manufacturer has always been Hegener & Glaser of Munich, West Germany. Their first MEPHISTO was written for an RCA 1802 microprocesor by Thomas Nitsche, a brilliant computer scientist who is also an accomplished artist. Nitsche had worked on a mainframe program called ORWELL (and later a parallel version called PARWELL), and was quick to realise the commercial potential of his work.

Figure 11.2 The MEPHISTO "MUNCHEN" with the Almeria program

His MEPHISTO 1 program was launched in 1980, enabling Hegener & Glaser to stake a firm claim in the German market. Armed with a capable program and strengthened by the fact that in Germany one prefers to buy German made products, Hegener & Glaser grew steadily year by year, until by the end of the 1980s the company had 85 percent of their home market. Since West Germany is probably the world's biggest market for chess computers, Hegener & Glaser became extremely successful and is now a public company.

The earliest chess computers required the user to employ algebraic notation to enter the moves: E2E4, C7C5, and so on. Although this method is still employed today in a number of products, particularly those at the lower price points, chess enthusiasts soon became more demanding. In 1980 Fidelity paved the way for the future by launching chess computers with sensor board technology. To make a move one merely had to press the piece down on its "from" square and "to" square — a membrane keyboard detected the move. This technology continues to be popular, though many manufacturers also have chess computers with magnetic pieces, using reed switches beneath each square to detect the movement of a piece. The first product to be marketed with magnetic pieces was the magnificent "Auto Response Board," launched in 1980, which contained the SARGON 2.5 program written by the Spracklens.

During the early 1980s various chess robots came onto the market. Novag manufactured an elegant looking machine which initially sold at around $2,000, but the mechanics were not too reliable and the price was rather high. Milton-Bradley then launched the "PHANTOM," which moved its pieces from beneath the playing surface using two concentric electromagnets mounted

Figure 11.3 The Fidelity "PHANTOM"

on a mechanism which could move horizontally and vertically. The Phantom was entertaining to watch, partly because of the way that it captured its opponent's pieces — the captured piece would slide, via the shortest path, to a special location at the edge of the board, and the capturing piece would then take its place. Milton-Bradley subsequently sold the rights to produce the Phantom to Fidelity, who still have the product on the market.

While chess computer manufacturers have always attempted to put better and better technology (and gimmicks) into their products, they have also made efforts to strengthen the play of their chess programs for each new selling season. As part of this effort most manufacturers have hired the best known names in the field of microcomputer chess program design. Dan and Kathe Spracklen's programs were originally marketed by Chafitz Inc. under the name SARGON. Later the Spracklens worked for Fidelity, providing both 6502 and 68000 based programs that were the world's best for a number of

Figure 11.4 Dan and Kathe Spracklen

years. Recently they have moved on from Fidelity and now work for Saitek (formally Scisys), one of the three Hong Kong manufacturers who are still in the chess computer business after a whole decade. Co-author David Levy started in the commercial field as a consultant to Texas Instruments on the "Video Chess" cartridge for the 99/4 home computer. When that project finished he worked with Scisys, and later moved to Cassia (now Newcrest Technology Ltd) who market under the "Sphinx" brand name. Another International Master, Julio Kaplan, has worked with Scisys/Saitek since the early 1980s. David Kittinger has been programming for Novag for about the same period of time. And the best chess programmer of them all, Richard Lang, has been providing the strongest MEPHISTO programs since 1985.

The commercial constraints imposed on chess programmers force them to make the most of hardware which, to a mainframe programmer, appear extremely limited. At one end of the scale there is the 4-bit chess program algorithm designed by David Levy in 1980. This algorithm has been programmed into various Hitachi 4-bit micros containing only 2K words of ROM and 80 bytes of RAM. The program plays fully legal chess, it knows about castling, en passant captures and pawn promotion, and it does not put pieces on squares where they can be taken for nothing (or for a lesser piece). The program also understands something about center control and advancing its passed pawns. In fact it plays a very reasonable game of chess, considering the hardware at its disposal.

Moving up from 4-bit chips, there have been some rather good programs written for single-chip 8-bit processors. The Hitachi 6301 has been a popular choice for commercial chess programmers. This chip comes with various memory configurations — its ROM can be as little as 4K bytes or as much as 16K, its RAM can be 128, 192 or 256 bytes. Programs for the larger configuration version have reached an Elo rating of 1585, corresponding to a U.S. rating of around 1685.

The two most popular microprocessors among those striving to produce the strongest programs are the 8-bit 6502 and the 16/32 bit 68000/68020/ 68030 family (and there is a 68040 just coming available). Logically one would assume that the 68000 must be a better vehicle than the 6502 for just about any kind of software, including chess programming, but that is not necessarily the case. The 6502 has some instructions which could almost have been designed with chess in mind, and the strongest 6502 program at the end of 1989 — Ed Schroeder's REBEL — was on a par with Lang's MEPHISTO program running on a 68000. In fact, in the 1989 ACM Computer Chess Championship in Reno, Schroeder's program, running on a bit-slice 6502, won its individual encounter against Lang's program, running on a 68030! (A couple of days later Lang's program beat DEEP THOUGHT!)

How does one explain such discrepancies? Why is it that the best program written for a 6502 can defeat the best program written for a 68030, and how can the 68030 program be good enough to win against DEEP THOUGHT in the same tournament? In my opinion the principal reason is that one produces the best results one can with whatever hardware is available. Ingenuity by a good programmer can sometimes be more important than the power of the chip with which he is working. MEPHISTO certainly uses less hardware power than DEEP THOUGHT, but while DEEP THOUGHT searches more deeply, MEPHISTO understands more about the positional aspects of chess. In the game in which MEPHISTO triumphed over DEEP THOUGHT it was because MEPHISTO took control of the game and never released its grip. By the time the tactics started, DEEP THOUGHT's position was beyond repair. I believe that as of November 1989, MEPHISTO was fundamentally stronger than CRAY BLITZ, whose Cray Y-MP processors have a computing power which is awesome in comparison with the "lowly" 68030.

It is interesting to examine the rate of progress in microcomputer chess, over the period since SARGON first competed in human tournaments. At the beginning of 1980 SARGON made a USCF performance rating of 1736. At the end of 1989 MEPHISTO was given an official USCF rating of 2376. These two figures correspond to an average rate of improvement in commercially available chess programs of 64 rating points per year. If we examine the Swedish rating list for commercially available chess computers and software, published in each issue of the ICCA Journal, we find that over the period from December 1984 to December 1989, the Elo rating of the strongest commercially available machine increased from 1801 to 2159, an average increase of approximately 72 points per year. This leads us to two conclusions:

1. The average rate of improvement per year has increased faster during recent years than it has done over the longer term, in other words the rate of progress has accelerated.

2. Since commercially available micro processor based products have been improving at an average rate of approximately 72 points per year, and the world's very best programs have been improving at a slightly slower rate of approximately 50 points per year, the gap between the MEPHISTOs of this world and the DEEP THOUGHTs is closing at the rate of approximately 22 points per year. Should this trend continue, the World Computer Chess Champion will be a micro before the turn of the century.

What has stimulated so much progress in chess programming on a micro-computer? The incentive for those companies which manufacture chess computers is the desire to be able to advertise their products as having the strongest programs. The right to say that one's program is "World Champion" is worth millions of dollars (literally) to the manufacturer who wins that title. World Microcomputer Championship tournaments have been held almost every year since 1980, and the manufacturers who vie for the title make every effort to improve their strongest program in the hope that it will win the crown. The first few years saw Fidelity the dominating force, with programs written by the Spracklens: London 1980, Travemunde and Hamburg 1981, Budapest 1983. Then in 1984, in Glasgow, there was a four way tie between FIDELITY, MEPHISTO, CONCHESS (programmed in Sweden by

Ulf Rathsman) and Richard Lang's program. By the following year Lang was working for Hegener & Glaser, and the World Champion title has been his every year from 1985 to 1989: Amsterdam 1985; Dallas 1986; Rome 1987; Almeria 1988; Portoroz 1989. In Portoroz, Yugoslavia, the Championship was played in the very same hall where Bobby Fischer competed in his first international tournament 31 years earlier.

Throughout this period the Spracklens, Lang, Kittinger, Kaplan and others tried each year to wring the utmost in improvements from their code, in an effort to create a program that could win the next World Championship title. It is this competitive struggle which has been the impetus for the best chess programmers who are working with microprocessors, and those who have succeeded have reaped ample rewards.

Another reason for the great progress in microcomputer chess has been the availability of computing power at a price that most people in the Western world can afford. The chess programmers of the 1970s needed regular, free access to multi-million dollar mainframes in order to ply their art. Nowadays anyone with $200 or more to spare can buy a computer and start to write a chess program. There is a wealth of printed information available on the subject, ranging from simply written articles on the general principles of chess programming to much more advanced papers devoted to the minutiae of tree search, evaluation or other aspects of the subject. The fact that millions of people now have the chance to write a chess program, means that some of them will produce strong programs and a few of them will find good, original

Figure 11.5 Richard Lang, MEPHISTO's programmer, in Edmonton, 1989

ideas that push forward the frontiers of knowledge in this field. Although those with their Commodore 64s or IBM PC clones do not have the same computing power as programmers working with Crays or with special purpose chess hardware, the sheer weight of numbers will eventually result in a tiny percentage of these programmers surpassing the feats of those who program the more powerful machines. As a natural consequence of this phenomenon, I believe that by the year 2000 there will be a dedicated chess computer retailing for less than $250 which plays at the strength of a grandmaster. And if all that you want is a mere international master, it will fit into a cigarette pack and cost $50.

The reader can obtain an excellent perspective of the strength of the microprocessor-based programs by following through the following five games played in the last several years.

White: **FIDELITY**
Black: **Gorman (2461)**
American Open, Los Angeles 1987
Sicilian Defense

1 e2–e4 c7–c5 2 Ng1–f3 a7–a6 3 c2–c4 e7–e6 4 Bf1–e2 Qd8–c7 5 O–O Ng8–f6 6 e4–e5 Nf6–g4 7 d2–d4 c5xd4 8 Qd1xd4 h7–h5 9 Qd4–e4 Nb8–c6 10 Bc1–f4 b7–b6 11 h2–h3 Ng4–h6 12 Nb1–c3 Bc8–b7 13 Ra1–d1 Nh6–f5 14 Nc3–d5 Qc7–d8 15 Bf4–g5 Nf5–e7 16 Nd5–f4 Qd8–c7 17 Qe4–d3 O–O–O 18 Qd4–d6 Rd8–e8 19 Qd6xc7+ Kc8xc7 20 a2–a4 Ne7–f5 21 Be2–d3 Nf5–d4 22 Nf3xd4 Nc6xd4 23 Bd3–b1 Nd4–c6 24 Nf4–d3 Rh8–g8
Preparing an interesting tactical idea.

Figure 11.6 After 24 ... Rh8–g8

25 Rd1–c1 f7–f6!? 26 e5xf6 g7xf6 27 Bg5xf6 Nc6–d4 28 g2–g3 Nd4–e2+
29 Kg1–h2 Ne2xc1 30 Rf1xc1

The smoke has cleared and Black has emerged with a small advantage in material, added to which is the established wisdom that commercial chess computers cannot play endgames well. Or can they?

30 ... Bb7–c6 31 Bb1–c2 d7–d6 32 Nd3–b4 Bf8–h6 33 Rc1–f1 Bc6–b7 34 f2–f4 Re8–f8

Black aims to capitalize on the fact that White's knight is out of play and his kingside looks shaky.

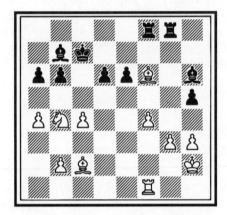

Figure 11.7 After 34 ... Re8–f8

35 Bc2–h7 Rf8xf6 36 Bh7xg8 h5–h4 37 Bg8–h7 a6–a5 38 Nb4–c2 e6–e5 39 f4–f5 h4xg3+ 40 Kh2xg3 Bh6–f4+ 41 Kg3–g4 Rf6–h6 42 Bh7–g8 Bb7–g2

Finally justifying his 34th move! Black picks up material.

43 Rf1xf4 e5xf4 44 Nc2–d4 f4–f3 45 Bg8–d5 Bg2xh3+ 46 Kg4xf3 Kc7–d7 47 Bd5–e6+ Kd7–e7 48 Nd4–b5 Bh3–f1 49 Nb5–c7 Ke7–d8 50 Nc7–b5 Kd8–e7 51 Nb5–c7

FIDELITY is naturally satisfied with a draw, being slightly down in material, but Black wants more.

51 ... Rh6–h2 52 Nc7–d5+ Ke7–d8 53 Nd5–f4!!

This is what Black overlooked when he went for the win at move 51. Now 53 ... Rh2xb2 loses quickly to 54 f5–f6, threatening 55 f6–f7 Kd8–e7 56 Nf4–g6+ and the f-pawn promotes.

53 ... Kd8–e7 54 Nf4–d5+ Ke7–f8

Again Black disdains a draw — after 54 ... Ke7–d8, White would have repeated the position with 55 Nd5–f4.

55 Nd5xb6 Rh2xb2 56 Nb6–c8 Bf1–g2+ 57 Kf3–e3 Bg2–c6 58 Nc8xd6 Bc6xa4 59 c4–c5 Ba4–b5 60 Nd6xb5 Rb2xb5 61 Ke3–d4 Kf8–e7 62 Be6–c4 Rb5–b8

63 Kd4–e5 a5–a4 64 c5–c6 a4–a3 65 f5–f6+ Ke7–e8 66 c6–c7 Rb8–a8 67 Ke5–d6 a3-a2 68 f6-f7+ **Black resigns.**
After 68 Ke8–f8 Bc4xa2, only a rook sacrifice by Black will stop the c-pawn.

White: **FIDELITY**
Black: **Desjardins (2272)**
World Open, Philadelphia 1988
Sicilian Defense

1 e2–e4 c7–c5 2 Ng1–f3 Nb8–c6 3 d2–d4 c5xd4 4 Nf3xd 4 Ng8–f6 5 Nb1–c3 e7–e5 6 Nd4–b5 d7–d6 7 Bc1–g5 a7–a6 8 Nb5–a3 b7–b5 9 Bg5xf6 g7xf6 10 Nc3–d5 f6–f5 11 Bf1–d3 Bc8–e6 12 Qd1–h5
So far all this is well known theory.

12 ... Ra8-c8 13 O–O f5–f4 14 c2–c4 Rh8–g8 15 c4xb5 Be6–g4 16 Qh5xh7 Rg8–g7 17 Qh7–h8 Nc6–d4 18 b5xa6 Rg7–g6 19 Rf1–c1 Rc8xc1+ 20 Ra1xc1 Rg6–h6 21 Qh8–g8 Rh6–g6
Black is trying to draw by repeatedly attacking the white queen, but FIDELITY finds a neat way to capitalize on its passed a-pawn.

Figure 11.8 After 21 ... Rh6-g6

22 Nb5–c7+ Ke8–e7
If 22 ... Qd8xc7 23 Qg8xf8+ Ke8xf8 24 Rc1xc7 and the a-pawn promotes.

23 Qg8xg6 f7xg6 24 a6–a7 Ke7–f7 25 a7–a8=Q Qd8–g5 26 Qa8–d5+ Kf7–g7 27 Nc7–e8+ Kg7–h6 28 Ne8xd6 Nd4–f3+ 29 Kg1–h1 Bf8xd6 30 Qd5xd6 Qg5–h5 31 Qd6–f8+ Kh6–g5 32 Qf8–d8+ Kg5–h6 33 h2–h3 Bg4xh3 34 Qd8–h8+ **Black resigns.**

White: **Blees (International Master, 2445)**
Black: **FIDELITY**
Hilversum 1989
Queen's Indian Defense

This game was played in a match between a team of 12 computers and a team
made up of the participants in the 1989 Dutch Championship. The humans
won by 9-3.

1 d2–d4 Ng8–f6 2 c2–c4 e7–e6 3 Ng1–f3 b7–b6 4 a2–a3 d7–d5 5 c4xd5 e6xd5
6 Nb1–c3 Bf8–d6 7 Bc1–g5 c7–c6 8 e2–e3 O–O 9 Bf1–d3 Rf8–e8 10 Qd1–c2
h7–h6 11 Bg5–h4 Bc8–g4 12 h2–h3 Bg4–d7 13 Nc3–e2 c6–c5 14 g2–g4 c5–c4
15 Bd3–f5 b6–b5 16 g4–g5 Qd8–a5+ 17 Ke1–f1 h6xg5 18 Nf3xg5 Bd7xf5
19 Qc2xf5 Nb8–d7 20 Rh1–g1 Qa5–d2 21 Ng5–f3 Qd2–d3 22 Qf5xd3 c4xd3
23 Ne2–c1 d3–d2 24 Nf3xd2 Ra8–c8 25 Kf1–e2 Rc8–c2 26 Nc1–d3 Nf6–e4
27 Ra1–d1 Nd7–b6 28 f2–f3 Ne4xd2 29 Rd1xd2

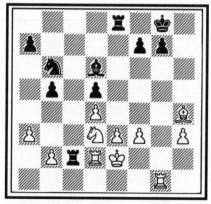

Figure 11.9 After 29 Rd1xd2

29 ... Re8xe3+!!
A bolt from the blue. If 30 Ke2xe3 Nb6–c4+ forking king and rook. It is so
obvious once you have seen it.

30 Ke2–d1 Rc2xd2+ 31 Kd1xd2 Nb6–c4+ 32 Kd2–c2 Re3xf3 33 Bh4–f2
Shell shocked, White allows another little combination which nets a further
pawn.

**33 ... Nc4xb2 34 Nd3xb2 Rf3xf2+ 35 Kc2–c3 Rf2–f3+ 36 Nb2–d3 Bd6xa3
37 Kc3–d2 f7–f6 38 h3–h4 Rf3–h3 39 Rg1–g4 Rh3–h2+ 40 Kd2–c3 Ba3–d6
41 Rg4–g1 a7–a5 42 Rg1–a1 Bd6–c7 43 Ra1–c1 Rh2xh4 44 Kc3–d2 Bc7–d6
45 Rc1–c8+ Kg8–f7 46 Rc8–c6 Bd6–e7 47 Kd2–e3 Rh4–e4+ White resigns.**

White: **Judith Polgar (playing 25 games simultaneously)**
Black: **MEPHISTO ALMERIA**
Nurnberg 1989
Caro-Kann Defense

1 e2–e4 c7–c6 2 d2–d4 d7–d5 3 e4xd5 c6xd5 4 c2–c4 Ng8–f6 5 Nb1–c3 e7–e6
6 Ng1–f3 Bf8–b4 7 c4xd5 Nf6xd5 8 Bc1–d2 Nb8–c6 9 Bf1–d3 O–O 10 O–O
Nd5–f6 11 Bd2–g5 h7–h6 12 Bg5–h4 g7–g5 13 Bh4–g3 a7–a6 14 a2–a3 Bb4–e7
15 Qd1–d2 b7–b5 16 h2–h4 Nf6–h5 17 Bg3–h2 Bc8–b7 18 h4xg5 h6xg5
19 Bd3–e4 Nc6–a5 20 Be4xb7 Na5xb7 21 Ra1–e1 Nh5–g7 22 Nc3–e4 f7–f6
23 b2–b4 Qd8–d5 24 Ne4–c3 Qd5–b3 25 Re1–e3 Ng7–f5 26 Re3–d3 g5–g4
27 Nf3–e1 Ra8–c8 28 Nc3xb5 Qb3–c4 29 Nb5–c3 Kg8–f7 30 d4–d5 e6–e5
31 d5–d6 Nb7xd6 32 Nc3–d5 Qc4–c1 33 Qd2–e2 Rc8–c4

Figure 11.10 After 33 ... Rc8–c4

34 Nd5xe7 Kf7xe7 35 Bh2xe5 f6xe5 36 Qe2xe5+ Ke7–d7 37 b4–b5 Rc4–c5
38 Rd3xd6+ Nf5xd6 39 Qe5–g7+ Rf8–f7 40 Qg7xg4+ Kd7–c7 41 Ne1–d3
Qc1–g5 42 Qg4–d4 Rc5–d5 43 Qd4–a7+ Kc7–d8 44 Qa7–b8+ Kd8–d7
45 b5xa6 Qg5xg2+ and MEPHISTO announced mate in 2 moves.

White: **MEPHISTO ALMERIA**
Black: **J. Nooman (2350)**
Holland 1989
Slav Defense

1 d2–d4 d7–d5 2 c2–c4 c7–c6 3 Ng1–f3 Ng8–f6 4 c4xd5 c6xd5 5 Nb1–c3
Nb8–c6 6 Bc1–f4 Bc8–f5 7 e2–e3 e7–e6 8 Bf1–b5 Nf6–d7 9 Qd1–a4 Qd8–b6
10 Nf3–h4 Bf5–e4 11 f2–f3!? Be4–d3! 12 Nc3xd5!
Not 12 Bb5xd3 Qb6xb2 with advantage to Black.

**12 ... e6xd5 13 Bb5xd3 Qb6xb2 14 Ra1–b1!? Bf8–b4+ 15 Ke1–f1 Qb2–c3
16 Qa4–d1**
Threatening to trap the queen with 17 Rb1–b3.

16 ... Qc3–a3 17 Qd1–c2 h7–h6?
Better would have been 17 ... g7–g6 to control the f5-square.

**18 Rb1–b3 Qa3–a5 19 Nh4–f5 O–O?! 20 a2–a3! Bb4xa3 21 Rb3xb7 Nc6–b4
22 Qc2–d2 Nd7–b6 23 Qd2–e1!! Qa5–a4**

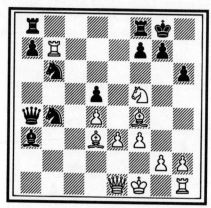

Figure 11.11 After 23 ... Qa5–a4

24 Nf5xh6+!
Here MEPHISTO ALMERIA announced mate in 7 moves. The game concluded:

24 ... Kg8–h8
Or 24 ... g7xh6 25 Qe1–g3+ Kg8–h8 26 Bf4–e5+ f7–f6 27 Rb7–h7 mate.

**25 Nh6xf7+ Kh8–g8 26 Bd3–h7+! Kg8xh7 27 Qe1–h4+ Kh7–g6 28 Nf7–e5+
Black resigns.**
28 ... Kg6–f5 29 g2–g4+ Kf5–e6 30 Qh4–e7 mate.

12

On Writing a Chess Program

Over the last 30 years, approximately 10,000 individuals from all over the world have participated in writing chess programs. Some have only been concerned with developing mate-in-x problem solvers, others with writing opening books, still others with constructing endgame databases. The vast majority, however, have wanted to create a world champion program though ultimately settling for much less. Several hundred programs have progressed to the point where they have participated in tournaments from Los Angeles to Lake Baikal, from Edmonton to Jerusalem. Seventy-five have competed in the twenty prestigeous ACM Championships dating back to 1970.

A number of outstanding scientists have devoted many years of their lives to writing chess programs. Former World Champion Mikhail Botvinnik, an electrical engineer by profession, started work on his program PIONEER in the 1960s and his work continues despite the serious handicap of inadequate computing facilities. Hans Berliner started at the same time. His first program J. BIIT appeared in 1970, his second PATSOC in 1983, and his third HITECH in 1985. Tony Marsland first became interested in the late 1960s. His program AWIT had its greatest success at the 4th World Championship in 1983 where it tied for second. Ken Thompson began with BELLE in the early 1970s, Hyatt in the middle 1970s. Even David Slate, whose programs have retired from active competition, continues his efforts which date back to 1968. Kathe and

Dan Spracklen began work on SARGON in the late 1970s and their interest has continued unabated. They have just left Fidelity International where they have been the driving force behind America's most successful commercial chess product, the CHESS CHALLENGER series, and they are currently with Saitek, another manufacturer of computer chess products. Others with long term programming interest include Don Beal of Queen Mary College in London, the entire KAISSA team including Mikhail Donskoy, Vladimir Arlazarov and George Adelson-Velsky, BEBE's Tony Scherzer who heads his own company SYS-10 in the Chicago area, and David Kittinger who has been the main programmer for the Novag series chess products.

To write a chess program requires a great burst of energy and concentration for a 2 or 3 month period. It is necessary to fit together many pieces of a large electronic puzzle that can never be entirely visualized. Addiction sets in soon after the first game is played, and while the suicidal pace of the first few months cannot be kept up, the programmer maintains a high level of energy and concentration for many years to come as the program gradually improves.

Once programming time has been set aside for the project, it is necessary to decide on computing facilities. The faster the better, but both IBM PC's or IBM's newer PS/2's (or compatibles) and Macintosh's Mac+, Mac SE, or Mac II are fine. If a Cray or large IBM mainframe is available, that's fantastic, but there may be a problem getting sufficient computing time. A multiprocessor such as a Sequent or N/CUBE or equivalent is also fine, although developing a single processor version of the program should be done before modifying the code for parallel search. If a small computer is used, it must come with a hard disk of at least 20 megabytes. A hardcopy printer is necessary to get program listings and records of games.

Memory size is not a major concern for programs without transposition tables. Chess programs have been written requiring less than 64k bytes of memory. Commercially available chess machines have been designed with a view to minimizing RAM (random access memory) which is more expensive than ROM (read only memory). As discussed in Chapter 11, programs with less than 1k of RAM have been designed and sold. Programs with transposition tables can use every bit of memory space available and that memory must be RAM. Thus many commercial chess machines cannot afford the luxury of transposition tables. To determine whether a chess program has a transposition table, it can be tested on the endgame position in 2i. If it recognizes that Ka1-b1 wins, that is, yields a score significantly greater than the one pawn advantage on the board, then it must have a transposition table.

An appropriate software package in which to develop the program must also be selected. Assembly language is used by a number of the best programs, but C is gaining in popularity. Turbo C and Microsoft C are especially popular programming environments. They come with good editors, compilers, assemblers, linkers, and debuggers, necessary ingredients for developing a chess program. It is interesting to note that for the last 3 years, every program participating in the ACM NACCCs has been programmed in either C or assembly language (CRAY BLITZ uses FORTRAN for I/O routines).

During the early 1970s, the question of what was an appropriate language for chess programs received considerable attention. Many felt that a strong chess program would not be developed until an appropriate language was developed, a language which had as primative terms words such as *attack*, *fork*, and *pin*. Such a language has not yet been developed, but the concepts of *attack*, *fork*, and *pin* are implicit in every chess program, encoded in ways that both man and machine understand, perhaps with an edge to the machine. The widespread use and success of low level languages is one of the biggest surprises to emerge from chess programming efforts. In the long run, computers will be designed to handle richer languages, while man will gradually adjust to the structure that computers impose on language. To date, however, the lack of a chess language has not hindered the development of chess programs.

The main advantage of C is its portability from one computer to another. Computers come and go over the lifetime of a chess program, and with C, the transition from one computer to another is easy. It is best not to pin down a program to depending on one particular computer. OSTRICH was written in Data General assembly language for Nova series computers which first appeared in the late 1960s. With Novas now obsolete, so is OSTRICH. The second advantage of C is that a program written in C can be compiled into code that executes almost as efficiently as programs written in assembly language. It is more efficient than PASCAL or FORTRAN, the most popular languages of the last two decades.

Chess programs have been developed by individuals working alone, although more frequently they are the result of a group effort with one dominant leader. The team, no matter what the size, needs a programming whiz. Every program that has won the world championship has been a team effort with at least one programming whiz. KAISSA's was Donskoy, a computer science graduate from Moscow State University. CHESS 4.7's was Slate although Atkin was also very capable. BELLE's was Thompson while Condon was the circuit design whiz. CRAY BLITZ was designed by two whizzes, Hyatt and Nelson. Nelson is considered one of the best Cray assembly language programmers in the world. DEEP THOUGHT has Hsu, although his forte at circuit design may even surpass his programming expertise.

A strong chess player is also important to a team but not as crucial as a programming whiz. Again, surveying the world champion programs: KAISSA's Donskoy is a fair player and he received chess advice from Bitman, a master. CHESS 4.7's Slate is an expert and Atkin is a class B player; they never felt a need to add stronger expertise to their team. BELLE's Thompson is a class B player and over the years he has received advice from a number of strong players including masters Ed McCormick and Mike Valvo. CRAY BLITZ's team includes Bert Gower who is a master, and DEEP THOUGHT's team includes Murray Campbell who plays at strong expert level. Table 12.1 gives a listing of several prominent programs and an estimate of the ratings of their main programmer and main chess expert. These ratings are the current ratings of the individuals listed; some had lower ratings when they began their chess programming. Hyatt and Hsu were very weak players when they began their work and their ratings were off scale; they have improved as their programs improved.

The weakest player ever to develop a strong chess program was Claude Jarry. Jarry developed L'EXCENTRIQUE while an undergraduate student at McGill in the late 1970s. L'EXCENTRIQUE's shining moment came at the 1980 World Championship in Linz, Austria where it defeated the reigning World Champion CHESS 4.9 in the first round. Jarry, a fantastic programmer, knew so little about chess that the only way he could tell whether L'EXCENTRIQUE was winning or losing was by reading the score provided by the program after each move. His success dramatizes another lesson of computer chess: a programmer can develop a program much better than himself.

Advice from a strong chess player can hinder a project unless the player has a keen comprehension of computers. Without some understanding of the correlation between chess concepts and the amount of programming work to implement them, a strong player can waste a programmer's time. In the past, many strong players were unable to understand the complexities of the search process sufficiently well to suggest realistic ways to improve tactical play.

It is in the preparation of opening books that the contribution of a master or grandmaster can be particularly useful or disappointingly counterproductive. Openings lines have to be chosen very carefully so that upon leaving book the program is left in a comfortable position. For example, a master's favorite book line that sacrifices a pawn for positional advantages is often quite inappropriate. Too often, the program's positional play is not strong enough to win back the pawn. A book line that accepts a sacrifice is also a source of trouble. A computer playing Black in the Queen's Gambit Accepted may try to hold on to the extra pawn while forgetting to develop its pieces.

Testing and Debugging Chess Programs

Most of the time spent developing a chess program is spent testing and debugging. Endless hours are consumed playing games with the program, hunting for bugs and looking for ways to improve play. More can be learned by observing the program in defeat than in victory, but watching it being humbled by a far superior player is of little help. To get a true feel for the program's strength, it is necessary to play with a clock. Commercially available programs that play master level chess can serve as sparing partners. When the program has played several hundred games it is ready for serious competition in either human or computer tournaments. Beside testing a program by playing games, there are sets of positions which serve as tests. In Chapter 8, a set of 16 endgame positions from Fine's *Basic Chess Endings* were presented. Once upon a time they served as an excellent test, but now they are too easy. The Bratko/Kopec set of 24 test positions has been used by a number

Table 12.1 Ratings of chess programs, their principal programmers, and their chess experts

Program, Rating	Princ. Prog.,Rating	Chess Expert, Rating
DEEP THOUGHT, 2580	Hsu, 1200	Campbell, 2200
HITECH, 2413	Berliner, 2400	Berliner, 2400
CRAY BLITZ, 2300	Hyatt, 1400	Gower, 2200
CHESS CHALLENGER, 2250	Spracklen, K., 1700	Kopec, 2500 & Baczynskyj, 2500
BELLE, 2200	Thompson, 1700	Valvo, 2500 & McCormick, 2200
BEBE, 2200	Scherzer, 1400	Scherzer, 1400
PHOENIX, 2200	Schaeffer, 2100	Schaeffer, 2100
NOVAG, 2150	Kittinger, 2000	Kittinger, 2000
CHESS 4.9, 2100	Slate, 2050	Slate, 2050
KAISSA, 1800	Donskoy, 1600	Bitman, 2300

of programmers. The set features tactical positions in which there is a move leading to a material advantage and "lever" positions in which there is a pawn advance that pries open the position. Kopec's set is good because while small,the problems are rather varied. The largest set of test position comes from Reinfeld's *Win at Chess*. Three hundred different tactical positions are presented; of the 299 positions with solutions, DEEP THOUGHT solves 296 in 3 minutes or less, makes the correct move but for the wrong reasons in another, and fails to solve 2.

A good debugger is essential for program development. There is no chess program that doesn't have a bug or two, and almost never is a game played without at least one bug surfacing. At first, bugs cause crashes, but after several months of work, they become more subtle. Curing one bug often creates another. Because of the complex interaction between parts of the program, a chess program must be constructed a little at a time, with each addition thoroughly checked out before the next one is added.

Debuggers come with both Turbo C and Microsoft C, but the programmer should build in additional debugging aids. Every minute spent adding debugging features to a chess program pays off in rich dividends in time saved later. It should be possible to step through the search one move at a time looking for problems. Logging search to a disk file is also useful, although logging a search of ten million positions may consume a big chunk of memory. When a crash occurs, getting a computer to repeat its search is often very difficult. Many parameters must be reset to values that are not known. Parameters concerned with time are especially a problem. Transposition tables are impossible to reset. If more than one computer is involved, the problems are even more severe.

During the course of a search, a program should print all kinds of information. At the end of each iteration, the principal continuation should be printed, as well as the score of the continuation, the number of nodes searched, and information on time consumed. From time to time, the program should print something, anything, on the screen just to inform those watching that the program is still alive. Otherwise, there is no way to know whether a crash has occurred or the program is just taking a long time to make up its mind.

While there are 100,000,000 people on earth who enjoy a good game of chess, the percentage involved in chess programming is very small. However, as hardware improves and software packages and programming languages become more versatile, the game of chess may become the game of programming chess. The joy of watching one's own program play is infectious and it could well spread to the younger generation who feel as at home with computers as the older generation does with cars.

13

Stop Press

As this book is going to press a milestone was clearly reached in the history of computer chess. On April 27th 1990, in Munich, West Germany, former World Champion Anatoly Karpov gave a simultaneous exhibition against 24 opponents. He lost one game, to a MEPHISTO chess computer! This is the first time that a holder of the (human) World Championship title has ever lost to a computer. Even though Karpov was playing 23 other opponents at the same time, it is a significant event.

In chess history there have been other occasions when a game played in a simultaneous exhibition has proved momentous. In 1925, when he visited Moscow for a Grandmaster tournament, the Cuban World Champion Jose Raoul Capablanca lost a game against a young boy called Mikhail Botvinnik, who became rather well known as a result. Twenty-three years later Botvinnik became World Chess Champion. In 23 years time will it be MEPHISTO?

White: **Karpov**
Black: **MEPHISTO PORTOROZ**
Munich, April 27, 1990
Slav Defense

1 d2–d4 d7–d5 2 c2–c4 c7–c6 3 Ng1–f3 Ng8–f6 4 Nb1–c3 d5xc4 5 a2–a4 Bc8–g4
6 Nf3–e5 Bg4–h5 7 f2–f3 Nf6–d7 8 Ne5xc4 e7–e5 9 Nc3–e4 Bf8–b4+ 10

Bc1–d2 Qd8–h4+ 11 g2–g3 Qh4–e7 12 Bd2xb4 Qe7xb4+ 13 Qd1–d2 Qb4xd2+
14 Ke1xd2 e5xd4 15 Ne4–d6+ Ke8–e7 16 Nd6xb7 Nb8–a6 17 Bf1–h3 Ra8–b8
18 Nb7–a5 Rh8–c8 19 f3–f4 f7–f6 20 e2–e3 d4xe3+ 21 Kd2xe3 Na6–b4
22 Ke3–f2 Nb4–d3+ 23 Kf2–g2 Nd3xb2 24 Rh1–e1+ Ke7–d8 25 Nc4–d6
Rc8–c7 26 g3–g4 Bh5–g6 27 f4–f5

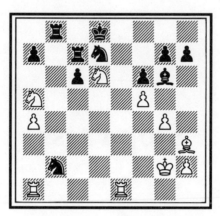

Figure 13.1 After 27 f4–f5

It now looks as though Black's 23rd move fell into a 9-ply trap, which costs
MEPHISTO a piece, but in fact Black's position was already difficult.

27 ... Nd7–e5 28 f5xg6 h7xg6 29 Ra1–b1 Rb8–b4 30 g4–g5 Kd8–e7 31 Re1–e4
Rb4xe4 32 Nd6xe4 Nb2xa4 33 Rb1–a1 Na4–b6 34 Ne4–c5 Ke7–e8 35 Na5–b7
Ne5–f7 36 g5xf6 g7xf6 37 Ra1xa7 Ke8–e7 38 Ra7–a6 Nb6–d5 39 Kg2–g3
Nf7–e5

With correct play this position is virtually impossible to win for White. Even
though he is a piece up, Karpov has only one pawn on the board and in order
to win the game he must find some way to promote his h-pawn. His major
problem in this respect is that the h-pawn promotes on a black square, but
Karpov's bishop is on a white square. This means that if the knights and rooks
are traded off, Karpov cannot win the game even if he were to get all of Black's
remaining pawns for nothing! The ending with dark squared bishop and h-
pawn and nothing else on the board is a draw so long as the black king is near
enough to h8, which in this case it is.

Karpov presumably continued this game in the hope that he could find
some way to win more material.

40 Bh3–g2 Nd5–e3 41 Bg2–h1 g6–g5 42 Nb7–a5 Ke7–d6 43 Nc5–e4+ Kd6–e7
44 Ne4–c5 Ke7–d6

MEPHISTO is naturally happy to repeat moves, since it will be satisfied with
a draw. Karpov still wants more.

45 Nc5–b7+ Kd6–d7 46 Ra6–a8 c6–c5 47 Ra8–h8 Kd7–e6 48 Na5–b3 Ne3–f5+ 49 Kg3–f2 Ne5–d3+ 50 Kf2–e2 c5–c4 51 Nb3–a1 Nd3–f4+ 52 Ke2–e1 c4–c3 53 Na1–c2 Rc7–c4 54 Ke1–d1 Rc4–c7 55 Rh8–e8+

Possibly the fatal mistake. Correct was 55 Bh1–e4.

55 ... Ke6–f7

Figure 13.2 After **55 ... Ke6–f7**

56 Re8–d8 Kf7–e7 57 Nc2–b4 Nf5–e3+
Black can draw by 57 ... Rc7xb7!? 58 Nb4–c6+ Ke7–f7 59 Nc6–e5+ Kf7–e7

Figure 13.3 Karpov in Munich, April 1990

60 Ne5–c6+ etc. Instead of 59 ... Kf7–e7 Black could try 59 ... f6xe5 60 Bh1xb7 Nf5–e3+ 61 Kd1–e1 (*not 61 Kd1–c1 Nf4–e2+ 62 Kc1–b1 c3–c2+* and the pawn promotes) 61 ... c3–c2, but then 62 Ke1–d2 restrains the black c-pawn. Instead MEPHISTO finds a stronger continuation in 57 ... Nf5–e3+.

58 Kd1–e1 c3–c2 59 Nb4xc2 Rc7xc2 60 Rd8–d2 Rc2–c1+ 61 Ke1–f2 Ne3–c4 Black achieves nothing with 61 ... Ne3–g4+ 62 Kf2–g3 Rc1–g1+ 63 Bh1–g2 Ng4–e3 64 Kg3–f2 when it is not clear how Black wins, if at all.

62 Rd2–d4 Nf4–e6 63 Rd4–e4 Rc1xh1 64 Re4xc4 Rh1xh2+ So now MEPHISTO has a two pawn advantage and the rest is silence.

65 Kf2–g3 Rh2–b2 66 Nb7–a5 f6–f5 67 Rc4–c3 Ke7–f6 68 Na5–c4 f5–f4+ 69 Kg3–f3 Rb2–h2 70 Rc3–c1 Rh2–h3+ 71 Kf3–e4 g5–g4 72 Rc1–e1 Rh3–b3 73 Re1–g1 g4–g3 74 Rg1–g2 Rb3–c3 75 Nc4–d2 Rc3–e3+ 76 Ke4–d5 Kf6–f5 77 Nd2–f1 Re3–d3+ 78 Kd5–c4 Rd3–d4+ 79 Kc4–c3 Kf5–g4 80 Rg2–g1 Kg4–f3 81 Nf1–d2+ Kf3–f2 82 Rg1–f1+ Kf2–e2 83 Rf1–g1 Rd4–d3+ White resigns.

Additional Reading

The leading source of material on computer chess is the *ICCA Journal*. It has published quarterly since 1977, initially as the *ICCA Newsletter* and then renamed the *ICCA Journal* in 1983. Professor Jaap van den Herik has served as editor for the last seven years. His address is the University of Limburg, Faculty of General Sciences, Department of Computer Science, P. O. Box 616, 6200 MD Maastricht, The Netherlands.

Advances in Computer Chess has published five volumes in 1977, 1980, 1982, 1986, and 1989. Volumes 1 and 2 were published by the University of Edinburgh Press, Volumes 3 and 4 by Pergamon Press, and the latest volume by Elsevier Science Publishers B. V. (North Holland), P. O. Box 103, 1000 AC Amsterdam, The Netherlands.

Other publications where material has appeared include (1) the *Machine Intelligence* series, first published in 1967 by Oliver & Boyd of Edinburgh and published most recently by Oxford University Press, Walton Street, Oxford 0X2 6DP, United Kingdom, (2) *Artificial Intelligence*, published monthly by Elsevier, and (3) the *IEEE Transactions on Pattern Analysis and Machine Intelligence*, published monthly by the IEEE, 345 East 47th Street, New York, New York 10017-2394. These three publications cater to a wider range of topics than just computer chess, encompassing the many aspects of artificial intelligence.

Books on the subject have appeared with Botvinnik's *Computer Chess and Long Range Planning*, published in 1970 in English by Springer-Verlag being the first. Others are listed here. Following the listing of books on computer chess is a listing mainly of research papers but including as well several books referred to in the text.

Books on Computer Chess

Adelson-Velsky, G. M., Arlazarov, V. L., and Donskoy, M. V., *Algorithms for Games* Springer-Verlag, New York, 1988.

Botvinnik, M. M., *Computers, Chess, and Long Range Planning*, Springer-Verlag, Berlin and New York, 1970.

Ebeling, C., *All the Right Moves: A VLSI Architecture for Chess*, MIT Press, 1987.

Frey, P., (Ed.) *Chess Skill in Man and Machine*, 2nd ed., Springer-Verlag, New York, 1977.

Levy, D. N. L., *Chess and Computers*, Batsford, London, 1976.

Levy, D. N. L, and Newborn, M. M., *All About Chess and Computers*, Computer Science Press, Potomac, Maryland, 1982.

Levy, D. N. L., *Computer Chess Compendium*, Springer-Verlag, New York, 1989.

Newborn, M. M., *Computer Chess*, Academic Press, New York, 1975.

Spracklen, D. and Spracklen, K., *SARGON III Computer Chess*, Hayden Software, Lowell, Massachusetts, 1984.

Other Publications, Books, and Research Papers Referred to in the Text

Aldelson-Velsky, G. M., Arlazarov, V. L. , Bitman, A. R., Zhivotovsky, A. A., and Uskov, A. V., "Programming a computer to play chess," *Russian Math. Surveys*, vol. 25, 1970, pp. 221–262.

Akl, S. G., Barnard, D. T., and Doran, R. J., "Design, analysis, and implementation of a parallel tree-search algorithm," *IEEE Transactions on Pattern Recognition and Machine Intelligence*, 1982, pp. 192–203.

Anantharaman, T., Campbell, M., and Hsu, F., "Singular extensions: adding selectivity to brute-force searching," *ICCA Journal*, vol. 11, no. 4, 1988, pp. 135–143.

Arlazarov, V. L., and Futer, A. V., "Computer analysis of a rook endgame," *Machine Intelligence 9*, (Hayes, J. E., Michie, D., and Mikulich, L. I., Eds.) University of Edinburgh Press, Edinburgh, Scotland, 1978.

Berliner, H. J., "Computer chess at Carnegie Mellon University," *Advances in Computer Chess 4*, (D. Beal, Ed.), Pergamon Press, 1986, pp. 166–180.

Berliner, H., and Ebeling, C., "The SUPREM architecture: a new intelligent paradigm," *Artificial Intelligence*, vol. 28, 1986, pp. 3–8.

Bernstein, A., De V. Roberts, M., Arbuckle, T., and Belsky, M. A., "A chess playing program for the IBM 704," *Proc. Western Joint Computer Conference*, vol. 13, 1958, pp. 157–159.

Bettadapur, P., "Influence of ordering on capture search," *ICCA Journal*, vol. 9, no. 4, 1986, pp. 180–188.

Bratko, I., and Kopec, D., "A test for comparison of human and computer performance in chess," *Advances in Computer Chess 3*, (Clarke, M. R. B., Ed.),Pergamon Press, 1982, pp. 31–56.

Clarke, M. R. B., "A quantative study of king and pawn against king," *Advances in Computer Chess 1*, (M. R. B. Clark, Ed.), University of Edinburgh Press, 1977, pp. 108–115.

Condon, J. H., and Thompson, K., "Belle chess hardware," *Advances in Computer Chess 3*, (Clarke, M. R. B., Ed.), Pergamon Press, 1982, pp. 45–54.

Condon, J. H., and Thompson, K., "Belle," *Chess Skill in Man and Machine*, 2nd Edition, (Frey, P., Ed.) Springer-Verlag, 1983, pp. 201–210.

de Groot, A. D., *Thought and Choice in Chess*, Mouton, The Hague, 1965.

Ebeling, C. and Palay, A., "The design and implementation of a VLSI move generator," *IEEE 11th Annual International Symposium on Computer Architecture*, Ann Arbor, 1984, pp. 74–80.

Edwards, D. J. and Hart, T. P., The alpha-beta heuristic, M. I. T. Artificial Intelligence Memo, no. 30, (revised), October 28, 1963 (Originally published as The Tree Prune (TP) Algorithm, December 4, 1961.)

Fine, R., *Basic Chess Endings*, David McKay, Philadelphia, 1941.

Gillogly, J. J., "The Technology Chess Program," *Artificial Intelligence*, vol. 3, 1972, pp. 145–163.

Greenblatt, R. D., Eastlake III, D. E., and Crocker, S. D., "The Greenblatt chess program," *Proceeding of the Fall Joint Computing Conf.*, San Francisco, 1967, pp. 801–810.

Herik, H. J. van den, Herschberg, I. S., and Nakad, N., "A reply to R. Sattler's remarks on the KRP(a2)KbBP(a3) database," *ICCA Journal*, vol. 11, no. 2/3, 1988, pp. 88–91.

Hyatt, R. M., "Using time wisely," *ICCA Journal*, vol. 7, no. 1, 1984, pp. 4–9.

Hyatt, R. M., Gower, B. E., and Nelson, H. L., "CRAY BLITZ," *Advances in Computer Chess 4*, D. Beal (Ed.), Pergamon Press, Oxford, 1985, pp. 8–18.

Hyatt, R. M., "Parallel search on the Cray X-MP/48," *ICCA Journal*, vol. 8, no. 2, 1985, pp. 90–99.

Kister, J., Stein, P., Ulam, S., Walden, W., and Wells, M., "Experiments in chess," *J. Assoc. Comput. Mach.*, vol. 4, 1957, pp. 174–177.

Knuth, D., and Moore, R., "An analysis of alpha-beta pruning," *Artificial Intelligence*, vol. 6, 1975, pp. 293–326.

Komissarchik, E. A., and Futer, A. L., "Computer analysis of a Queen endgame," *ICCA Journal*, vol. 9, no. 4, 1986, pp. 189–200.

Korf, R. E., "Iteratively-Deepening-A*: An optimal admissible tree search," *Proceedings of the Ninth International Joint Conference on Artificial Intelligence*, Los Angeles, California, 1985, pp. 1034–1036.

Kotok, A., *A chess playing program for the IBM 7090*, B. S. Thesis, MIT, AI Project Memo 41, Computer Center, Cambridge Mass, 1962.

Marsland, T. A., and Campbell, M., "Parallel search of strongly ordered game trees," *Computing Surveys*, vol. 14, no. 4, 1982, pp. 533–551.

Marsland, T. A., Olafsson, M., and Schaeffer, J., "Multiprocessor tree-search experiments," *Advances in Computer Chess 4*, (D. Beal, Ed.), Pergamon Press, Oxford, 1985, pp. 37–51.

Marsland, T. A., and Popowich, F., "Parallel game-tree search," *IEEE Transactions on Pattern Analysis and Machine Intelligence*, 1985, pp. 442–452.

Michie, D., "Brute force search in chess and science," *ICCA Journal*, vol. 12, no. 3, 1989, pp. 127–143.

Michie, D., and Bratko, I., "Ideas on knowledge synthesis stemming from the KBBKN endgame," *ICCA Journal*, vol. 10, no. 1, 1987, pp. 3–13.

Nefkens, H. J. J., "Constructing data bases to fit a microcomputer," *ICCA Journal*, vol. 8, no. 4, 1985, pp. 219–224.

Nelson, H. L., "Hash tables in CRAY BLITZ," *ICCA Journal*, vol. 8, no. 1, 1985, pp. 3–13.

Newborn, M., "PEASANT: an endgame program for kings and pawns," *Chess Skill in Man and Machine*, (Frey, P., Ed.), Springer-Verlag, New York, 1977, pp. 119–130.

Newborn, M., "Recent progress in computer chess," *Advances in Computers 19*, (Yovits, M., Ed.), Academic Press, New York, 1979, pp. 58–118.

Newborn, M., "A parallel search chess program," *Proc. of the 1985 ACM Ann. Conf.*, 1985, pp. 272–277.

Newborn, M., "A hypothesis concerning the strength of chess programs," *ICCA Journal*, vol. 8, no. 4, 1986, pp. 209–215.

Newborn, M., "Unsynchronized iteratively deepening parallel alpha-beta search," *IEEE Trans. on Pattern Analysis and Machine Intelligence*, vol. 10, no. 5, pp. 687–694, 1988.

Newborn, M., "Computer chess: ten years of significant progress," *Advances in Computers 29*, (Yovits, M., Ed.), Academic Press, New York, 1979, pp. 197–250.

Newell, A., Shaw, J. C., and Simon, H. A., "Chess playing programs and the problem of complexity," *IBM Journal of Research & Development*, vol. 4, no. 2, 1958, pp. 320–335.

Pearl, J., "Asymptotic properties of minimax trees and searching procedures," *Artificial Intelligence*, vol. 14, 1980, pp. 113–138.

Reinefeld, A., Schaeffer, J., and Marsland, T., "Information acquisition in minimal window search," *Proc. 9th Int. Joint Conf. on AI*. 1985, pp. 1040–1043.

Reinfeld, F., *Win at Chess*, Dover Publications Inc., New York, 1958.

Schaeffer, J., "The history heuristic," *ICCA Journal* , vol. 6, no. 3, 1983, pp. 16–19.

Schaeffer, J., "Improved parallel alpha-beta search," *1986 Proc. of the FJCC*, 1986, pp. 519–527.

Shannon, C. E., "Programming a computer for playing chess," *Philosophical Magazine*, vol. 41, 1950, pp. 256–275.

Shapiro, A. *The role of structured induction in expert systems*, Ph. D. Thesis, Machine Intelligence Research Unit, Edinburgh, 1983.

Shapiro, A. and Michie, D., "A self-commenting facility for inductively synthesized endgame expertise," *Advances in Computer Chess 4*, 1986, pp. 147–162.

Slagle, J. R., and Dixon, J. K., "Experiments with some programs that search game trees," *J. Assoc. Comput. Mach.*, vol 16, 1969, pp. 189–207.

Slate, D. J., and Atkin, L. R., "CHESS 4.5 - The Northwestern University Chess Program," *Chess Skill in Man and Machine*, (P. Frey, Ed.) Springer-Verlag, 1977, pp. 82–118.

Slate, D. J., "A chess program that uses the transposition table to learn from experience," *ICCA Journal* , vol. 10, no. 2, 1987, pp. 59–71.

Stickel, M. E., and Tyson, W. M., "An analysis of consecutively bounded depth-first search with applications in automated deduction," *Proc. of the 9th International Joint Conf. on Artificial Intelligence,* Los Angeles, California, 1985, pp. 1073–1075.

Stiller, L., "Parallel analysis of certain endgames," *ICCA Journal*, vol. 12, no. 2, 1989, pp. 55–64.

Thompson, K., "Computer chess strength," *Advances in Computer Chess 3*, (Clarke, M., Ed.), Pergamon Press, 1982, pp. 55–56.

Thompson, K., "Retrograde analysis of certain endgames," *ICCA Journal* , vol. 9, no. 3, 1986, pp. 131–1986.

Turing, A. M., "Digital computers applied to games," *Faster than Thought,* (Bowden, B. V., Ed.), Pitman, London, 1953, pp. 286–310.

Zellner, H., "The KPK database revisited," *ICCA Journal*, vol.12, no. 2, 1989, pp. 78–82.

Zobrist, A. L., *A hashing method with applications for game playing*, Technical Report 88, Computer Sciences Department, University of Wisconsin, Madison, Wisc., 1970.

A

The International Computer Chess Association

The International Computer Chess Association (ICCA) is the official world governing body for computer chess. It organizes regular chess tournaments in which the only particpants are computer programs. In addition, the ICCA publishes a quarterly journal and organizes a regular conference on Advances in Computer Chess.

Until the late 1970s, there was no official governing body for activities in computer chess. Nevertheless, a small team consisting of Ben Mittman and your two co-authors, acting by default, had a hand in the organization of virtually all computer chess competitions. Newborn and Ken King, both then at Columbia University, organized the very first computer chess tournament in New York in 1970. That event was held as part of the Annual Conference of the Association for Computing Machinery (ACM), an organization that has continued its support of computer chess activities for over two decades.

In 1971 the ACM tournament took place in Chicago, organized by Mittman with help from Newborn. Mittman was Director of the Vogelback Computing Center at Northwestern University where the winner of the 1970 tournament "lived." By chance it happened that David Levy was planning a trip to the United States and his visit coincided with the tournament in Chicago. He was invited to act as tournament director and commentator, a role which he held for 10 years.

The early ACM tournaments reflected an increasing interest in computer chess. During the 1973 ACM tournament, Mittman exclaimed to his cohorts: "Gee. This is great fun. What can we do next?" In reply Levy suggested a World Championship for computers, mirroring the human World Championship in which the reigning champion defends his title after a 3 year period of tenure. We were fortunate to find support for the event from the International Federation of Information Processing Societies (IFIPS), whose own tri-ennial conference was due to take place in Stockholm in the summer of 1974. This conference became the venue for the 1st World Computer Chess Championship, won by the Soviet program KAISSA. The World Championship has taken place every 3 years since 1974, with a European city hosting the events in 1974 (Stockholm), 1980 (Linz) and 1986 (Cologne), and a North American city being the host in 1977 (Toronto), 1983 (New York) and 1989 (Edmonton).

In 1976 a Dutch chess programmer, Barend Swets, proposed that an official governing body be set up. A few months later a computer chess enthusiast, Doug Penrod, published the first issue of the *Computer Chess Newsletter* from his home in Santa Barbara, California. Penrod published letters from people interested in computer chess, as well as some games played by chess programs. He even obtained three games played by Bobby Fischer against the Greenblatt chess program.

In 1977, at the 2nd World Computer Chess Championship held in Toronto, Swets' idea came to fruition and the ICCA was born. Mittman was elected President, Newborn Vice President and Ken Thomspon Secretary-Treasurer. Penrod, who was terminally ill at the time, was pleased to hand over the *Computer Chess Newsletter* to the ICCA. It was renamed the *ICCA Newsletter* and Mittman took over as its first editor. In 1983, it became the *ICCA Journal* and its editorship was assumed by Jaap van den Herik, professor of computer science at the University of Limburg.

In 1983 Newborn took over as President, Johann Enroth of Sweden as Vice President and William Blanchard as Secretary-Treasurer. In 1986 Levy became President and was re-elected in 1989, as were the other members of the ICCA board: Tony Marsland as Vice President and Jonathan Schaeffer as Secretary-Treasurer.

The ICCA organizes two world championship events. In addition to the tri-ennial World Computer Chess Championship in which any kind of computer program is eligible to take part, there is an annual World Microcomputer Chess Championship. The microcomputer events give amateurs and professional programmers the chance to show their mettle. These events have done much to stimulate rivalry in the world of commer-cially available chess computers, and as a result the strength of the best micro-based programs is now close to matching that of the best mainframes and special purpose chess engines.

The venues of the micro tournaments have mainly been in Europe: London (1980), Travemunde and Hamburg (1981), Budapest (1983), Glasgow (1984), Amsterdam (1985), Dallas (1986), Rome (1987), Almeria (1988),

Portoroz (1989). Anyone wishing to take part in this event should contact the ICCA via one of the addresses given below.

Another activity which the ICCA has recently taken over is a regular conference on Advances in Computer Chess. Five of these conferences have been held previously on an ad hoc basis, starting with the first one in Oxford in 1975. The proceedings of these conferences have all been published under the title: *Advances in Computer Chess*. The organizer is: Don Beal, Computer Science Department, Queen Mary College, Mile End Road, London E1, England.

The ICCA has secured sponsorship for two special awards in computer chess. The West German company Hegener & Glaser, who manufacture the MEPHISTO range of chess computers, has endowed two ICCA awards. The prize of a top-of-the-line MEPHISTO chess computer has been presented annually since 1988, for the best publication on computer chess. A scholarship, worth $5,000 to the winner, is also given each year to the programmer under 19 years of age who writes the best chess program. The first MEPHISTO Scholarship was awarded in 1989 to two West German programmers.

Anyone interested in joining the ICCA should send their membership fee ($25 US or 50 Guilders or equivalent plus bank charges and exchange commissions), which includes a subscription to the *ICCA Journal*, to either:

Professor Jonathan Schaeffer
Computing Science Department
University of Alberta
Edmonton, Alberta
Canada   T6G 2H1

Professor H. J. van den Herik
University of Limburg
Faculty of General Science
Dept. of Computer Science
P. O. Box 616
6200 MD Maastricht
The Netherlands

B

Results of Major Tournaments

World Championships

Year	City	Winner	Runner-up
1974	Stockholm	KAISSA; Donskoy, Arlazarov; ICL 4/70	CHESS 4.0; Slate, Atkin; CDC 6600
1977	Toronto	CHESS 4.6; Slate, Atkin; CDC Cyber 176	DUCHESS; Truscott, Wright, Jensen; IBM 370/165
1980	Linz	BELLE; Thompson, Condon; PDP 11/23 w/ chess hardware	CHAOS; Alexander, Swartz, Berman, O'Keefe; Amdahl 470/V8
1983	New York	CRAY BLITZ; Hyatt, Gower, Nelson; Cray X-MP 4/8	BEBE; Scherzer; Chess Engine
1986	Cologne	CRAY BLITZ; Hyatt, Gower, Nelson; Cray X-MP 4/8	HITECH; Berliner, Ebeling, Goetsch, Paley, Slomer; SUN w / chess hardware
1989	Edmonton	DEEP THOUGHT; Hsu, Anantharaman, Browne, Campbell, Jansen, Nowatzyk; SUN w/chess hardware	BEBE; Scherzer, Scherzer; Chess Engine

ACM North American Computer Chess Championships[1]

Year	City	Winner	Runner-up
1970	New York	CHESS 3.0; Slate, Atkin, Gorlen; CDC 6400	DALY CHESS PROGRAM; Daly, King; Varian 620/i
1971	Chicago	CHESS 3.5; Slate, Atkin, Gorlen; CDC 6400	TECH; Gillogly; PDP 10
1972	Boston	CHESS 3.6; Slate, Atkin, Gorlen; CDC 6400	OSTRICH; Arnold, Newborn; DG Supernova
1973	Atlanta	CHESS 4.0; Slate, Atkin, Gorlen; CDC 6400	TECH II; Baisley; PDP 10
1974	San Diego	RIBBIT; Hansen, Crook, Parry; Honeywell 6050	CHESS 4.0; Slate, Atkin; CDC 6400
1975	Minneapolis	CHESS 4.4; Slate, Atkin; CDC Cyber 175	TREEFROG; Hansen, Calnek, Crook; Honeywell 608
1976	Houston	CHESS 4.5; Slate, Atkin; CDC Cyber 176	CHAOS; Swartz, Berman, Alexander Ruben, Toikka, Winograd; Amdahl 470
1977	Seattle	CHESS 4.6; Slate, Atkin; CDC Cyber 176	DUCHESS; Truscott, Wright, Jensen; IBM 370/168
1978	Washington	BELLE; Thompson, Condon; PDP 11/70 w/ chess hardware	CHESS 4.7; Slate, Atkin; CDC Cyber 176
1979	Detroit	CHESS 4.9; Slate, Atkin; CDC Cyber 176	BELLE; Thompson, Condon; PDP 11/70 with chess hardware
1980	Nashville	BELLE; Thompson, Condon; PDP 11/70 w/ chess hardware	CHAOS; Alexander, O'Keefe, Swartz, Berman; Amdahl 470
1981	Los Angeles	BELLE; Thompson, Condon; PDP 11/23 w/ chess hardware	NUCHESS; Blanchard, Slate; CDC Cyber 176

[1]Called the ACM United States Computer Chess Championship until 1975, when it was renamed the ACM North American Computer Chess Championship.

ACM North American Computer Chess Championships (Contd.)

Year	City	Winner	Runner-up
1982	Dallas	BELLE; Thompson, Condon; PDP 11/23 w/ chess hardware	CRAY BLITZ; Hyatt, Gower, Nelson; Cray 1
1983	New York[2]		
1984	San Fran.	CRAY BLITZ; Hyatt, Gower, Nelson; Cray X-MP 4/8	BEBE; Scherzer, Chess Engine, and FIDELITY EXPERIMENTAL; Sparcklen, Spracklen, Fidelity Machine[3]
1985	Denver	HITECH; Ebeling, Berliner, Goetsch, Paley Campbell, Slomer, SUN w/ chess hardware	BEBE; Scherzer, Chess Engine
1986	Dallas	BELLE; Thompson, Condon;	LACHEX; Wendroff, Cray X-MP PDP 11/23 w/ chess hardware
1987	Dallas	CHIPTEST-M; Anantharaman, Hsu, Campbell; SUN 3 w/ chess hardware	CRAY BLITZ; Hyatt, Nelson, Gower, Cray X-MP 4/8
1988	Orlando	DEEP THOUGHT 0.02; Hsu Anatharaman, Browne, Campbell, Nowatzyk; SUN 3 w/ chess hardware	CHESS CHALLENGER EXP; Spracklen, Spracklen, Nelson, Fidelity Machine w/ Motorola 68030 microprocessor
1989	Reno	HITECH[4]; Ebeling, Berliner, Goetsch, Paley Campbell, Slomer; SUN w/ chess hardware	DEEP THOUGHT[4]; Hsu, Anatharamam, Browne, Campbell, Nowatzyk, 3 SUN 4s w/ 2 chess processors per SUN
1990	New York[5]		

[2]Not held as the ACM's NACCC that year but as the 4th World Computer Chess Championship.
[3]BEBE and FIDELITY EXPERIMENTAL finished in a tie for second place.
[4]HITECH and DEEP THOUGHT finished in a tie for first place.
[5]Scheduled to take place November 11–14 at Supercomputing '90 at the New York Hilton.

World Microcomputer Championships

Year	City	Winner	Runner-up
1980	London	CHESS CHALLENGER	BORIS EXPERIMENTAL
1981	Travemunde/Hamburg	FIDELITY X	CHESS CHAMPION MARK V
1983	Budapest	ELITE A/S	MEPHISTO X
1984	Glasgow	Four way tie: ELITE X, MEPHISTO S/X, PRINCHESS, PSION CHESS	
1985	Amsterdam	MEPHISTO AMSTERDAM I	MEPHISTO AMSTERDAM II
1986	Dallas	MEPHISTO DALLAS 3	FIDELITY "2533"
1987	Rome	MEPHISTO	CYRUS 68K
1988	Almeria	MEPHISTO	FIDELITY
1989	Portoroz	MEPHISTO	FIDELITY
1990		Scheduled for Lyons	
1991		Scheduled for Vancouver	

Index